Further
Particulars

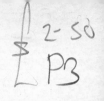

D1390416

Further Particulars

C. H. ROLPH

Oxford   New York

OXFORD UNIVERSITY PRESS

1988

Oxford University Press, Walton Street, Oxford OX2 6DP

Oxford New York Toronto
Delhi Bombay Calcutta Madras Karachi
Petaling Jaya Singapore Hong Kong Tokyo
Nairobi Dar es Salaam Cape Town
Melbourne Auckland

and associated companies in
Beirut Berlin Ibadan Nicosia

Oxford is a trade mark of Oxford University Press

First published 1987
First issued as an Oxford University Press paperback 1988

British Library Cataloguing in Publication Data

Rolph, C. H.
Further particulars.
1. Rolph, C. H.
Rn: Cecil Rolph Hewitt   I. Title
364'.092'4   HV7911.H45
ISBN 0–19–282143–1

Library of Congress Cataloging in Publication Data

Rolph, C. H. (Cecil Hewitt), 1901–
Further particulars.
Includes index.
1. Rolph, C. H. (Cecil Hewitt), 1901–
2. Great Britain — Biography.   I. Title.
CT788.R542A34 1988   941.082'092'4 [B]   86–5386
ISBN 0–19–282143–1

Set by Dobbie Typesetting Service
Printed in Great Britain by
The Guernsey Press Co. Ltd.
Guernsey, Channel Islands

To my much-loved children and the equally cherished people they married, all of whom have been spared any mention in this book. They should be relieved about this. In case any of them is not, this seems the best place in which to offer public atonement, at the same time congratulating them all on their escape.

ACKNOWLEDGEMENTS

I want to record here my gratitude to the Department of Printed Books at the Imperial War Museum for details of the 1940 pamphlet *If The Invader Comes* (and of its disputed authorship); to the Librarian at the University of Sussex, as well as to A. D. Peters & Co, writers' agents, for their permission to reproduce a tape-recorded interview with Dame Rebecca West; to the Home Office for leave to publish a report submitted by myself in 1969 after a glimpse of the prison parole systems in Australia and New Zealand; and to John Grigg for allowing me to reproduce a letter he sent me in 1969 about the meaning of Easter, which I am still confident that (eventually) I shall understand.

CONTENTS

CHAPTER ONE

As I was saying, when you reach your seventeenth birthday the law of England admits you as a grown-up. It was already taking this view in 1918, when I did it, and despite many other age limits that have since been changed, it is 17 now. Of course at that time the man of 17 had another four years to wait for the right to vote, marry in defiance of his parents, make a will, or drive a bus. But at 17 I had put all those things behind me, convinced that life offered only one acceptable role, niche, vocation, or fulfilment. In common with some millions of others, I was to be a writer.

And in tune with life's universal irony, the supply of writers increases as the likelihood of getting published withers. In 1918 it seemed a rarer ambition, or perhaps it was an ambition that people kept more to themselves. Most people, it appeared, were still content to read what a select few were writing. I recall that I seldom saw myself as a writer of novels (throughout the war I had been under the spell of Dostoevsky, Gogol, Bennett, Dickens, George Eliot, and the Brontës), or of short stories, plays, or poems. By elimination I had arrived at something between the essayist, the historian, the polemicist, and the crusader: Mill, Macaulay, Bright, Blatchford, Wells, Shaw. Never Marx or Engels: I hoped *never* to be a bore and would have hated to be widely misunderstood. The worst of all fates (I tried to assure myself) would be to become a Set Book.

But I was by this time (December 1918) in the process of being only too well understood by my employers, Spreckley White & Lewis of 13–15 Cannon Street, City of London, manufacturing wholesalers of ladies' and children's coats, skirts, and dresses. I had been there two years as a counting-house clerk, and I had only recently understood why this long-established and much-respected

firm could be said to be 'manufacturing' anything. Much
of its labour force comprised tailors, cutters, and
needlewomen, all known as 'outworkers'. They lived in
the East End and worked in their little slum tenements.
They came to 13–15 Cannon Street, a grey and rather grim-
looking six-storey building in the shadow of St. Paul's
Cathedral, for their cloth and measurements, they took
them away, and they were not seen again until they
returned with the finished garments. Every Friday some
of them came for their pay, which (everyone said below
the salt) was criminally small. They were of both sexes,
of all shapes and sizes, their ages ranged from about
14 to about 80, and they all looked foreign or Jewish
or both. They were not employees of the firm, and they
had no insurance or pension rights—they were indeed
to have no employees' rights until the decision of an
Employment Appeals Tribunal sixty years later. Some of
them, I found, couldn't speak English, and these were
sometimes accompanied by a relative or friend who
believed he could.

On Fridays it was my job to go to the Midland Bank in
Threadneedle Street and get the money for their wages;
after which it was my weekly embarrassment, as I
crouched over my ledger in the counting-house, to be
acutely aware of them queueing at the cashier's desk to get
their money. The queue stretched from old Mr Edwards's
desk, on the other side of a frosted glass partition dividing
him from us, out of the counting-house and right across
the adjoining Cloth Department to the big double swing-
doors giving on to the street. Outside the counting-house,
the queue spoke in whispers as it waited. Inside, it was
silent. All its members were lifelong queuers. Most of them
came from countries where you queued to get into the
world and queued to get out.

After a few months I became aware that the weekly
queue always included a strikingly pretty girl of about 16
who (I told myself) would be beautiful, literally beautiful
in the absolute sense which we all secretly acknowledge
but never see realized, if it were not for the sallowness of

her complexion. Reluctantly, I allowed that the legs and arms were rather thin. She was very small, I should say not more than five feet tall. And as if to emphasize her tiny stature she always wore completely flat shoes and, most unusually in those days, no hat. Nor did she bunch up her hair on the top — she pulled it tight from a central parting like the Mona Lisa's, and I think she may be one of the reasons, perhaps the main reason, why I have only been able to pretend that I like the Mona Lisa. But I know that what caught my attention more than all this was that she always had with her a small suitcase, which served as a seat for any older person (and some were very old) in front of or behind her in the queue.

I don't remember how long she thus engaged my attention. Sometimes I had a mad impulse to speak to her, the madness of which became apparent after one minute's calmer thought. The counting-house of Spreckley White & Lewis was not a place in which you made advances to girls; and even if it had been, I was not the kind of youth who made them. But one autumn evening when 5.30 came, and the counting-house clerks were all noisily brushing the turn-ups of their trousers as an indication to the satraps behind the glass partition that they were ready to go home, there had been some hold-up and the patient queue of outworkers was still there. There were always disputes as to how much they had earned, and perhaps this time they had been specially difficult. My diminutive Mona Lisa was still some yards from the cashier's desk, for she had, as she often did, given up her place in the queue to someone whose time was more precious. Recklessly and unusually, I decided then and there that I would wait for her. The patience of these waiting outworkers, I thought, was pathetic — it was another half-hour before she was paid. And then as she at last left the counting-house, to find me waiting for her at the outer swing-doors, she saw something that rooted her to the spot. It was by now after 6 p.m., and the evening incursion of Mrs Mopps had taken possession, an occasion that even I had never seen before. To the girl's manifest astonishment, they were sprinkling

wet tea-leaves all over the floor, from buckets in which
the staff's afternoon teapots had been emptied. As she
watched them she caught sight of me, and with no
hesitation whatever she came and asked me what they
were doing. Thus, after all, it was she who spoke first.

I didn't know what they were up to, but it was plainly
necessary to find out. The wet tea-leaves kept the dust from
flying. The day's deposit of fluff and other debris in the
cloth department was considerable, and as the busy brooms
churned it into a noisome brown paste with the tea-leaves,
we stood witnessing an early example of waste-recycling
which had the secondary effect of bringing us together.
(Once or twice since I have seen it done in hospital wards.)
With a lissom movement of easy gallantry, I took her bag
from her.

'May I walk along with you?' I said. I held open the door
to the street. She didn't say I could, but neither did she
hold on to the bag. She went down the steps to the crowded
Cannon Street footway — and then waited. There she stood,
a tiny yet resolute figure among the homeward-hurrying
crowds, and behind her loomed the vast bulk, outlined
against the setting sun, of St. Paul's Cathedral. I can
remember that I could scarcely believe my senses; I was
wondering what to do next. I must have conveyed to her
that I wanted to talk to her, and that a place where we
could talk was the small public garden of the cathedral,
not more than 200 yards away. And I must have won her
assent without difficulty (though it wasn't the way she
wanted to go), for a few minutes later, having exchanged
barely a word more, we were sitting on a bench in St. Paul's
Gardens. There I learned that she had long been aware of
me in the counting-house, and I registered my very first
adolescent shock of romantic excitement. Anything, from
that moment, would have seemed credible.

As we talked, she told me how in the late nineties her
Jewish parents had come to London as refugees from the
Ukraine. And I recalled proudly how my father had often
told me that, during the European anti-Jewish pogroms of
that time, all refugees arriving in this country were given a

leaflet headed 'THE POLICE OF THIS COUNTRY ARE YOUR FRIENDS' (he used to say that many of them, on reading it or being told what it said, used to break down and weep). She was born here in 1902, and I realized that I was listening disappointedly for an interesting foreign accent, to match her dreamily exotic appearance. Instead I was listening to the period voice of the East End cockney, of Bethnal Green, Shoreditch, Spitalfields—and Brick Lane, where she lived. And I call it the period voice because I am quite certain that in the seventy years which have since elapsed the London dialect has undergone a woeful loss of character, and its sharpness and vitality and expressiveness have been smothered as it has spread throughout the entire south-east of England. Not that it was ever anything but ugly and abrasive and, as it were, reactionary; marking perhaps the earlier stages of a resentful working-class struggle against compulsory education, a defiant retreat into nostalgic and contorted Sam Wellerism. It was all right for stand-up comics, for Gus Elen and Marie Lloyd and Edgar Wallace's Kiplingesque British Army. It was strong, not easily mimicked (though everyone seemed to believe it was easy), and strictly local to London—not to the East End but to all the inner suburbs except perhaps Mayfair, St. John's Wood and Bayswater. And what it has become is a flat and featureless pseudo-cockney, frequently sloppy and epicene, which is handed on in schools, nourished on television, bleated from pulpits, and accepted as standard managerial English in business and industry; the ghost of a murdered patois. All attempts to phoneticize it can only flatter it.

Her name was Naomi (her surname I simply couldn't grasp), and she, her parents, and two sisters all toiled as outworkers for the wholesale clothing trade. Their pay varied from threepence to fivepence an hour. They belonged to no trade union and I can see that even now, as then, they would lose their jobs if they did. An employer who had to pay them a 'rate for the job' would see no future in lending them sewing-machines or sending vans round the country collecting their finished work—as many manufacturers did and still do. Shocked and miserable, I had come across

my first evidence that there was slavery in England, and it
led to one of my earliest attacks of high-minded radicalism.

I don't know what poor Naomi thought of me, but her
responses to my questionings had transformed her from an
interestingly pretty girl into a case history. I have no recollection that she ever spoke to me again, or I to her. Probably
she made no further appearances in the counting-house
queue. I suspect that she told her parents about me, perhaps
to account for lateness that evening, and was replaced in the
queue by someone else from the family. But I have to record,
with embarrassment, that having heard her speak and
registered my secret rage that she should have been saddled
for life with this ugliest of all versions of my native tongue,
I immediately lost interest in her as a girl and now recall her
merely as a method of producing unpleasing noises. It was
as if one had dared to follow a likely-looking girl for a mile
and then discovered that she had no face. She none the
less remains a milestone on my road to social maturity.

By this time (1917) I was trying to sell general articles,
paragraphs, sketches, short stories, and 'anniversary'
pieces — the latter being memorial tributes to people and
events in the news ten years earlier, or fifty years or a
thousand; classic unsolicited 'feature page' fill-ups of the
kind which cram the waste-paper baskets of every newspaper
and magazine in the land — and the chances of acceptance
then were far better than they are now. For two shillings I had
bought from a book-barrow in Leather Lane, Holborn, a
tattered copy of *Haydn's Dictionary of Dates and Universal
Information* — 'containing the history of the world to the
autumn of 1895'. (Incidentally from the same barrow a fortnight later I got for two shillings and sixpence the two-
volume sixth edition (1775) of Dr Johnson's *Dictionary*;
and I still have it, splendidly rebound and of no earthly use
except as a booklover's bonus and a source of pedantic and
scholarly whimsy.) Haydn was a mine of information about
great historical events, great frosts, floods and disasters,
great scandals, great fires. It was a kind of *Guinness Book of
What Happened When*. It was the work of a Mr Joseph Haydn,

of whom I know nothing except that he died in 1856 and was not therefore the immortal Joseph Haydn who invented the symphony orchestra and the string quartet; and that he had, to quote his own Preface to the First Edition, 'persuaded himself that this Dictionary of Dates will be received as a useful companion to all biographical works, relating as it does to things as those do to persons'. Dear Mr Haydn, you earned me many a guinea.

My counting-house duties seemed to have been prescribed for a slower pen than mine. I was left with nothing much to do for hours at a time. My allotted place at a long desk (shared by two other clerks) was tucked away in the darkest corner of a partitioned-off room about the size of a squash-court. And because the location of the counting-house was thus seemingly an afterthought, it had oddities like the underside of a staircase which sloped above my head and induced, by involuntary practice, much care and thought in standing up suddenly. In that corner I must have scribbled enough would-be essays and articles to fill a whole shelf of books. What they filled, instead, was an endless series of office waste-paper baskets; and it was in relation to these that I committed a tactical and continuing error of such monumental idiocy that I should be glad, looking back after all these years, to find that my memory had played me false. It hasn't. The waste-paper basket was always half-filled with rejected drafts of letters and memoranda. Everything in that office was handwritten, in what would now be regarded as 'period copperplate', and its spelling and symmetry had to be faultless. To get away with the smallest alteration, a counting-house clerk needed the skill of a highly successful forger. Any unacceptable draft was cancelled with a ruthless diagonal stroke from the pen of Mr Edwards, and it joined the growing daily collection in the w.p.b. The backs of these rejected efforts were, for me, an inexhaustible supply of scribbling paper. If I produced a final effort that seemed to me satisfactory, then I wrote it out at home in copperplate, on lined paper of my own, and sent it off to an editor. But because I lived in the City I was within walking

distance of half the editorial offices in the country and
could save myself the postage costs which confine most
freelance scribes to a reasonable output.

Editors in those days were getting much of their copy
in handwriting. Among the lesser scribblers, the typewriter
was still as much a luxurious gimmick as the word
processor is today. But like a fool I consigned my
abandoned drafts to the office w.p.b; and there, unknown
to me, they were being periodically discovered (and read)
by the formidable Mr Edwards, who sometimes needed to
retrieve a draft letter for consideration. Among them he
must have found an impassioned polemic about the
underpayment of outworkers in the clothing trade.

It was this, I shall always maintain, that got me the sack.
If there were other faults, they were of a kind that was
common to us all. Mine alone was the distinction of
writing angry articles about sweated labour in the clothing
trade and leaving them in the firm's waste-paper baskets.
It was the end of my rag-trade career. The next one, given
my disenchantment with bookkeeping, figures, accounts,
and the unacceptable face of capitalism, may be found
scarcely more credible.

CHAPTER TWO

I
T was January 1919. Effectively, the Kaiser's war had
ended two months before, though we all understood
that 'the Peace' would not be signed for a long time;
and of my minuscule contribution to its 'victorious' climax
I have written elsewhere. Both in Fulham, where I had
ended my school-days, and in the East End, now five
minutes' walk from my home in the City, there lived
thousands of refugees working under the conditions of
poverty, squalor, and exploitation which (I had learned at
school) had long ago been abolished through the efforts of
men like Shaftesbury, Rowntree, and Francis Place. I was
a serious-minded youth, determined to be thought
serious-minded, and much given to long solitary walks,
in the course of which I tried to see myself as the object
of much curiosity and speculation.

I was also becoming, at about this time, a puzzled reader,
or rather a vigorous sampler, of works like Burton's
Anatomy of Melancholy and Marx's *Capital*. To the latter,
much discussed with my elder brother Harold, I owed the
capacity to speak of dialectical materialism as though I
knew what it meant, and a growing habit of informing
others that religion was the Opium of the People.

Three unrelated events remain in my memory from that
year of my adolescence, one of them quaint, the other two
fateful. First, Signor Paderewski, whose Chopin-playing
I had just started collecting on expensive HMV one-sided
gramophone records (one-sided — think of it, and eight and
sixpence a time), astounded everyone by becoming the
premier of his native Poland — in which capacity he lasted
five months. I had heard Paderewski play at the Albert Hall,
and he had so entranced me that I had adopted him as my
own personal genius for being entranced with. Second,
Mussolini established his Fascist party in Italy, and I thought
I understood the exciting new idea of the 'corporate state'

and a parliament representing professions and trades rather than districts with arbitrarily drawn boundaries. It was as easy and plausible, then, to be a fascist as to be a socialist, and as inevitable that the intolerance and ferocity of both ideologies should in due course damn them. Third, in Germany the Nazi party was founded, though not by Hitler. I suppose anyone as politically prescient as Harold and I considered ourselves to be should have felt the sudden shiver run down his spine. No shiver ran down ours. Instead, we had our idiot hopes fixed upon the emergence of communist 'republics' in Germany, Estonia, Budapest, Bavaria, and the Crimea. We had already decided that the teachings of Jesus, though they might have represented a reasonable ideal in AD 30 or thereabouts, were not practicable today. The communist ideal, on the other hand, was attainable, and the Sermon on the Mount could be its written constitution.

So it was with great anxiety that we read daily news items about the holy war now being whipped up against Lenin's Russia, which was the comfortably synecdochic name we now gave to the starry-eyed groups of revolutionaries whom everyone else was calling the Bolsheviks. Bolshevik was a hate-word, used as such by mass-minded Britons who neither knew nor cared that in Russia it was merely another word for majority. No one seemed to mind when, years later, we adored the Bolshoi Ballet though it had precisely the same etymological parents. Even for my brother and myself it happened, ludicrously, to invoke words like 'boll-weevil', 'botulism' ('sausage poisoning', which had killed thousands during the war and was regarded as German), and 'Bolsover', a rather odious character at Greyfriars School in the *Magnet* two-penny weekly which we still gratefully devoured. We wished they weren't so keen on calling themselves Bolsheviks.

And this is the moment, perhaps, to record that what finally disenchanted us both with communism, as eventually also with militant trade unionism, was the discovery that its rank and file were perpetually, chronically, and incurably engrossed in Getting More Money. We had seen communism and the trade unions as the one means by which working men and women throughout the world would destroy the will to make war. 'If you want to wage war,' they would now say to their masters, 'it's all yours, so long as you kill only each other. We've had enough of murdering our fellow workers because they live in other countries and can't speak English. The workers of the world have tumbled to it at last. No longer will they kill each other in order that Capital may survive, nor will they make the arms and munitions with which even you can go on doing it if you want to. You have been warned.'

We heard nothing like this from trade union leaders, though it was the familiar rhetoric (and still is) of countless parlour socialists. We never heard of a trade union (we told ourselves) calling upon its members to strike in defence of a threatened school or home, in opposition to some arbitrary act of state injustice, or in furtherance of anything other than an increase in wages or a decrease of working hours (both of which, of course, we nevertheless liked the sound of). It was probably unjust, but it was the strident voice of disillusionment.

On 1 February 1919 I became an audit clerk with a City firm of chartered accountants. They called themselves J. & A. W. Sully & Co., and I remember them with an affection which is heightened by gratitude for the marvellous toleration with which they retained me on their audit staff despite my chronic inability to understand accountancy. It was a job for which, I recall, I had but two qualifications. One was neat handwriting, acquired by imitating the characteristics I liked best in the handwriting of previous generations. The other was an ability to add up a long column of figures with a speed and accuracy that now seem to me fabulous. (I haven't done this for years, but although the need to do it has now been abolished by pocket calculators, I can still outstrip the check-out machines, or anyway their operators, in the supermarkets where I do my shopping.)

I have an absurd mental picture of my personal appearance at that time which, until quite recently, nothing would have induced me to recall, still less to reveal to others; and which helps further to illustrate the indulgence of my employers. I am thinking of the clothes I went about in, and their possible reflection of something in my character, then or now, which somebody else will have to explain. I wore a bowler hat, size 7½ (in these hatless days nobody will know, but that was an enormous bowler), which in addition to being so big was old and losing its shape, so that it would have looked like a large pudding on a rather flexible plate, were it not that its colour had become a kind of light black threatened by green. I commonly wore a very loose greenish tweed sports coat with (needless) leather elbows, and I was inordinately proud of a pair of cavalry officer's high-ankled boots, such as you could then buy in army surplus stores. In case all this was by itself insufficiently striking, I carried everywhere a black silver-knobbed swagger cane, usually under the arm like a bellicose sergeant-major. I found the recollection of all this both useful and corrective when, in due course, I had a son who conformed to the mores of his even more adventurous time by wearing a huge poncho (a blanket with a hole for his head) and a stetson hat. 'Control yourself', I thought: 'at his age you looked twice as funny.' And I know that his poncho period was much briefer than my own mixture of Stan Laurel and Harry Tate.

This was, I now see, a partial consequence of having no leisure companions. I lived over a City of London police station, whose neighbours were wholesale furriers, cloth warehousemen, and export merchants, and their premises were all as empty in the evenings and at weekends as were the deserted streets in which they bleakly propped each other up. My father, as the resident Chief Inspector of one of the four divisions of the City of London Police, was required (just as though we were in the depths of the country) to 'live over his shop'. My two brothers and I, all teenagers, regarded him with the deepest affection and a certain amount of fear, as indeed did most of the men under his command. My mother accorded him the same affection, but in her case the fear was easily vanquished by amusement. On the day in 1916 when we arrived at this odd but rather exciting new home (we had come from Fulham and were some hours ahead of the furniture van bringing along all we jointly possessed), he took us on an echoing tour of inspection through the empty rooms — huge, lofty, institutional, and solid-looking. He stopped and grouped us at the kitchen window, which for some reason was covered outside by a massive metal grille in the shape of the City coat of arms, incorporating the words 'Domine Dirige Nos.' 'And what does *that* mean, on a kitchen window?' asked Mother. 'God help us', he said earnestly, and it was as if the Corporation of London, our solicitous new hosts, had thought of everything. A bizarre version of a tired old joke, but Mother decided to join in the merriment and bide her time. Then we were bidden to look across the narrow lane (College Hill) at the beautiful church of St. Michael Paternoster Royal; which, or some of which, had stood there since the year 1219. This, said Father, was where Dick Whittington was buried, together with his fabulous cat. Four times Lord Mayor of London, he had restored the church in 1409, and it was destroyed in the Great Fire of 1666, his grave being among the relics to survive. A stone effigy of his cat was let into the wall when Sir Christopher Wren was rebuilding in 1694. (I think we disbelieved this cat story, even though a bas-relief cat is still to be seen in the wall. Someone must have put it there, but the spirit of Disneyland may be older than we suppose.) We discovered later that the Church of St. Michael acquired the subtitle Paternoster Royal because the thirteenth-century wine merchants in the neighbourhood (Whittington's executors) lived in an adjacent row of houses called Royale Lane, a corruption of Reole near Bordeaux, the source of their imported wines; and also because their sybaritic way of life prompted the thought, in a moment of anxiety, that they should establish a College of Priests from which prayers could be sent up for

their souls. They called it Whittington College and, until
the Reformation, there it stood on College Hill.

But back now to 1919. I was earning, or anyway being
paid, thirty-five shillings a week, and while this was twice
the wage I had been deemed worthy of by Messrs Spreckley
White & Lewis it left me almost dependent on my long-
suffering parents for clothes. My father's notion of what
was suitable clothing for a young City clerk was so bizarre
that nothing I could have worn could, I am persuaded, have
disturbed him. My mother's was expressed in a tight little
smile.

The thirty-five shillings a week as a junior audit clerk
seemed likely to remain unchanged for a very long time.
This is not to say that my employers were a mean lot, for
they emphatically were not; but there had not yet
developed the world-wide system by which everyone gets
a rise every year whether he is worth it or not, and whether
the firm is making or losing money, and all the prices
go up to keep pace with the wages bill. Inflation had
not yet been officially adopted as a kind of game in
which everyone, reverting to childhood, tried all day
to jump on his own shadow. We had yet to see the collapse
of Weimar Germany's economy, and to witness the new
system under which you bought a tin of beans with a
piano. But there was poverty even in the gentlemanly
profession of accountancy, as the following incident will
illustrate.

One of my first audit jobs was a tour of the retail
branches of a dairy company called Welfords Ltd., whose
office was in Maida Vale and whose shops were fronted
with red and white tiles and shiny grey paint. I was under
the temporary tutelage of a senior audit clerk called Mr
Tootal. He was fresh from six years as an able seaman in
the Royal Navy and, I was to learn, had had a pretty terrible
war—of the kind unforgettably portrayed, many years
later, by Nicholas Monsarrat in *The Cruel Sea*. He was then
about 40, had a white, hawk-like face, an almost bald head,
a rolling walk (you would have put him down as a
merchant seaman on shore-leave), and a pipe which needed

relighting every forty-five seconds. (I think this was because he had formed the habit, perhaps in the Navy, of deeply inhaling every puff, and after half a dozen of these he had to put the pipe down while he recovered.) He also had, and certainly needed, a priceless sense of humour. I remember asking him one morning whether the chairman of Welfords was likely to look in upon us one day, for I knew that there were difficult questions he needed to raise at 'top level' and they were unlikely to be welcome. The chairman's attitude to audit clerks (a loveless brood anyway) had sustained the legend that he had been known to eat several before breakfast. Mr Tootal inhaled several puffs and expelled them through his nose. 'I have grave hopes', he said at last.

His salary was four pounds ten shillings a week, and he had two children. On our first day at a Welford's dairy shop (we merely 'sampled' the books at the branch shops), after a morning's unremittingly conscientious book-ticking, he announced that it was lunch-time and that he would be going to the nearest Lockhart's for a snack that probably wouldn't appeal much to me. The only Lockhart I had ever known anything about was the son-in-law of Sir Walter Scott, who wrote an unreadable biography of Robbie Burns. Lockhart's cookshops, I now discovered, were a chain of working-men's caffs, much invoked in lower middle-class circles as a pathetic example of even lower middle-class eating habits. In the same grey area of peasant catering were places like the John Pearce Dining-Rooms, where the tables had marble tops with wrought iron supports (like the ones on our mangle at home), and the solitary waiter was always a shuffling fat man in an off-white apron; and the individual 'good pull-up for carmen', the virtual disappearance of which must, I now realize, date from the supersession of the horse-drawn van which, in those days, crowded every central London street. The carman has also vanished from many of today's dictionaries (the *Concise Oxford* and *Longman's*, for example, know him not); and what he drove was not what we call a car, but a four-wheeled wagon hauled about our urban streets by splendid horses with

great tufted fetlocks. The pull-up, still recognized by
the *Concise Oxford* but not, for example, by *Longman*
or *Collins*, often had high back-to-back settles for its
patrons, bare hardwood tables and a much-favoured dish
known as 'baby's 'ead and two veg' (the baby's head being
a steak-and-kidney dumpling, and very good it usually
was).

Mr Tootal pushed open the door of Lockhart's Men's
Dining-Room and preceded me into the steam and fug.
There were two possible seats at one of the crowded settles,
though you needed a practised eye to see them as they had
been pre-emptively occupied by other patrons spreading
themselves out as their previous occupants left. A youth
in a black apron detached himself from the shop counter,
stood before us, and tilted his head in an attitude of
perfunctory enquiry. 'Bread roll, cheese, and cocoa', said
Mr Tootal doggedly. The youth looked at me. 'Same again',
I said, and off he went. 'Look, you don't have to have the
same as me', said Mr Tootal. 'I have what I can afford.'
He explained that the bread, cheese, and cocoa gave him
the maximum nourishment for fivepence and that it was
what he always had. Always? Well, Saturdays and Sundays
at home he made up for it. He made no secret of his
dilemma. He would much prefer to eat on his own, but
if I insisted on being with him (and he could hardly turn
me adrift or give me the slip) I would have to accept the
fact that married senior audit clerks were constrained by
their salaries to lunching on bread and cheese and cocoa.
I ventured the view that it would be even cheaper to bring
his bread and cheese from home, an easily packed lunch
at less than half the cost. And where would he eat it, he
demanded? (It was midwinter.) For fivepence he got a seat
in the warm, a hot drink, and room to read his book. I was
convinced. Did he, I asked awkwardly, want to read now?
Yes, but he wouldn't while I was with him. Ostentatiously,
I opened a much-folded copy of the *New Statesman*, about
three weeks old and bequeathed to me by my brother and
mentor. Without a glance at it, he took out a pocket edition
of *The Long Trick*, by Bartimeus—which I *did* glance at

with interest because I had read it during the war. (I wonder if anyone now remembers that nerve-twisting naval story of the Kaiser's war, a blueprint for an even better book of thirty years later, J. P. W. Mallalieu's *Very Ordinary Seaman*?)

I stuck with the bread and cheese and cocoa for four days (not always in the same café, but always in a Lockhart's somewhere); and at last I broke new ground with sausage and mash (eightpence). Mr Tootal seemed not to notice. I grew attached to Mr Tootal. He had integrity without priggishness, he believed in doing a fair day's work, and he laughed at my jokes. A stranger to accountancy when the war ended, he had enrolled at a London County Council evening institute to study bookkeeping and accounts, while working in the daytime as an assistant in a hardware shop. He must have been one of the few who completed those LCC courses, embarked upon with such resolution in September every year and usually abandoned after the first trying month or so. He comes no more into my story except as an exemplar, never to be forgotten, of what I still resolutely regarded as 'the dignity of labour'. I still think that it was the first time I had seen it in operation.

And while I'm in 1919 I want to record what seems to me an odd piece of musical history, in which a prominent part was played by two pretty girls and which is therefore (such was my timorous attitude to all girls, pretty or not) etched in authenticity. It was in the London office of J. & A. W. Sully & Co., 19–21 Queen Victoria Street, that I was forced into my first close acquaintance with girls. In the 'general office', which was in fact a kind of reception-cum-ante-room, there worked two very bright teenaged typists, who seemed to be eternally typing draft balance sheets on enormously long typewriter carriages. They were called Miss Poulter and Miss Eyles. No one called them by their first names, though among the junior clerks (and a few of the less austere seniors) they answered to the nicknames Polly and Fanny. I came to like them both immensely, unaware that (as these creatures commonly do) they were training me, bringing me out, and deriving immense private amusement from it. I think Miss Eyles was also triumphantly aware that in her case my liking was earning itself a stronger name; which, however, tapered off when I left the firm.

One morning in 1919 these two girls and I discovered that our musical fancy had just been caught by the dance tune which today is called 'In The Mood'. (It certainly wasn't then.) Today every jazz expert, including all the books of reference, will tell you that 'In the Mood' was composed and first published in 1938 by Joe Garland, an American saxophonist, and first recorded in that year by the Edgar Hayes band. A slightly different arrangement, they add, was published and recorded in the following year by Glen Miller. But back in 1919 those two girls and I had heard it played by cinema orchestras — which in those days filled in the gap between the two big films with a spotlit performance on the stage, for which they engaged expensive soloists and augmented their other ranks; and Fanny, at least, had begun hearing it in dance-halls. I clearly remember teaching them both its catchy time-beat and watching them tap it out with pencils, and with growing skill, on their desks. It must have been what the jazzmen today call a 'riff' (an 'ostinato played over changing harmonies') which began life as a kind of folk-tune, of unknown authorship. There is no surer aid to the placing of a date or the recollection of a tune than to recall exactly when the two first coincided. For me, 'In The Mood' belongs with Ibáñez's *Four Horsemen of the Apocalypse*, Arthur Mee's *Children's Newspaper* (for whose third issue I wrote a small article), and André Messager's suite *Monsieur Beaucaire*, which the cinema orchestras liked playing in the intervals and which the Stoll Picture Theatre orchestra seemed to play all the time. None of these can enter my mind at any time without the others.

There were three recreational events wherein, during that extraordinary year 1919, I found myself involved to an extent which, as things turned out, took a firm hold on my life. Two of them were new books, each introduced to me by someone I met in the course of my accountancy work (I liked calling it this, though it entailed nothing cleverer than making ticks in ledgers, cash-books, journals and bank passbooks.) My employers' clients included what must have been a high proportion of religious and philanthropic societies, among them the Wesleyan Methodist Missionary Society (in Bishopsgate), the British and Foreign Bible Society (Queen Victoria Street), and the Shaftesbury Homes and Arethusa Training Ship (High Holborn). Each of these three places remains photographically in my mind for special reasons of its own. May I introduce you to the Wesleyan Missionaries?

The Wesleyan Methodist Missionary Society's rather splendid premises in Bishopsgate always seemed to me an affront to the principle of 'support by voluntary contributions'. They conveyed the impression, just as banks and insurance companies more understandably and designedly do, of having Too Much Money. Inevitably they made me think of the tiny cloth bags, with draw-string tops, in which my childhood buddies and I had reluctantly dropped the pennies with which we were weekly dispatched to our Methodist Sunday school. I supposed that wealthy Wesleyans left money in their wills for the Methodist missionary work, and that there were other sources of benevolence. But an undue pro-portion of it all seemed to me to go on the administration by which the Word was being spread among the heathen. It must have been one of the functions of my employers to keep a censorious eye on this proportion, but at my level of involvement I never heard of any queries being raised. I have since recognized one of the dilemmas confronting such organizations. If they conduct their world headquarters business in tin huts, I now tell myself, or in converted corner pubs, derelict chapels, or seedy Victorian villas (in all of which I have sat on various pressure-group committees), supporters may well feel less confident about the effective handling of their donations and subscriptions. Presenting an appearance involves 'Keeping up Appearances'.

But another important consequence for me was that the Methodists' boardroom in the Bishopsgate headquarters contained a beautiful little two-manual organ—I never knew why, but supposed that board meetings perhaps ended, or even began, with one or two hymns. Anyway, for half an hour at the end of each day during the twice-yearly visits in which I would spend a whole week putting ticks in the Wesleyans' beautifully kept account books, I was allowed to practise on this organ. And then, when it was time for me to go home, there would be a brief chat with the resident caretaker, Mr Steadman, who (it turned out) as well as being a Methodist lay preacher was an ardent socialist and spent his every spare penny on books. He was also one of the most companionable people I have ever known and a man from whom (I often remind myself) I learned the first rudiments of conversation and the art of listening—which, none the less, I have never been very good at.

One day in the autumn of 1919 he showed me his latest acquisition, a compendium of the articles and essays then flowing from the neatly epigrammatical pen of Dean Inge of St. Paul's. Its title, fully justified by its contents, was *Outspoken Essays*. To my great surprise and delight, Mr Steadman offered to lend it to me. I don't doubt that I had been enacting, for his benefit, my current role of discriminating and sophisticated young reader, the insecure basis of which must have been laughably apparent to everyone but myself. But I found the book absorbing, and soon afterwards bought a copy of my own. Its original sources, the *Edinburgh Review*, the *Hibbert Journal*, and the *Quarterly Review*, were mere names to me. Its two main essays (as I saw them), 'Cardinal Newman' and 'Survival and Immortality', I have read dozens of times in these past sixty years, each time with slightly increased admiration and much increased perplexity. They have for me the quality which, as in reading metaphysical poetry, one knows to conceal some vital but eternally elusive truth; and one accordingly goes on hunting for it. Dean Inge, whom I was to meet occasionally and briefly in later years, was known widely as the Gloomy Dean because he affected to foresee, and seemed likely to welcome, the end of democracy. But he seems to me, still, one of the great thinkers of our time. For many years he wrote a brilliant weekly article in the *Evening Standard*, always bristling with quotations and always illuminating something in the week's news with a radiance, sometimes benign but more often acerbic, of wit, simulated surprise, and profound scholarship. Once at a public dinner for journalists A. P. Herbert, introducing him as the speaker, described him as 'not merely a pillar of the Church but a couple of columns in the *Evening Standard*'. *Outspoken Essays* is one of the few among my many books that I can always find within seconds and one of the few rereadable books which, in my old age, will never send me to sleep. The other literary event was Jeeves. Dr Inge and P. G. Wodehouse would have been an oddly assorted couple to meet in one memorable year, but in fact they were not an assorted couple at all. They erupted like simultaneous volcanoes in my reading life.

I was working at the British and Foreign Bible Society in Queen Victoria Street, an even more splendid building than that of the Methodists in Bishopsgate, a place of broad curving marble staircases with mahogany and brass handrails, of lofty and stately rooms stocked with heavily impressive furniture. In the Accounts Department was a Mr Scaife, to whom I used to report on the first day of an audit. He was always friendly but solemn, and he wore a lapel badge which I now believe to have proclaimed him a Rotarian though he never told me what it meant, and I never liked to ask him in case it was something like the Brotherhood of Cheery Sparrows. (I have an irrational hatred of lapel buttons, will never wear my name-card at conferences and conventions, and contemplate men who wear service medal ribbons on their waistcoats as if they and I belonged to separate biological species.) Mr Scaife was an authority on P. G. Wodehouse, with whose enchantingly idiotic phrases his conversation was liberally sprinkled—without attribution.

He told me that I would be unable to work in the auditors' accustomed room, a small committee room, because for the time being the Secretary was using it. And the Secretary, who was a very large man, fitted into my usual chair 'as if it had been built round him by someone who knew that they were wearing armchairs tight round the hips that year'. I said at once 'That's Wodehouse', for I had seen it quoted somewhere, probably in a book review; and sure enough it was *My Man Jeeves*, which had just been published and had allowed a barely deserving public to meet this shimmering, immortal valet for the first time. Mr Scaife and I had discovered a harmony that made us almost blood-brothers. Thus introduced, I believe I can safely say that I never looked back.

Before I leave Mr Scaife and Jeeves and the B&FBS (the strange device that was emblazoned in gilt lettering on the leather covers of all its account books), I have to recall that he was the last man but one whom I ever saw writing with a quill pen. The last one was Sir Henry Dickens, KC, Common Serjeant at the Old Bailey in the 1930s, who maddened everyone in Court No. 3 by using an extra large, ultra squeaky and slow-moving quill with which to make his judge's notes during every trial. A much-loved man, dear old Sir Henry Dickens, then in his eighties; but the quill pen was beloved only by visiting antiquarians and Americans, who adored it. Mr Scaife was a real penman. His handwriting, which may still, I suppose, be open to reverent inspection at the Queen Victoria Street offices of what is now more simply called The Bible Society, was to me of an importance second only to Jeeves; for I assiduously copied it — and I dare to think that I was soon doing it quite well.

There are people who attribute the disappearance of handwriting (for it is all but dead) to the arrival of the ballpoint pen. Older grumblers blame the fountain-pen. I can report that as late as 1921 we clerks were not allowed to use fountain-pens. They took the character out of writing, we were told. They also leaked and made a mess of books, papers, fingers, clothes, and handbags. You could pay £25 for a fountain-pen, and you could get one for a shilling (it was called a 'Blackbird'). The posh one was 'self-filling', which meant that you filled it yourself. You replenished its internal bladder with ink by raising a little lever (which normally rested along the side of the pen) with your fingernail, thus closing the bladder and expelling all the air. You then submerged the nib in a bottle of ink, sometimes knocking the whole thing over, and by pressing the little lever back into place you slowly opened the bladder and sucked the ink into it. What, by comparison, was not self-filling was the kind of pen which came with a little glass dropper, a kind of syringe topped with a depressible rubber bulb. The top halves of such pens screwed off so that the fresh ink could be squirted in. Lack of squirting experience led to many mishaps.

No employer I worked for would countenance any of this. Pens were intended to renew their ink by being dipped into little pots, ink-wells; but sometimes the pots were embedded in large containers with a base as big as a dinner-plate, whose purpose was to reduce the danger of being knocked over. We were all dippers. (I still know dippers, though I sometimes wonder where they manage to find their ink-wells when they have the misfortune to break or lose them.) But at the risk of sounding like a growling reactionary I shall maintain that the dippers were always better writers than the wielders of fountain-pens, even of those exquisitely refined things which in recent years have been advertised as writing instruments . . . and as I write this, the newspapers have just published (22 September 1984) photographs of the infant Prince Henry's birth certificate, on which the handwriting is totally illegible; and people have been writing to the editors asking what on earth has happened to both loyalty and calligraphy. The loyalty was much in evidence for other reasons and in other ways, but the calligraphy had gone . . . for ever? Not yet, I believe. There is a Society of Scribes and Illuminators and there is a Society for Italic Handwriting, and between them they may yet save one of the bench-marks of civilization.

Then came the third and equally seminal event in this *annus mirabilis*. It took place at the offices of the Shaftesbury Homes and Arethusa Training Ship in High Holborn, then known as Fordham House. For some reason which I forget, but probably because Fordham House was the home of about a dozen orphaned or homeless boys who were destined for a seafaring life when they were old enough, the biggest room on the ground floor at Fordham House contained a full-sized billiard-table, probably a gift from one of the society's benefactors. It was always kept in superb condition. The senior audit clerk who was my mentor at this audit was not only a good companion (and a good accountant) but also an accomplished billiards player. His name was Shackleford. I have forgotten his first name, if indeed I ever knew it. First names were not then the thing, and we all knew him as Shack. And it was on that table, after working hours, that Shack undertook my education in the only game which, as it turned out, I was ever to be any good at.

The process was later taken up by some of the policemen living in the 'section house' (i.e. barracks) to which my father's quarters were a kind of appendage; none of whom, I secretly decided in due course, had really discovered much about the game but all of whom played it with gusto, crashing shots, billiard-balls leaping in terror on to the floor and cue-tips flying off into space. Shack had a graceful, almost terpsichorean style of play and knew pretty nearly (but not quite) all there was to know about the complicated behaviour of a billiard-ball which is rolling in one direction and spinning in another. The spell of the game is still upon me. I do not understand how people play it with spectacles on, but I see them doing it on television and suppose that I too readily gave up trying. I shall not now resume. But I can watch the young snooker millionaires of today with a knowing eye and with an envy which, to my own recurring astonishment, concerns their skill and not their millions.

I am about to leave 1919. Before I go I want to recall not only that it was on 11 November of that year that the two minutes' Armistice silence was first observed in Britain, but that I was probably among the first Britons to observe it in shirt-sleeves in a crowded street. The previous day I had been packed off to Reading, and had just begun a fortnight's book-ticking at the biscuit factory of H. O. Serpell & Son. (They always gave each of the audit clerks, at the end of the annual fortnight, a huge tin of Serpell biscuits, a crammed cubic foot of assorted goodies. I don't know why they did this, and fought back any suspicions because both Serpells and my employers seemed always, to me, *sans peur et sans rapproche*.) During the morning of 11 November 1919 I had nipped out to buy a bottle of aspirins for my senior, who was suffering from a hangover he had recklessly (but characteristically) ensured for himself in the hotel bar the night before. Because I thought my quest would be a brief one I didn't bother about a jacket — we always worked in shirt-sleeves whatever the time of year. Outside, it was cold, blustery, and wet, and I saw no sign of any shop in which you would expect to find aspirins. Instead of turning back to get a jacket, I hurried on and on, dimly aware that I was probably getting lost and sharply aware that I was certainly getting cold.

Suddenly I noticed that everyone within sight was standing stock still and that an unearthly silence was descending upon us all. I remembered then that it was Armistice Day and realized that the long-discussed two minutes' silence was upon us. It had begun no doubt with the firing of rockets (we had called them 'maroons' throughout the war, when they were used as an air raid warning); but I didn't hear them that day in Reading — their bangs must have been drowned by passing traffic noises. As the engines were shut off in all the cars, vans, and buses, as all conversation stopped, as every kind of industrial and domestic machinery sank into silence, the effect was almost frightening, as of a vast echo dying away into a cosmic distance and leaving us all ossified for ever. I thought of Conan Doyle's story *The Poison Belt*, in which the earth passes through a vast formation of toxic space-dust. Those two minutes, during which we were intended to be thinking about war and peace, were the longest two minutes I have ever known, including all the periods spent outside headmasters' studies; and my own mind was entirely absorbed, as it has always been on crowded occasions, in the contemplation of people's observance of each other.

For example, one man in my line of vision, arranging his belongings so as to begin the silence in comfort, dropped his umbrella. The volume of sound was astonishing, as if a microphone had been planted there to pick up the effect. All eyes were upon him as he stooped to regain his umbrella. Half-way down he became aware of them, and, it seemed, realized his awful prominence. He remained half bent for some moments, frozen by his wretched isolation. And then very slowly, almost imperceptibly, he straightened himself so as to look like the rest of us. The umbrella observed the silence from where it had fallen. The silence seemed to isolate each of us, like little Lowry figures on our crowded canvas. Now and then a cart-horse shook its harness vigorously, a loud jangle that recalled to my mind Tolstoy's tense account of the eve of Borodino, as the cavalry waited throughout that long night of *War and Peace* . And somewhere in the distance a small dog was barking incessantly . . . until a deafening bang overhead brought us all to life again.

Against all this mass organized solemnity, I have completely forgotten whether I ever got the aspirins, and whether my senior's hangover had impeded his own response to a ceremony which was to lapidify the entire nation for those two minutes every year, until the practice was quietly dropped in 1940, to survive only as a feature of Armistice Sunday church services. But I believe that everyone's reaction, on that first of all Armistice silences, was much the same as mine, and was never repeated in its subsequent years.

As I left 1919, I was soon to say goodbye to the tick-tick-ticking which I had liked to call accountancy. And I can remember how the tick had been gradually assuming the

status of an imprint on the brain, an indelible mental image
as well as a professional tool and trade mark. (To this day,
when I have spent some hours weeding a garden, as I close
my eyes in bed I see the spread-out leaves of dandelions
and daisies like a wallpaper pattern. They are there
for hours. The doctors call them hypnagogic images.
Similarly, as an audit clerk I saw formations of ticks as
I waited for sleep.) Why did we, why do we, call it a tick,
this tiny certification of accuracy or of approved location,
which I was now giving up as another man might
relinquish a spade, a handsaw, a Stillson wrench or a
paintbrush? I once listened to a passionate dispute between
two of my seniors, a factual and etymological argument,
as to what was a tick and what was not. One of them was
saying, in effect (as the *Oxford English Dictionary* says
today) that a tick was 'formed by two small strokes at an
acute angle'. The other man, a budding partner in the firm
and indeed a son of the principal, thought that every
member of the staff should use a distinctive tick, so that
ticking errors could be attributed to their perpetrators. He
himself used a Greek 'E', which was much scorned by
everyone else as a symbol of élitism. Its obvious defect was
that you couldn't always tell which line it was supposed
to be standing on. The *OED* man maintained, rightly I
suppose, that the whole purpose of the tick was that it
should be a kind of directional arrow, having an apex or
point so that there could be no doubt where it stood or
to what it was a pointer. They nearly came to blows, and
the embryo journalist in me was enchanted by a possible
story about two men fighting over a tick. Well, it had taken
little more to precipitate terrible wars, hadn't it? And
during Hitler's war there came one of the great Ticks of
history. It is recorded that when Churchill and Stalin
met in Moscow on 9 October 1944, and had got as far as
dividing up the Balkans, Churchill made a sudden
proposition. 'How would it do', he said, 'for you to have
90 per cent predominance in Rumania, for us to have 90
per cent in Greece, and go 50–50 in Jugoslavia?' He pushed
the paper on which he had written these figures towards

the Soviet leader. Stalin 'took his blue pencil and made a large tick on it,' wrote Churchill in his memoirs, 'and the post-war fate of millions was sealed'.

But if it happened today, I could help them. I could show them that the tick started life, in England *circa* 1840, as a quotation mark, forerunner of the inverted comma. Then it became a mercantile indication that the item ticked had been looked at, compared with something, and found good. By the time it got to America it had been debased as a 'dot or dash' (*Funk & Wagnall*, *Webster*), or 'a light mark' (*Heritage*). Today, *Collins* even gives you a little drawing (✓) showing a dawning affinity with the square root sign. None of them seems to know its etymology, or even to think it worthwhile to say 'etym. doubtful'. Tick of unknown origin, farewell. I leave you without regret.

CHAPTER THREE

BUT not before I have recorded my gratitude to one of the oddest eccentrics I have ever known (I believe we should all be grateful to eccentrics anyway), a man who, because he lived on a different mental plateau from the rest of us, would neither have known nor cared what kind of impression he was making upon me. It was in fact an impression, in two important respects, which was profound and lifelong. If I now have another fifty years to live, which seems improbable, I shall not forget him. His name was Bert Trotman, and he was the son of the managing director at Welfords Dairies Ltd, doing a rather simple clerical job which seemed to our auditors' eyes to have been specially created for him. When I met him he was about 38, sandy-haired, with eyebrows and eyelashes that were nearly white. He was almost a hunchback. The left side of his face was permanently distorted and pulled his mouth up into a kind of hypotenuse. I understood that he was a 'seven months' child', had not been expected to live, and had already since the age of 20 had three strokes. He was unmarried. To me, though I never said so to anyone (I grew rather fond of him) he was like a cross between Barnaby Rudge and J. D. Beresford's Hamdenshire Wonder. He was uncannily and disturbingly intelligent and perceptive, and not a comfortable companion.

The two new faculties with which he permanently infected me, and I use the word 'infected' deliberately, were an intense love of Liszt, Wagner, and Sibelius, and a secret and always shamefaced readiness to accept the likely existence (it didn't last) of an occult world in which there were ghosts, poltergeists, and clairvoyance. (I don't remember that there was said, at that time, to be any spoon-bending.) One evening in the Maida Vale offices, when I had stayed late in the vain pursuit of some elusive figure which had been unbalancing the accounts, he took

me out for comfort to a nearby pub, where we intended
to restore my good spirits and self-esteem. We sat in a
corner and talked occultism in low voices. I remember
feeling half reckless, half convinced, and wholly excited.
I knew I was in the presence of some spiritual aberration
which I should never understand; and that Bert Trotman,
though possibly half mad, was entirely and frighteningly
matter-of-fact. And that evening I acquired from him my
one and only ghost story, which has for me remained to
this day credible and unexplained. I ask leave to tell it here
for the first time, exactly as I heard it.

He was on a boating holiday near Ipswich, in company
with an older man, a senior member of the firm called Mr
Mayhew, who had a weekend place near Bramford. Mr
Mayhew was in fact a displaced company chairman whose
dairy had been swallowed up by Welfords some years
before, and he was doing a nondescript job in the head office
until he reached retiring time. One evening in an Ipswich
boatbuilder's shed, much frequented by the locals of the
waterside, they heard a group talking about a recent failure
to solve the 'haunted house' mystery which had long
condemned to dereliction a one-time hotel at Bramford.
No man, they were saying, would go into that building
after dark for fear of its dreadful and unknown dangers.
No one seemed to know exactly what these were. It was
known that early one morning twenty years before, when
it had already been empty for years, a murdered man had
been found by the caretaker, in one of its first-floor
bedrooms. His body was tied or strapped to a Windsor
rocking-chair in the centre of the otherwise empty room,
and it bore no signs whatsoever of any cause of death. The
caretaker had called a passing milk-man making his early
morning round, and together they tried to revive the man.
Failing in this they went out to call the police. When the
police arrived the body had gone — but *the chair was still
rocking*. No such body was ever found. Since then the keys
of the house had passed from one estate agent to another,
all of them declining to do more than instruct possible
purchasers as to its whereabouts. For some years the owner

had been offering a £100 reward to anyone who would go into the place at night, find out what if anything was wrong, and expose the absurdity of the whole story. Whatever was wrong, it seemed, was to be discovered only at night. He resolutely refused to have the place demolished, convinced that what needed demolition was the inhibiting ghost story, which kept on acquiring fresh horrors as the years went by. Trotman and Mayhew decided to earn the £100.

Three nights later they borrowed mooring-lamps from the longshoremen and set off on foot for Bramford with the keys of the house, accompanied by Mr Mayhew's bulldog. The house, almost hidden in giant shrubs, was filthy and cobwebbed, its doors all creaked as haunted house doors should creak, and of course as soon as they were inside the dreaded room their lamps went out. Then, standing in the dark, by this time rather shaken, they heard the dog running round the room and panting as it continually collided with the wainscot. After a few minutes it stopped, and there was silence. At last Trotman got his lamp alight again, to find that the dog was dead, with no mark of injury upon it. In the middle of the bare floor was a large Windsor rocking-chair.

It was rocking, slowly, and without a sound.

They got out as quickly as their unsteady legs would take them. They ran noisily down the echoing stairs, slammed and locked the front door, and had hurried in perplexed silence for about a mile before they suddenly remembered the dog. Were they sure it was dead? Could they, even so, leave its corpse in the house, to become a part of the legend? *Perhaps to disappear?* Reluctantly, each shamed by the other, they went slowly back. They climbed the stairs with leaden limbs, and pushed open the creaking door of The Room. The dog still lay motionless. It was dead. Mr Mayhew grabbed it convulsively, and turned to go. Then they saw that the chair was still rocking, but rather more than when they had left it fifteen minutes earlier. Their second exit, more resolute even than the first one, took up less of their time. They never went back.

All of which is normal enough, once you have left
the usual sort of normality behind. It's what follows that
will be found hard to believe. And of course it is my own
lonely certainty of it which, for me, isolates the story
as incapable of rational explanation. Many years later, it
must have been about 1941, I met a much aged Mr Mayhew
at a London conference organized by the Ministry of Home
Security to work out a scheme for the protection of
domestic animals during and after air raids. He remembered me, or said he did. I took the opportunity to test his
memory (and Bert Trotman's accuracy) about the haunted
Bramford hotel, which I had never forgotten. Without
hesitation he gave me an earnest account of it, corroborating
Trotman in every single detail except in saying that the
dog was a Boston terrier and not a bulldog. (I should have
thought them easy enough to distinguish.) I have retained
no theories about the affair. I have retained only a sombre
little corner of the mind which offers uneasy lodgement
for the occult, and a shifty but ineradicable distaste for
rocking-chairs.

It was Bert Trotman whose parents owned a freehold box
at the Albert Hall. I think they may have inherited it, for
it seemed to mean nothing to them and they never used
it. By long custom it had become almost his prescrip-
tive property. Bert Trotman was intensely — almost
grotesquely — musical, an accomplished organist (I never
heard him at the piano), and in frequent demand for church
services. He played without music: he knew by heart every
tune in the church hymnals and a great deal of Widor,
Pachelbel, Haydn, and the Bachs (of whom his favourite
was C.P.E.). As soon as he discovered my own response
to music he began to take me to Albert Hall concerts and
recitals. I sat in the undreamed-of splendour of the freehold
box and (mostly during the last two years of the Kaiser's
war) heard many of the great musicians of the day. They
included Fritz Kreisler, Jascha Heifetz, Mischa Elman,
Rafael Kubelik, Vladimir de Pachmann, Sergei Rachmaninov,
Lotte Lehman, Eva Turner, Frederick Lamond, Albert

Sammons, William Murdoch, Percy Grainger, and Pablo
Casals (I enjoy rolling off their names, as a kind of tribute
to the memory of Bert Trotman. Anyone bored by music
would have been bored by him. In such company, he could
have bored for England.) Sir Landon Ronald was conducting
his famous long series of Sunday afternoon concerts. To
most of them I went alone, Trotman being usually
occupied elsewhere. And I was slightly ashamed to find
that, although the enjoyment of music is normally a
gregarious thing, I was much more at ease when he wasn't
there. His intensity was almost insane, his propinquity
even in a private box acutely embarrassing. I think I couldn't
have sat beside him in the public part of the hall.

But he had sealed my fate as an addict of all the great
classical composers and equipped me with the apparatus
for eventually appreciating Stravinsky, Shostakovich,
Messiaen and Britten. He had two blind spots, as
inexplicable as Bernard Levin's indifference to Verdi: he
could stand neither Berlioz nor Delius. I find that totally
bewildering. I wonder what he would think today of
Stockhausen, Webern, Cage, and even Peter Maxwell
Davies; but I believe I know.

It was, in the oddest way, a romantic musicality that
played a large part in inclining me towards the police
service; a wish, in fact, to emulate my father, who had
been a fine flautist and had habituated me to the company
of musicians, members of many bands and orchestras.
Accordingly I knew all the members of the City of London
Police band, which in those days was the equivalent of any
band in the Brigade of Guards — though it was many years
since he had, on promotion, reluctantly ceased to be a
member. Many of the bandsmen were musicians from line
regiments. As much as I could, and more than had the full
approval of my father, I went with them everywhere. I
often asked them anxiously if I was a nuisance or an
embarrassment to them, but they were a tolerant lot, made
me welcome, and almost I think adopted me as a mascot.
I expect it to seem odd to anyone more critically musical
than I; and it is a further oddity, no doubt, that I have

always enjoyed rehearsals more than public performances, delighting not only in the backstage shirt-sleeved informality which enabled me to feel part of the proceedings, but also in the gradual dovetailing of the various instrumental parts (from which, of course, you can learn so much). I had discovered in childhood that what I used to call 'important music' was seldom to be enjoyed, like popular melodies, at first hearing, or second, or third. You had to work at it, and the rewards were immense. I never passed through any stage in which, as Noel Coward found, *Pelléas et Mélisande* sounded like *Parsifal* without the jokes. I came to love them both and have remained faithful.

So in September 1921 I found myself a probationer constable in the City of London Police. That is now sixty-four years ago, and I recall every detail of the day exactly as if it had happened last week. It was a police force with tremendous prestige; I'm not quite sure why. City magnates and mandarins were said to be very proud of it. It had a minimum height standard of six feet. Shortly before that time it had had two sporting teams which, on their own, represented England in water polo and tug of war respectively. The water polo ascendancy was nearing its end, for at about that time there arrived in this country the unbeatable Australian crawl stroke, which all the youngsters learned at school and which left our men splashing ineffectually. The tug of war team, whose members weighed about twenty stone apiece, went on pulling over other teams of giants for a few more years, after which there remained a comforting afterglow in which we all felt like giants who would one day reassert ourselves. (We never did.)

In particular I remember wondering if I really knew what I was supposed to be doing, had any clear idea of how long I would go on doing it, whether this was really the 'bread-and-butter job' which would earn me the leisure time for writing, and if I was at last in the right job. As it turned out the answer to each of these questions was no. Fourteen other men had joined with me, and I realize as I write this that I could (but won't) give a good description of each one of them, recalling especially his voice, his walk, and—if he had one—his laugh. I am not sure, by the way, that even the police have ever recognized that a person's laugh is as inimitable and distinguishable as his fingerprints. Above most other means of identity, I know a man by his laugh. Which reminds me that one man was sacked before he had completed our month's tuition in the 'school of instruction', because he turned out, a bit belatedly, to be a bigamist. He was also the only one among us who never laughed, and since then I have often wondered whether in fact bigamists have anything to laugh about.

One thing I remember that we all laughed about was our first appearance in helmets. Very odd things, helmets, with a history divided between protecting the heads of miners, sappers, and soldiers (and especially twelfth-century knights, who wore 'helms' coming down over their shoulders and may one day, I suppose, be imitated by modern policemen on riot duty who show an increasing and provocative tendency to defend themselves) and frightening people by making oneself look a foot taller. Even in those days there was a constant police argument about the merits of the helmet and the peaked cap, and the never-ending pretence that the helmet was a protection in a fight or struggle. It wasn't. In a struggle it was the first thing to come off, and there was no way of stopping it. Nor was there usually any time to recover it and pop it on again, so that it could again be sent flying. I was always an anti-helmet man. It was an invitation to ridicule, and seems to be seen as such by all stage and film producers, whose policemen's helmets are always at least one size too big, always come down over the ears, and always help to stamp the wearer as a self-important clown. If a drama producer insists on police helmets he should be supplied with a helmet man, just as a film director has a continuity girl, to ensure that his policemen don't look idiotic (unless he wants them to). It was always noticeable that, in almost every fresh intake of police recruits, it would be a man from the Household Cavalry who knew how to put his helmet on, clear of his ears and with the peak just clearing the bridge of his nose. Lesser men took weeks to learn; and a pantomimic few, alas, never did. But when we first caught sight of our own helmeted reflections in shop windows, we always hoped fervently that we wouldn't meet anyone we knew. Think of Colonel Calverley in *Patience*:

> When I first put this uniform on,
> I said as I looked in the glass
>   'It's one to a million
>   That any civilian
> My figure and form will surpass.'

The police memoirs which now follow will be brief, atypical, and lacking excitement; not attempting, and certainly not inviting, comparison with the countless books of reminiscence by former police officers (some original, some ghosted), the majority of which, by confining themselves to real-life crime stories, sustain a popular belief that police work is mainly about the solution of insoluble crime problems. And on the subject of 'what police work is about' I wish to offer a few commonplace observations before moving on to more stirring matters.

Of course it's about the preservation of what we nowadays call Laura Norder; and the mere existence of a police system is itself a tribute to the remarkable achievement, not only that order should have got established by the law but that law should have been established through the realization of order. Side by side they have unsteadily sustained each other, so to speak, through countless crises. Law and order mean together, however, very much more than the attempted control of crime and criminals, though that self-evident aspect of police duty supports a huge nationalized industry, employing legions of lawyers, magistrates, judges and their clerks, prison officers, probation officers, social workers, and an army of civil servants; all essential to its network of suppliers, to the economy, to employment, and to the image of authority. The police in 150 years, starting as an execrated body of spies and Bumbles, have acquired the persona of the village headman, someone to be called upon in thousands of minor emergencies which no one could have foreseen as bobby-on-the-beat matters. In 1935 I had to compile an official police 'instruction book', to replace a tattered handbook fifty years old which confided to the City of London policeman how and when to blow his whistle or 'spring his rattle', how to enforce the laws about stage-coaches and the driving of cattle, how he must look out for broken or dirty street lamps, and why he must never stand (or, for that matter, sit) gossiping with servants. One detail of my remit was that I must try to specify the numerous emergencies and minor crises in the lives of the citizenry which called for or justified some kind of police action, or the production of some excuse for not doing anything. I found that it would have been easier to set down the things which the police were not to do. In the end, I did neither. I took refuge in a waffling paragraph which is still in antiquarian circulation and which I have just re-examined (after fifty years) with a self-conscious grin and the growing hope that no one ever really sees it any more.

The year 1921 may not seem very long ago to have begun police duty in the streets of London. Many people have adult memories going much further back. But how many people today would believe that in the early mornings at that time I saw the entire roadway of Blackfriars Bridge, one of the widest bridges in the country, covered by trotting sheep on their way to Smithfield Meat Market? The law required that they should be kept to the left of the road 'so as to obstruct the thoroughfare as little as possible', and their drovers were forbidden to 'suffer them to spread over the thoroughfare'. But their drovers were stolidly suffering them to go where they liked so long as it was in the direction of Smithfield, and no one seemed to take much notice. In the line of tramcars following them over the bridge, few people seemed to be looking up from their early morning papers. A heaving acre of scrambling, woolly-backed aimlessness, the sheep were kept on the trot by the uncannily intelligent sheep-dogs and, in the distance, two or three men in cloth caps, big scarves and leggings, all carrying long sticks which they never used except to point to a dog. The sticks could lawfully be fitted with 'a goad or point of no greater length than a quarter of an inch', but the animals must not be struck 'on or below the hock'. These men were 'licensed drovers'. They wore (compulsorily) arm badges issued to them after much enquiry by the Corporation of London, who were my employers too. Sheep sometimes came over London Bridge also, and I have seen them filling Cheapside and Newgate Street, then to veer symbolically away from the Old Bailey corner and scamper down Giltspur Street to Smithfield and their Last Journey. I believe all this must have stopped by 1925, the huge refrigerated vans having by that time taken over this poignant little Via Dolorosa.

Still to be seen some years even after that were the horse-drawn vanloads of vegetables or flowers bound for Covent Garden Market. These came clip-clopping through the dark City streets all night long, every night except Saturday, and the same horses were used with such regularity that one came to recognize them by their markings. And an inevitable effect of the regularity was that the carman, up on his reasonably comfortable seat, warmly wrapped like any Pickwickian coachman, was often fast asleep for most of the journey. The horses knew every step of the way. By some regularly recurring miracle they got over all crossroads without mishap, and the amount of sleep their drivers got depended entirely on the duty-bound rectitude of the numerous policemen through whose little bits of territory the vans had to pass. This rectitude was of four kinds or degrees, each expressing itself differently. The sternest kind of policeman would stop the horse, wake up the carman, take his name and address, and tell him that he would be prosecuted for 'driving to the common danger' (this was a Police Act phrase). It was said that this always had the effect of keeping the man awake, at least for the remainder of that morning's journey. The second kind would step out quickly from the footway and give the poor horse a mighty slap on its nearside haunch, jolting it into a trot and throwing the carman heavily back in his seat — they were always slumped forward while dozing. The effort of finding the reins and frantically jamming on the foot-brake was far more potent than any alarm clock. The third kind would gently take the halter and lead the horse into a cul-de-sac, at the end of which it would come gratefully to a stop and go to sleep itself. In this event, horse and man would sometimes slumber for hours, to be wakened by the arrival of early City workers for the day's business. What happened to these carmen on arrival hours late at Covent Garden, where the morning's business was long over and the roadways occupied only by cabbage leaves, onion skins, and damaged carnations, I never discovered. But the fourth kind, and I confess that I belonged to it, pulled out a truncheon and banged it heavily on the driver's footboard. Such a driver, realizing his luck, would wriggle into position, touch his cap, grin, and grope for the reins with a sort of flustered propitiation. What I wished I had the power to do was to unharness the horse, tie it to the back of the van, put the man in the shafts and make him pull the lot. But the horse wouldn't have got any sleep.

Many of the City streets at that time were paved with stone 'setts', a kind of rectangular cobblestone constructed on the principle of producing as much din as possible when traversed by iron-shod hoofs and metal-rimmed cart-wheels. Two kinds of vehicles competed for the distinction of making the more row: traction-engines, which were numerous, and horse-buses, which were nearly but not quite extinct. I think the horse-bus won, because even its iron-rimmed wheels could not drown the appalling rattle of its windows. I never discovered, though I tried for years, why the window-frames of horse-buses were fitted with loose glass. Motor-car windows weren't; and, contrary to much modern assertion, motor cars were quite numerous

on the roads by 1921 and had been since about 1910. Road
noise in the 1920s was different in quality from today's:
it was worse for the ear. And the hospitals were allowed
(as ordinary householders were not, having lost the
privilege in 1888) to lay straw right across the roadway to
deaden the sound of passing vehicles. I forget how often
the straw was taken up and renewed, and whether that
frequency was prescribed by any regulations. But some of
it got pretty malodorous before anyone did anything about
it, what with the horse droppings, the litter, and the
repeated soakings with rain. Throughout the Kaiser's war,
when the imposing Fishmongers' Hall on London Bridge
Approach was turned into a hospital for officers, the
roadway outside was always straw-covered, and it was
wonderfully effective. As a vehicle came on to the straw
its passage suddenly became ghostly. During my police
service all the stone setts were gradually supplanted by
wood blocks and then, everywhere, by Tarmac. The horses
and the old buses would have had a better and quieter time
on Tarmac.

But in the twenties we saw a new exploitation of the
motor-bus (and what a period phrase that has now become;
outclassed only by the police description of a bus as a motor
metropolitan stage carriage). This was the sudden
proliferation of small bus companies, some of them one-
man businesses, which were stigmatized as 'pirate' buses
because they were in cutthroat competition with the
London General Omnibus Company and a few smaller but
accepted enterprises. I rather objected to the term 'pirate'.
Was a single hardware shop, I asked myself, a pirate
because it dared competition with Robert Dyas? Was the
little corner grocer a pirate threatening the life of
Sainsbury's? The little chemist a menace to Boots? Oh,
it was said, any operator like this was in charge of a
potentially lethal vehicle; he had the safety of the public
in his hands. And not Dyas, Sainsbury's, Boots? The word
'spiv' wasn't then invented (nor does any dictionary seem
to know where it came from, and when), but if it had been
in use then, these men would have been spivs. . . .

There is no doubt that because in those days public servants, like bus drivers, railwaymen, postmen, and milkmen, still wore uniforms, the descent to universal scruffiness not having yet begun, there was something outrageous and socially frightening about a man in shirt-sleeves and no tie driving a bus with people in it. What could be legitimately frightening was the swerving and cutting-in at bus-stops, where the competition was fiercest, to say nothing of the stop-me-anywhere tactics of the 'pirates' and the way their conductors hung out and hauled running passengers aboard in mid-stream. There was a Chocolate Bus Company, with buses biliously coloured accordingly, whose drivers were specially daring and impudent. It is my recollection that these gadfly busmen, having acquired the police licence which couldn't lawfully be denied them, were then harassed by the police in a manner and to an extent that had never been thought necessary in the case of the London General Omnibus Company. They were prosecuted for numerous breaches of the Hackney Carriage Acts which had never been noticed when committed by the LGOC. Yet they differed from LGOC buses then, as they would differ from London Transport buses now, in their anxiety to carry passengers rather than to evade them. They were got rid of by a Home Office Order of 1924, and the streets were less exciting but (marginally) safer.

The City of London at that time regarded itself (maybe it still does) as the busiest traffic centre in the world; and, unaccountably I thought, seemed proud of it. Because of it the huge encircling Metropolitan Police force, from whose area most of the City's traffic originated and converged, commonly asserted that the City didn't know how to cope with its traffic. This was a non-stop controversy, and it ran until in the 1930s automatic traffic-lights had been everywhere installed. Then it faded into a kind of tribal memory imperfectly clothed in *badinage*, like Bannockburn or the Wars of the Roses. All police forces, everywhere, have blamed their neighbours for traffic snarl-ups, but today when things go wrong they unite in hostility to electronics, the machine, and the computer. What survives is an eager and mainly masculine interest in specific kinds of motor vehicle, and at the time I am here concerned with we were all fascinated by the Austin Seven, which had arrived to a chorus of mixed acclaim and derision in the summer of 1922. It was a revelation, and none of us foresaw that it was also a revolution. In the ensuing fifty years I have driven many Austin Sevens and their successors the Minis, and was glad to be still around when with just pride they celebrated their half-century.

The City streets were still crowded with horse-drawn vehicles of all kinds, and until they were banned in 1934 they consorted valiantly with the growing volume of motor traffic. I shall always remember what seemed to me the uncanny skill of their carmen; how almost any of them could be turned completely upon its own axis (as no motor car has ever done), the horse playing its own intelligent part in the manœuvring that this always entailed in a narrow City lane. When the first 'articulated vehicle' appeared, its front part was known as a 'mechanical horse'; and special provision had to be made under the Road Traffic Acts for its inability to behave anything like a real one.

The last horses to go, I believe, were the ones that took the fish carts to and from Billingsgate Market; which was odd, because it was here that they had by far their most arduous job to do and that their relief was the most urgent. When I saw them in the early mornings, so early that it seemed to me like the middle of the night, straining and stumbling up the steep roadways of Monument Street, Fish Street Hill, Botolph Lane, and St Mary at Hill, where the stone setts were eternally wet and slimy with fish scales, I felt almost as sorry for them as I always did for myself, on duty in that shouting inferno of esoteric abuse, exasperation, experienced bustle, and resourceful profanity.

Billingsgate Market I shall always remember for its pathetic population of 'scats', a small army of unemployed (and probably unemployable) casuals who loitered about the market at the busy time in the hope of earning an occasional sixpence. They earned their sixpences when one of the regular market fish-porters (aristocrats in the whole system and second only to the buyers, who were rich men with country houses) was about to pull a barrow laden with wet fish up one of the short steep hills to the cart stands in Eastcheap or Great Tower Street. He would need an extra hand on the barrow, and he took the first comer from among the 'scats' who were waiting to pounce. Some of them, in fact, had a regular liaison with a porter who knew them. I have never come across this meaning for the word 'scat' in any other context, though some policemen tended to use it in referring to any kind of vagrant or street eccentric. And in this sense it has found its way into no dictionary, not even Partridge admitting it as recognized slang. Everyone in the market used it. 'Seen any scats, guv?', I have been asked by a porter at the bottom of a market hill. 'Blimey, they're never 'ere when you want them.' But more usually the scats were waiting to run forward and be chosen, as soon as a laden barrow emerged through the huge and ornate market gates. 'Up the 'ill, guv?' they would all shout in ragged unison. 'Up the 'ill?' In police circles 'Up the 'ill' had long had the meaning of an offer of any kind of short-term help.

I was in fact more interested in such representatives of the City of London's submerged tenth than in the mandarins who have given the City its reputation, its status, its Dick Whittington aspect in popular mythology. I shall say a word or two about these in the next chapter, where I can so arrange them as to reflect each other's luminosity. But here I want to introduce you to some of the watchmen, lamplighters, beggars, wandering evangelists, sandwich-men, and street traders who still lack a Henry Mayhew (he died in 1887) to present the world with a true portrait of their bustling urban lives.

Chronologically, my most active recollection of a licensed street trader concerns the one I officially encountered at the corner of Cheapside and Foster Lane one day in the autumn of 1923. He had a large wooden tray supported on his abdomen by shoulder-straps, and on the tray there lay numerous fat bundles of German mark

notes. 'One million marks for a tanner', he was shouting
to incredulous passers-by. 'Come on there, chance of a
lifetime, tanner a million marks.' People were buying them
as fast as he could take their money, fumble for change,
and slip rubber bands round the quantities they asked for.
Speaking over the heads of his puzzled but eager customers,
I asked him where he had got them, and at once felt the
public hostility stirred up by the bobby who interferes with
what seems a harmless bit of enterprise displayed by a
barrow boy. For harmless it was. The value of the
Reichsmark, it turned out, was at that moment ten
thousand million to the pound sterling. British soldiers on
leave from the Rhineland were bringing home kitbags
stuffed with these pathetically worthless pieces of paper,
encouraged to do so by quick-penny East End operators who
were giving them £10 a sackful, and then employing street
traders to sell them at a huge profit on the London streets.
In the City, which was fussy about street traders, there
were certain things they were not allowed to sell at all
(fireworks, cigarettes, drinks, and some less subversive
things), and other articles they could legally sell without
even needing a street trader's licence. Among the latter
were newspapers and magazines, but not Reichsmarks.
What this man was doing was certainly not within the law,
but I contented myself (since, having interfered, I had to
do a face-saving *something*) and riled the bystanders by
sending him away. The next day I learned that so many
street traders had been arrested in the City for selling
Reichsmarks that there had been a high-level decision to
let them get on with it, since the whole enterprise couldn't
be more than a nine days' wonder. Instead of nine, I recall,
it lasted about three. But in those three days the City of
London's lunch-time strollers had bought themselves some
eloquent little tokens in the developing story of currency
inflation and monetarism.

Some of the big clothing wholesalers like Dent Allcroft
& Co. and I. & R. Morley Ltd. (respectively noted for gloves
and stockings) employed night-watchmen outside as well
as inside their City warehouses in places like Wood Street,

Milk Street, and Foster Lane, Cheapside. One of these was a fussy and earnest little man called George Bacon (by his family, not by the police, who called him Jeff because his colleague *inside* the building was so much taller than he that together they looked like two current comic-strip characters called Mutt and Jeff). I called him George because he became rather a protégé of mine, a persecuted little man — the bobbies subjected him to countless practical jokes in the still watches of the night — and I found him an unexpectedly interesting chap to talk to. He had a large red nose, whose redness was innocent of origin, and a huge white moustache, and in the winter always wore a coachman's cloak which, since it was far too big for him, swept the ground as he went his rounds 'punching' the clocks which recorded his vigilance. The cloak was the cause of much merriment among the police. But at least it served to identify him reassuringly when you caught sight of him in the dark distance, and might otherwise have wondered who was prowling in Wood Street at that hour of the night. Apart from being a Christian fundamentalist to whom the entire Bible was the Word of God, and totally uninhibited in his declarations of faith whatever the company and its likely reaction, he was a bibliophile with three special heroes — Pepys, Coleridge, and Boswell. His mind was uncritically crammed with their quotable wisdom and he could recite the whole of *The Ancient Mariner* at will. I suppose his age was about 60. I don't know what kind of adversity would reduce such a man to that position, or whether any special adversity was needed — there were two million unemployed and no dole; but he never talked of it or complained about it. I gathered from my colleagues, and they told me of it with endless amusement, that he had 'taken rather a shine to me'; and I have mentioned him at some length because, when I got married in 1926, he had somehow discovered where the wedding was to be and had turned up at the church, dressed in a little frock-coat, a trilby hat, and a wing-collar, though as a night-watchman he should properly have been in his bed. I still think of him with a kind of puzzled respect and affection; and I am aware that having known that very odd little man has been in an unmistakable way an enrichment. Perhaps I may be allowed to record just one of his many topical aphorisms. He deeply disapproved of A. J. Cook, the miners' leader, the Arthur Scargill of the twenties. 'Whenever that man opens his mouth,' he said, 'it is to subtract from the sum of human knowledge.'

For very different reasons, I think with affection of Bill the City lamplighter, whose surname nobody knew. He was older and fatter than George, walked very carefully with his feet turned out at a quarter-past-nine, had jowls that hung down over his coat collar, and carried his lamplighter's pole across a shiny broadcloth patch let into the shoulder of his coat. All the street lamps in the City in Bill's time were gaslit, and he had been lighting them (that is to say, the forty or so within his jurisdiction) for so many years that he had become as much a part of the City of London as Gog and Magog, St. Paul's, and the Bank of England. More, he had been photographed and then sketched, to be used in the famous Veritas gas mantle advertisement in which a lamplighter has accidentally struck a mantle as he turns with the pole on his shoulder. He sees to his wonderment that it remains unbroken. 'Blimey,' he says, 'it must be a Veritas.' Bill's claim to our attention is that it was his chosen duty to tell anyone who would listen that his beloved City of London, rebuilt with such loving care after the Great Fire of 1666, was now falling down and could be made to stay up. Wherever one of his lamps, he said, was sited somewhere near any kind of stone upright, and he was thus obliged to raise his eyes, he would see that the stone upright was cracking right down the middle. Sometimes a mere hair crack, sometimes a crevice you could put your little finger into. It was the work of the Fleet river and the Wallbrook, said Bill, both of which still ran under the poor old City on their way to the Thames and were gradually rotting its foundations. You couldn't put up these damn great buildin's, he said, on water. It was asking for trouble. We often told him that the Fleet and the Wallbrook were confined to underground conduits, but he seemed not to hear.

So when one hot night in the summer of 1927 he excitedly told a constable in Leadenhall Street that there were new cracks in the smart façade of the Commercial Union Assurance Company's six-storey building in Cornhill the constable nodded kindly and said there, there. But Bill shuffled anxiously from one policeman to another as he toured his lamps, until at last he met me (I was now a sergeant) on the north side of Cornhill almost opposite the Commercial Union; and he begged me to cross the road with him and look. Sure enough the face of a stone angel, the keystone of the arch over the main doors, had a half-inch vertical split down its nose and chin. And from inside, as we stood and listened, there came ominous creaking noises. I telephoned the Fire Brigade at Cannon Street Fire Station. '*Looks* like coming down?' said the fireman. 'We can't turn out just because somebody thinks a building *looks like* falling down.' We arranged that when it started I would break the glass in the nearest fire-alarm post and pull the handle. Meanwhile we closed Cornhill to all traffic at both ends. It was nearly an hour before I heard a party-wall start to give way at the west side of the building, adjoining a huge excavation about to be built on by another insurance company (and this, it turned out, was the cause of all the trouble — and of an enormous subsequent lawsuit). Almost as I tugged the handle I heard the distant answering firebells as the appliances turned out in Cannon Street, a quarter of a mile away. After about another hour the Commercial Union building collapsed across Cornhill with a roar that seemed to last five minutes. We just had time to see the heaps of office furniture, the filing cabinets, the typewriters and the desks and chairs, and the beds and wardrobes from the resident caretaker's quarters on the sixth floor, arranging themselves among the rubble before everything was hidden in a huge cloud of dust, which also hid us from each other . . . Cornhill was completely closed to traffic for five months, day and night.

But Bill the lamplighter, prophet of the City's doom, was vindicated at long last. He took no pleasure in it. He was never heard to say 'I told you so.' I am glad he didn't

live to see what the *Luftwaffe* did to his lamplit territory
in 1940, when night after night huge buildings spread
themselves and their contents across the streets, with no
waiting about for cracks to develop or firemen to accept
invitations. I genuinely believe that daft nightmare of
annihilation would have broken his heart.

There were quite a number of street beggars in the City
in the twenties, particularly around Throgmorton Street,
Copthall Avenue, Tokenhouse Yard, and Lothbury. The
attraction, no doubt, was the daily 'street market' run by
the Stock Exchange, which every afternoon crowded the
roadway of Throgmorton Street with prosperous-looking
men in black jackets and striped trousers, their faces
perennially sunburned by weekends of golf and yachting,
and their business as mysterious to me as the genealogy
of the Dalai Lama. What was slightly less mysterious about
them was the obvious assurance with which they totally
obstructed the roadway, knowing that they would never
be 'moved on', and thus afforded cover for the beggars who
would otherwise be so conspicuous in those highly
Mammonistic surroundings. Beggars at that time were still
regarded without much pity, and still rather deplored as
an anachronistic legacy from the Napoleonic Wars, a proof
that there would always be some people, especially ex-
servicemen, too feckless to work and too dishonest to
qualify (or too lazy to apply) for poor relief. If any of us
arrested a beggar and charged him under the Vagrancy Act,
his whereabouts had to be reported to an anti-beggar
organization called the London Mendicity Society. This
had started life in 1818 as the Society for the Suppression
of Begging, when the penniless and cast-off victors of
Waterloo and the Peninsular War were roaming the streets
of a grateful Britain in a state of utter destitution. Nor was
there anything benevolent about the London Mendicity
Society, unless you can call it benevolent to protect your
rich subscribing members, as it most effectually did,
against mendicity. It did a useful job in cataloguing the
numerous professional begging-letter writers, whose

eloquence often confused mendicity with mendacity; and
I suppose that today it would have to divulge, on demand,
particulars of those whose names it had thought worthy
of inclusion in its books. In the 1930s this society was
enquiring into the bona fides of 150,000 beggars every year.

   It seemed to me that my police colleagues sorted
themselves into three main classes in this matter. Those
in the largest one carefully looked the other way when they
caught sight of some obvious beggar plying his calling,
unless the plying was being done with unusual abandon.
Those in the middle one would 'take him inside', where
he would be charged—and fingerprinted so that his
criminal record, if any, could be supplied to the Mendicity
Society, which reciprocated with a list of his begging
convictions from its own records (these weren't on his
criminal file). Those in the third and much the smallest
class would discreetly give him a coin or two, having first
made sure that such culpable involvement was unobserved.
The first time I saw this done was by far the most
memorable. I was in the company (as a sergeant) of a much-
feared inspector who bore the improbably Dickensian name
of Eli Crook. He was a very tall and thin, almost emaciated
figure, white-faced, bony, and unsmiling, an implacable
disciplinarian of whom it was cruelly said by the rank and
file that the only time he had ever been seen to laugh was
when he saw a dog run over. One afternoon in Bartholomew
Lane, behind the Bank of England, a shuffling little 'scat'
whom I knew as a virtuoso beggar actually hobbled across
the road to us and, to my horror, asked Inspector Crook
if he could spare him the price of a cup of cocoa. Surely
the heavens must now fall? I crouched. They stayed up.
Eli Crook looked round almost furtively, and then stepped
backwards into Capel Court, a cul-de-sac near where we
stood. He lifted the tails of his heavy greatcoat, peeled off
his brown kid gloves, fumbled in his trousers pocket, and
produced a coin which he didn't allow me to see. 'Here
you are, old chap', he muttered. 'Off you go!' I was
stunned. 'If a man comes cadging to a police inspector,'
said Eli Crook awkwardly, 'he's genuinely up against it.'

And, curtly acknowledging my valedictory salute, he abruptly left me. I'm sure he never knew, and would have been totally unmoved if he had known, but without actually liking him much (you *couldn't* really like him) I greatly admired Eli Crook. I envied him his two most salient qualities, I suppose: an effortless sense of authority and an unshakeable commitment to the Christian faith. The public got far more than their money's-worth out of Eli Crook.

But not even he, though he was a Plymouth Brother, found it possible to approve of the 'sandwich-men' who haunted the boundaries of the City; though most of their sandwich-boards seemed to proclaim that The Wages of Sin was Death, that The Wicked would Descend into Hell, that God was Love and that Millions Now Living would Never Die. This last was the discovery of a Judge Rutherford (Judge was his Christian name, not his status), one of the inexhaustible supply of American evangelists who bring their stentorian messages of hope to these benighted islands. The sandwich-men haunted the boundaries because in the City of London you mustn't walk about, or even stand, with a sandwich-board unless you have the consent in writing of the Commissioner of Police. In case you might find yourself doing this without due thought, let me explain (or let the *Concise Oxford Dictionary* explain) that a sandwich-board is 'one of two advertisement boards carried by sandwich-man', while a sandwich-man is conceived as 'walking in street with sandwich-boards hanging before and behind'. (Yes, he is easier to draw than to define.) At that time he got about a shilling a day, and brought his own sandwiches to munch at lunch-time; though I never saw one so narrowly shop-floor minded as the one in the *Punch* cartoon, who carried his boards upside down until he had finished eating.

I don't know how numerous they were before 1867, but in 1867 they came under statutory control. They then required police permits if their purpose was to 'advertise' anything, a requirement which sustained much police argument as to what else you would carry a sandwich-board

for. And ever since then the faces of successive
Commissioners of Police have been firmly set against
them. No City permits have ever been issued, though in
the surrounding Metropolitan Police district, where the
people in the streets have more time to read, the police
have always been fairly indulgent. Therefore they haunted
the City boundary, nipping across when no policeman was
in sight and sometimes, *mirabile dictu*, penetrating as far
as the Stock Exchange, where their message about people
descending into Hell was not too well received.
Occasionally one of my sterner colleagues, spotting one
of these mercenary missionaries, would 'take him inside'
and spark off once again the age-old controversy about the
meaning of 'advertising'. If you carry in the street a placard
saying 'Vengeance is Mine Saith the Lord', are you
advertising? Of course you are, says the *Concise Oxford*:
you are 'making something generally or publicly known'.
Nonsense, says *Collins*: if you mean 'warn' or 'caution',
the word 'advertise' is obsolete. *Longman* thinks
advertising is all about selling things or services, praising
them in the mass media, and so on. *Nuttall* thinks it is
giving notice generally to the public (which could easily
and properly include anything about Divine Vengeance),
or 'making conspicuous'—without saying what gets the
conspicuousness. In the end the sandwich-man, who had
usually been sitting in the police station muster room
during this semantic uproar, would be told to go away and
in future frighten only the Metropolitan Police area.

The City of London moves, or moved, partly on the
backs of such people. They all contribute to its 'image'.
But it is time for me to turn to some of the other and more
tailored backs upon which, if one is to be fair, the City
was more recognizably borne along: the Lombards, the
Lazards, the Joels, the Rothschilds, the Clores, and the
Rowlands.

CHAPTER FOUR

I HAD told myself that I would not, in these re-miniscences, think in decades. 'What would you say', people ask each other, 'has been your best decade?' I find this unanswerable. I have never liked decimalizing my recollections, and somehow a decade might be seen as an even less suitable frame for thought when you are working your way through your ninth. But it has a sort of ready-made, or even lazy, tidiness about it, the kind of conventional time-slotting which enabled Franklin Roosevelt to write to Churchill on the latter's sixtieth birthday, 'It's fun to be in the same decade with you.' Accordingly, lining up my crowded decades, and leaving out the forties, which anyway drop out of human decency and expose a cauldron of depravity which most of us try (dangerously) to forget, I see that I have seven to choose from. And I know that my contemporaries see, perhaps will always see, the thirties as our truly significant period, the most fateful, formative, genetic, breathless, and all the rest of it. Everyone writes about the thirties. Of course that may be because so many of our best writers and poets and sages were young in them. To me, if I accept after all this decimal nostalgia, and I now begin to see that I shall, our century seems to climax in the twenties.

When Julian Symons produced his ruthlessly percipient book *The Thirties*, I resisted its invitation to see that period through his eyes as a time of aborted artistic promise, founding all our hopes and self-deceptions and failed altruism in a decade of unheeded writers and poets and artists. It was in one's teens, I told myself, that one talked of poets as unacknowledged legislators. Stevenson had it right when he talked about 'the bitterness of arts — you see a good effect, and some nonsense about sense continually intervenes'. But now when I look at the twenties I find that it was there that all the planting out took place. For me it all began with H. G. Wells and his *Outline of History*, and no other book from that didactic little man illustrates so excitingly the sweep of his mind. Then there came Lytton Strachey's *Queen Victoria*, *The Waste Land*, *Babbitt*, *A Passage to India*, *The Magic Mountain*, *St. Joan*, *The Great Gatsby*, *An American Tragedy*, *To The Lighthouse*, *Goodbye to All That*, *The Good Companions*, and *All Quiet on the Western Front*; and for me above all Tawney's *Religion and the Rise of Capitalism*. What a strangely assorted lot; but all in some way conceived during the war years, all with a message for my kind of malleable youth, and all combining to make the twenties the great period of New Writing. These people were actually alive, in my time, having similar day-by-day experiences to mine; not lying in their graves like my old favourites among the so-called classics. They made me into a book buyer, for it was only in the twenties, with the beginning of my police service and of a modest income from spare-time journalism, that I could get together any money for new books, as distinct from twopenny bargains on the barrows. And two books which I acquired as birthday presents, or presents of some kind, set in motion something in my grasshopper mind which is still in there, vainly trying to find comfortable lodgment: J. W. Dunne's *Experiment With Time* (which had the rather more important effect of launching J. B. Priestley on his extraordinary series of 'Time Plays'), and an unaccountably forgotten little book called *Three Men Discuss Relativity*, by J. W. N. Sullivan. I am quite certain that I never understood either of these books, but they gave me a dazzling glimpse of what there was to be understood; and I have since learned that this is what they did for most people (even, perhaps, for their authors). Accordingly, they combined to suggest, and they turned out to be right, that I should probably spend the rest of my life on the threshold of understanding.

I suppose there are many ways of striking up an acquaintance with a dean of the Anglican Communion. Mine was to pick one up out of the gutter. It was Dr W. R. Inge of St. Paul's, and he was making his way after evensong from the cathedral to his official residence at No. 4 Dean's Court, which was no more than two minutes' walk even for an elderly dean in gaiters. We all knew him by sight, but he never spoke to the police (with whom, accordingly, he was not universally popular). In particular, he didn't like it when some of our fellows, as they always seemed to me over-ready to do, gave him a smart military salute ('threw him up a beaver', they used to say). Not surprisingly, in the public streets this embarrassed him, though I can remember ecclesiastical mandarins who loved it, and he always affected not to have seen it. He seemed not to know what to do in response (similar dignitaries used to raise their hats).

As he stepped up on to the footway outside No. 4 he slipped and fell, rather heavily. Before I could get to him he was pulled to his feet by a passing youth, who then hurried on. I asked the Dean if he was hurt and he said, in a strange high-pitched stammer, that he rather thought he was. I supported him as he shuffled carefully into the hallway of No. 4, and just inside he sat on a very low chair with a high wickerwork back. For about a minute he sat looking at the floor, a thin white hand clasping each knee, and then he said no, he wasn't hurt at all. He stood up slowly and gestured towards the front door as an unmistakable intimation that I was to go. It was a courtly gesture, not at all imperious or offensive, but it was final.

A police difficulty about such episodes is the need to have some kind of record, in case there should be a sequel — an *ex post facto* discovery that the footway was in some way defective, even possibly a claim against the highway authority. If a bobby who happened to be there fails to make any report at the time, there will be no record. 'Oh, but there was a policeman there', someone will say. 'We saw a policeman help him into the house.' Who that policeman was will soon be discovered, and believe me it is not going too far to say that (in those days at any rate) such a 'neglect of duty' would probably be fatal to his prospects of promotion, be he never so bright. Is this not enough to explain the persistence, the officious nosiness, with which the bobby plies his victim with questions? True, I didn't need to ask who Dr Inge was. Already he was looking with distaste at my notebook. I knew his name, address, and occupation. But I should be expected to record his age.

Something in his expression made me hesitant about this topic. I would guess his age. Anyway it proved to be easy to find out that he was 68. I closed my notebook. As he was moving away I told him I should be expected to report the matter, and he stopped and half turned. 'Whatever for?' he snapped. I explained what for. He said testily that he didn't want anything reported, and tactfully I allowed him to see that he couldn't stop it. He was outraged. Couldn't a man fall over without becoming a police matter? I saw that he needed reassurance. Already no doubt he saw headlines in all the papers except the *Evening Standard*, which was then publishing the brilliant bi-weekly articles I have already referred to, and which alone would suppress the news that its distinguished essayist had fallen over. Rival papers, the *Evening News*, the *Star*, the tabloid dailies, all would make much of it. He always got a bad press. 'FALLEN DEAN', they would cry. 'GLOOMY DEAN BITES DUST'. 'CROPPER FOR INGE'. 'DEAN IN GUTTER'.

It was towards the end of August 1928; I remember this because it was close to my birthday. How much did it matter, at that moment, if a dean fell over? Sixty-five countries, including the USSR, had just signed the Kellogg–Briand Pact, all swearing that they would never again go to war and would settle future disputes by peaceful means. Can you, now, believe that such a thing ever happened? I urged Dr Inge to believe that I should not overshadow this kind of news by telling Fleet Street about his downfall, though I knew in my bones that anyone who had snapped it with a camera could have sold the picture (and kept the negative) for a nice lot of money; and in August the cathedral precincts were swarming with tourists photographing almost anything that moved. He must have felt comforted, for his manner slowly changed and at length he held out

his hand. I don't know how uncharacteristic this may have
been, though I came to know that he was a man in whom
a warm heart did constant battle with an icy shyness; but
as I shook hands with him I consciously forbore to mention
(though I was longing to do so) that I owned and treasured
a much-read copy of his *Outspoken Essays*. I'm not quite
certain after all this time, but I believe I dismissed the
impulse on the ground that it would seem like toadying.
But the fact that I didn't tell him may be responsible for
what has always seemed to me an astonishing sequel.

About five years later I had to call and see him officially
about a matter of police assistance at a cathedral ceremony.
Without his hat, and seated composedly at a desk, he
looked much more than five years older. But what
surprised me was that he had totally forgotten the episode
in Dean's Court. He took a detached, nodding, benign
interest in the story, almost as though I were making it
up as I went along. He clearly had no recollection of it
whatsoever. (*'Really?* How extraordinary. Was it snowing
at the time, frosty?' It was August, I reminded him. Did
he behave badly? 'I'm sure it was very kind of you. I'm
greatly obliged.' And so on.) This time I did tell him about
Outspoken Essays, and I can report with relief that he
hadn't forgotten those. But I don't believe that he felt the
book had been avidly read by a young man seeking
knowledge. I think he simply felt that it had been studied
carefully by the police.

I met him several times after that, always officially. I
am quite certain that each time he saw me as a total
stranger. And I have often wondered, defensively, whether
in fact that remarkable and profoundly scholarly
churchman wasn't a stranger to almost everyone.

If the twenties are to rank as my most memorable decade,
and of course by that I mean the decade I most want to
remember, they are much helped by the fact that they saw
the birth of the British National Opera Company, for which
we were all everlastingly indebted to Sir Thomas Beecham.
I don't know whether it should be possible to say, as you

listen to an orchestra playing Bach, Beethoven, Mozart, Haydn, or Delius, that you know at once who is conducting it; but it was always possible with Beecham. I try to allow for the feeling that one ought to be hearing it as conceived by the person who wrote it. But Beecham's conducting, even to my non-expert ear, was so original and dynamic, equally in hair-raising vigour and in the sweetest lyricism, that for me he is the great conductor of all time. His BNOC and his recordings have coaxed more money from my pockets than I could ever decently afford, and I fondly cherish the memory of the maestro.

But not of the man. One day in 1925 I was on patrol duty in Throgmorton Street, a job which involved the manipulation of bespatted stockbrokers and their clients' vehicles by way of maintaining some pretence that we were all on the King's highway, when an angry chauffeur hurried up to me at the corner of Old Broad Street, panted out that he wanted my help urgently, and hurried away without further explanation but with the obvious expectation that I would be following him. Before I could overtake him he had covered the length of Throgmorton Street and was beckoning me with one hand while he pointed with the other at a big grey car completely blocking the narrow entrance to Tokenhouse Yard. His own boss's car, it seemed, was on the far side of it, imprisoned there until the offender was removed. (I caught sight of a large red face glowering angrily at both of us through a distant windscreen.) Yes, he knew where the owner was, and the chauffeur too. They had told him he must wait a few minutes. He couldn't wait. His boss was due at the House of Commons, due this minute, overdue. Who was the owner, I asked as he hurried me to No. 6 Tokenhouse Yard? 'No idea, guv, but he's a pig, I can tell you that, and he's in there.'

I found that the owner was Sir Thomas Beecham, whom I recognized at once (as who would not?) when I saw him in the first-floor office of a firm of accountants who, I supposed, were advising him on some aspect of his notoriously adventurous finances. He glared at me.

Addressing his host, I asked if he knew who was the owner of the car. 'I am', said Sir Thomas very sharply. 'I've already said I'll be down in a minute.' I said it was a bit more urgent than that, and perhaps his driver could come down at once? Well then, he said, I must find the driver. I can't remember that I have ever been spoken to with such withering contempt.

He was dressed in his much-photographed double-breasted grey suit, the vertical white streak in his little beard looked like something dribbling down his chin, and he was holding a cigar at arm's length as he permitted himself to scrutinize me with his eyes nearly closed. He reeked of some perfume which, in its contest with the cigar, produced an odour that no words of mine could describe. I was just urging him to come down himself when my original informant put his head in at the door and shouted that the Beecham chauffeur had turned up. Sir Thomas sprang to his feet, grabbed his hat, brushed past me, and strode out with no word of farewell to his accountant. The accountant lifted his shoulders and glanced at the ceiling.

My proper course was obvious. As in the case of Dr Inge, I knew who he was, I could easily ascertain his address, and I should have reported him and his chauffeur for prosecution. The obstruction at the entrance to Tokenhouse Yard was not merely wilful and unreasonable in the eyes of the law. It was also bloody-minded in the eyes of anyone else. I thought about it. How long had he persisted in defying my request that the car be moved? A minute at the most. If he had been chatting me up amiably, as was usual in that stockbroker belt ('Oh certainly, Robert, I'll be down in a shake, too bad, very sorry' etc.) would I now be contemplating a summons? I would not. So he was to get a summons because I was resentful? Because he hadn't turned out to be the kind of Tommy Beecham I wanted him to be? The man my musician friends all thought so wonderfully witty and epigrammatic, the professional character with a universal licence to behave like a boor and be adored for it? I decided to forget it.

But I never have. Forgive it, then? The story illustrates again the risk that every bobby runs when he decides to do any forgetting. If Beecham had chosen to write to my Commissioner and complain of police incivility or harassment (I'm not sure that harassment had then been discovered, but let's suppose that it had and that people knew how to pronounce it), the absence of any report from me would have done me lasting injury . . . Three months later I bought a Columbia Graphophone Company album of 78s on which Beecham had recorded a miraculous performance of *Messiah*.

These episodes, Inge and Beecham, unimportant in themselves, could be matched in the experience of almost anyone who has done police duty in the City or West End of London. Their narration here is an attempt to show that they are potentially far more important to the bobby than to anyone else. Countless public complaints are made against policemen, some fully justified, some even revealing behaviour which is utterly outrageous. This was going on, to my knowledge, sixty years ago and I don't doubt that it goes on now. Boorish and surly shop assistants, by comparison, have always been so rare (I never meet any) that you can't help wondering why. The difference must lie in the consciousness of authority, an awareness which spoiled perhaps one in every ten of my police colleagues, certainly no more; the one who, to quote the eloquent Isabella in Shakespeare's *Measure for Measure* (I. ii. 117),

> Dressed in a little brief authority,
> Most ignorant of what he's most assured,
> His glassy essence, like an angry ape
> Plays such fantastic tricks before high heaven
> As make the angels weep.

Beecham, I suppose, must have made them weep sometimes, and I like to think that they wept then. But when he went to meet them face to face, perhaps with introductions to Bach and Mozart but without his cigar, monocle, perfume, and spats, they may have reminded him (quoting Karl Barth) that when they sing for God they sing

Bach, whereas when they sing for pleasure they sing Mozart and God eavesdrops. That would at least have stopped him saying it first.

I always saw it as a special problem for the City Police that their daily duties set them down among VIPs without much scope for ensuring that 'the right kind of men' were being thus deployed. In this sense they may be constructively compared with the surrounding Metropolitan Police, who have about thirty times as many to choose from as custodians of the Palace of Westminster and similar holy places. Some few of the City men, unavoidably, were much less suited than others for such official hob-nobbing, and there were occasions when the less suitable came into wonderfully abrasive contact with the City fathers. Typical of such encounters was that of Police Constable Mick O'Malley and Alderman Sir William Phoene Neal; the one a quick-tempered giant, a totally reliable companion in any danger, and a man you would rather have on your side than against you; the other a pompous old pseudo-Dickensian ass, cordially detested by everyone. Mick was probably the original bobby in the story about the mandarin's angry challenge 'Don't you know who I am?' and the reply 'No, and I shall want your address too.' He was cocky, and his cockiness took the form of telling his hearers, in any narrative, only what he had said and not the words of his discomfited adversary. His solitary gift was an instantly accessible vocabulary of profane epithets and injunctions, his sole means of emphasis in conversation. It was not good for stout and choleric City aldermen. Nor was it good, when reported to the Commissioner of Police and linked with Mick's divisional number, for Mick O'Malley. He left us at a speed which barely allowed him time to hand in his uniform. But most of the City fathers were very tolerant, rather touchingly determined to be proud of their police force, and very happy to sustain a kind of relationship that depended on one of two eventualities: not transgressing any law, and not being found out. It was a picture and a relationship that began to develop warts with the arrival of the motor car. (In the twenties the number of registered cars rose from 200,000 to over a million.) The Beecham episode was one of the harbingers of this decline.

There was a healthy mingling of the tribes whenever the Special Constabulary turned out in strength, as they did on big occasions like Lord Mayor's Day and ceremonial visits to the City by royalty or foreign potentates. They were a civic-minded and companionable crowd, mostly from a social milieu that differed from ours. But at times when the police were unhappy with their lot, which were not all that frequent, the Specials were seen as potential strike-breakers and (I thought) treated rather badly. During the General Strike of 1926 even the Special Constabulary were not numerous enough, and 140,000 ordinary members of the public were enrolled as a Civil Constabulary Reserve, recruited by the War Office but controlled by the police. I had some inside glimpses of all this at the time because I was employed as 'divisional clerk' (a job which had no official existence, but which eventually proved itself indispensable on the Parkinson's Law principle). And I thought at the time that, since the coal and rail strike had seemed so likely to turn into a nation-wide down-tools, the official reaction seemed incredibly slow-moving and improvised. The Civil Constabulary Reserve got no kind of street-duty instruction, and they didn't even have truncheons. It is one of the little-known facts of General Strike history that High Wycombe added to its stature as a furniture-making centre by providing them with lorry-loads of chairlegs for use as weapons in the coming struggle for power (which never came). I don't think there is a recorded instance of a chairleg being raised in anger. In fact it is interesting to recall, writing as I am during the 1984/5 coal strike and all its bitterness about police violence in warding off petrol bombs, bricks, and bits of flagstone, that after the General Strike of 1926 there were almost no complaints about police behaviour. But neither were there any petrol bombs or bits of flagstone.

I think everyone rather loved us for a few months, largely because a trade union orientated police service would have delivered over the people who were not on strike to the people who were; and in 1919, just before I became a bobby, it had looked for a time as if the police would form themselves into a trade union affiliated to the TUC. This is an idea which still raises its head from time to time, always to be smartly knocked down by Parliament and the Home Office. The last time it happened (in 1978) the solatium was a pay increase of such reckless munificence that you would expect the whole youth of Britain to be scrambling for admission to the service. They are not. But in 1926 when *The Times* invited its readers to give tangible expression to their sighs of relief, they subscribed £240,000 in a fortnight, and it turned into a National Police Fund which is still being administered by a Home Office Committee that will one day rank with the Maundy Money Office as a curiosity in Historical Handouts. However, by May 1927 the public, or anyway the Press, were ready once again for some police outrage or gaffe to enliven news columns that were getting dull. There is nothing so flaccid as a modern newspaper containing no culpable cops. The Arcos Raid was a godsend.

Somebody, probably a double agent, told M.I.5 (or perhaps in the first instance the police) that in the offices of Arcos, the USSR trading organization in Moorgate, it would find evidence of Russia's involvement in the fomentation of trouble in India. Mahatma Gandhi had just been re-elected President of the All-India Congress after six years in prison for preaching disaffection, and the USSR was understood to be offering him its fast-improving services as political impresario. The whole story was probably a pack of lies, its object the promotion of a piece of valuably ridiculous flat-footedness. One morning, having just come off night duty, I was trying to get to sleep in my bachelor cubicle at Moor Lane Section House when I was told, brusquely I felt, to get up, get into uniform quickly, and report to the officer on duty downstairs. This invasion of the single men's leisure hours was usually occasioned by a big fire, or some similar fast-moving catastrophe calling for extra men at once; and it was one of the means by which the single man was goaded into marriage, his only escape from barrack life—you couldn't 'live out' as a single man. Then with half a dozen bleary-eyed night-birds I was dispatched to the Arcos building on some utterly unexplained mission which nevertheless seemed unusually exciting and important. None of us had the smallest idea what went on in that respectable-looking building, which could easily have been a bank; but neither, it turned out, did M.I.5.

In Coleman Street, at the rear of the Arcos headquarters, we found a uniformed chief inspector and a group of senior CID officers all talking in undertones and trying (we thought) to look like good Europeans. Three or four of them had beards (rare in those days) and therefore looked as if they understood Russian. Uniformed constables were arriving in twos and threes from the other three divisions, all carrying their capes in case it came on to rain, and in the end there were twenty-four of us—six from each division, though our six seemed to be the only lot who had been hauled out of bed for the occasion: the others were all on duty anyway. We were told that certain officers were about to enter the Arcos building and search it, but whether for drugs, bombs, stolen property, firearms, scrap metal, contraband goods, spies, counterfeit coins, or white slaves we knew not. We were *not* told, but somehow got to know, that we were expected to arrest people coming out with bags or brief-cases or bundles of paper, so long as they were not police or M.I.5 officers (none of us knew then, without benefit of Alec Guinness and television, what an M.I.5 officer looked like). If we didn't know what they were, we were to stop them and find out. For the first time, we began to feel part of it all.

About ten men in plain clothes then pushed open the door of the building in Moorgate, and you could see them talking to a commissionaire inside. Then they split up and (we supposed) proceeded to search all the offices. They took an hour. They all came out again, empty-handed, unaccompanied by any Marxist-looking thinkers, and went away, four of them in a taxi. We didn't know at the time, but they had found absolutely nothing. After the usual interval, that is to say about fifteen or twenty minutes, during which someone decides that someone else had better make a decision, we were all sent away too.

As I tried to get off to sleep again I wondered who would authorize such a procedure. It obviously wasn't the police, who at the last minute had been brought in (I guessed) simply to see fair play and convince the Russkies that the British bulldog could do more than just scowl over the top of his Union Jack waistcoat. Later it came out that it was decided upon by three men: the Prime Minister (Mr Stanley Baldwin), the Foreign Minister (Sir Austen Chamberlain), and the Home Secretary (Sir William Joynson-Hicks), acting without informing the Cabinet. There was an unholy parliamentary row, stentorian insults were traded just as if it had all been happening at Question Time on Radio Four, and the newspapers went to town on the whole fiasco. 'RED FACES FOR POLICE', they said happily, with much meaningful manipulation of the word 'red'. I think it doubtful whether, as I eventually got off to sleep that day, my own face was even pink. MPs of course gave Mr Baldwin an unhappy time. Much goaded, he even read out to them the decoded texts of some Russian diplomatic correspondence, with the effect (it has since been believed) that Russian diplomatic codes were promptly changed to others much more complicated and difficult to read. What truly staggered me was the number of policemen said to have been present. And not merely present, but actually raiding the premises. Five hundred, said the *Daily Graphic*. Hundreds, said the *Daily News*. Mr A. J. P. Taylor in his *English History 1914–1945* (Oxford, 1965, p. 255) says '200 police raided the offices of Arcos'. And think of that — 200 of us crowding in through that swing-door in Moorgate, all looking for evidence about Mr Gandhi and the newly ascendant Joseph Stalin. What would we have found? Evidence, perhaps, that Lenin had been dead for three years, to be duly filed with the more poignant news about Queen Anne. It took hours to get to sleep again.

I leave the twenties at a funeral. I don't enjoy funerals, and Christian grief sometimes puzzles me, if the Christian death is to be properly seen as a deliverance, a fresh start, promotion. In 1929 the funeral of General William Bramwell Booth of the Salvation Army was the occasion of a huge procession, which came up Queen Victoria Street to the Mansion House, made a V-turn into Poultry and went back along Cheapside to St. Paul's Cathedral. It was headed by massed Salvation Army brass bands, picked musicians all; and as they neared the Mansion House, their vast volume of sound echoing among the City buildings, I stood rooted to the ground and shaking (I hope imperceptibly) like a man with malaria. They were playing an arrangement of 'What Is Life Without Thee?', the lovely aria from Gluck's *Orpheus and Eurydice* which Kathleen Ferrier has since made even more gloriously memorable. I supposed that the Salvationists, or anyway those of them who knew the Gluck aria, were really asking what was left for them now that William Bramwell Booth was dead, who had been their leader for twenty-seven years. On the other hand *Orpheus and Eurydice* was the only opera known to me with a happy ending and the lovers reunited. Each dominant note was emphasized by a blow on thirty big drums. And I recalled how, when I was a child of four, the big drums of the Grenadier Guards band marching in the Lord Mayor's Procession had seemed to thump dangerously on my very heart, so that I wondered whether people ever died of it. After that funeral I was thoughtful for a very long time.

I had come to regard the Salvation Army with a kind of guilty affection, a feeling of admiration for the many-sided social work I had now seen them doing, and a fierce partisanship engaged by the disposition of the police to deride their work because of its rather flamboyant association with 'religion'. That funeral of their departed leader stays in my mind as a deeply emotional tribute to a good man, and a constant reminder that Christianity is one of the bedrocks of the civilized world. But I still don't know how much the recollection owes to that huge concourse of slow-marching bandsmen, to their beautifully disciplined performance, to dear old Christoph von Gluck, or to the incomparable Ferrier. It's all so inextricably mixed up.

CHAPTER FIVE

NOT many men, in writing this kind of scamper through their decades, would dare to skip the thirties and the forties. Indeed skipping them altogether is not to be thought of, but they already support such a vast literature that I have the best of excuses for brevity. For much of the thirties I was on daily duty (during the Sessions) as 'inspector-in-charge' at the Old Bailey; concerned not with the prosecutions but with the preservation of order in the building and the safety and comfort of the judges, and (far more important) the safety and comfort of the City fathers who came there, as representatives of the Central Criminal Court Committee of the Corporation of London, to listen to the trials and have lunch. From this uncommitted viewpoint I was able to get a fly-on-the-wall picture of many famous criminal trials of the time, usually filled out by some inside knowledge not accessible to those in court: Clarence Hatry, who printed government bonds on a vastly greater scale than the governments knew about, Lord Kylsant of the Royal Mail Steam Packet Company and its false prospectus (the Kylsant shipping empire was tottering to its fall), Leopold Harris the fire assessor who set the fires going in order to assess them, Elvira Barney, who shot her lover and was found not guilty of doing it, Compton Mackenzie, who had drawn too freely on his Intelligence Service memories of the Kaiser's war (and was tried in camera), and many murder cases which at that time filled so much more newspaper space because the death penalty still hung over the scene — the black cap, the condemned cell, the gallows, the drop, the rope, the hysteria, the vigils, the devil quoting Scripture, and the potted Sunday biographies of killer, victim, killer's mother, judge, and hangman.

There can't be many of those trials which have escaped the published memoirs of judges, lawyers, journalists, policemen, and criminologists. There are none which I could revive here with profit or instruction for anyone. In any event, I recognize in myself (and here comes a confession) a built-in snootiness concerning the constant retelling of famous murder stories. I suppose they are as 'endlessly fascinating' as their authors and publishers usually claim, even though they always have a modest sort of sale and soon find their way into the remainder boxes. Unless they are superlatively well done, like Rebecca West's accounts of treason trials, they seem to me a squalid way of turning a penny or two. They have a near-monopoly of hushed courts, audiences hanging on words, deadly cross-examinations, slow-turning wheels, façades of respectability, guilty passion, and relentless enquiry, and of phrases like 'little-did-he-know', 'all-this-was-to-have-a-sequel', 'long-arm-of-the-law', and 'justice-never-sleeps'. They cause recurrent grief and the bitterest embarrassment to relatives of both accused and victim, sometimes many years after the wounds have almost healed, and they seek to live on that which they platitudinously condemn. Yet from among them all there must be set apart those angry writers, from Dickens, Zola, and Wilkie Collins to Arthur Conan Doyle and, in our time, Ludovic Kennedy and Montgomery Hyde, who have set out to expose injustices and vindicate the innocent.

What has seldom been done, except in isolated pockets among the learned periodicals, is to expose the shortcomings of our criminal justice system as they come to their wretched climaxes in a place like the Old Bailey. I am speaking of the unfeeling, or at least unconcerned, official treatment of witnesses, jurors, prisoners' relatives, and children, oppressing with a kind of transferred guilt all those brought together in that vast, busy, echoing, soulless place; the strange insensitivity which keeps a witness standing for hours in the witness-box until, with some rare flash of humanity, a judge or counsel or clerk or usher or *somebody* notices that the witness looks tired and he is asked if he would like a chair. (Every visiting American is astounded at this. One lady from New Jersey asked me if it might be possible, and convenient, for an English witness-summons to include a footnote saying 'Bring your own stool.') The cliché-ridden banality of many counsels' speeches, itself the product of generations of ham actors like Marshall Hall (there are and always have been brilliant exceptions), and clichés all repeated, with astonishing immunity, in 'submissions' to the judge, must bear some responsibility for the even sloppier prose in Press reports. The imitative cruelty of much cross-examination has all the thoughtful industry of a small boy pulling a captive fly to pieces or cutting up an earthworm with his new pocket-knife, a sight from which to avert the eyes and cover the ears. From the past fifty years I should like to instance, with great respect, three classic cross-examinations as models of forensic behaviour for as long as our present system may survive: Sir Norman Birkett questioning Alfred Arthur Rouse in the 'blazing car' murder in 1931; Sir William Jowitt, as Attorney General, questioning Lord Kylsant in the Royal Mail Steam Packet Company trial in 1934; and Lord Gardiner questioning all the defendants in the ETU ballot-rigging trial in 1961. All these defendants were trapped, helpless, and lying. All were treated with a scrupulous and incisive courtesy, a kind of kid-glove persistence, that was far more 'deadly' than all the blustering sarcasm so frequently paraded, and was far less likely to antagonize a jury into returning a perverse verdict.

There is said to be an 'art' of cross-examination, but in non-legal circles the expression itself is essentially misunderstood. It is of course the dramatic part of criminal court proceedings, reinforced by much hitching of gowns and adjustment of wigs and all the little histrionic movements that are supposed to impress juries (but never impress judges). In Terence Rattigan's play, when the Winslow Boy first meets the great advocate who, it is hoped, will defend him, the famous drawing-room interview is referred to as a cross-examination; but it is not, unless in the sense that it is an examination that makes two people cross. It is a bullying interrogation which the victim survives so well that the great man is able to announce that 'the boy is obviously telling the truth' and that he will 'take the case'. To most of us now, it seems, to cross-examine is to question someone very closely and persistently, assuming all the time that he is probably lying; especially if this is done with authority and the power to punish. It formerly meant to examine in a court of law (and nowhere else) a witness for the opposing side, in the hope of discrediting his evidence. In the courts it still does, but the dictionaries now admit also the popular meaning. And because our system mixes lawyers and laymen in a way that almost expects the latter to ape the former, it is quite common to hear a lay magistrate say to a defendant 'No, no, you can ask this witness any questions you like, but you *must not* cross-examine' — I have heard it a hundred times, and have wondered always at the tact with which the justices' clerk (though quite often a layman himself) would then extricate his Bench from its entanglement.

If indeed it is an art, its modern practitioners seem to me artists of diminishing merit, and that may be a good thing. It seems likely that the changes taking place in jury trial after the Civil War were accompanied by a growing indulgence as to how a witness could be treated — and therefore a growing cruelty. Judges even took over the business of cross-examination while counsel helplessly looked on. Jeffreys did it in nearly all the Monmouth treason trials, and especially the trial of Lady Alice Lisle, arraigned before him for giving a night's lodging to a couple of the fugitives from Sedgemoor. Jeffreys swore and railed at the witnesses in a way that achieved notoriety mainly because he was sending so many hundreds of prisoners to the gallows or to the stake — he wanted Lady Alice Lisle to be burned, but he was overruled and she was merely beheaded. By 1883, when Fitzjames Stephen — himself a distinguished judge — was writing his great *History of the Criminal Law of England*, he was able to report that cross-examination had become 'decorous and humane' in its 200 years of development. If so, it had slipped back by the time I got to the Old Bailey in the 1930s. Let me recall but one instance of it which no one who saw and heard it will be likely to forget.

The prisoner was a solicitor and an ex-Member of Parliament. There is no need to name him, and since his downfall he has regained public esteem and self-respect. Prosecuting him for the Treasury was Mr R. E. Seaton, who later became chairman of the County of London Sessions; today he would be a Crown Court judge, and I mention this circumstance because of the light it throws, or threw, upon the criteria by which our judges are chosen. The prisoner chose to go into the witness-box and give evidence on his own behalf—which he would not have been allowed to do in Jeffreys's time, or in Fitzjames Stephen's. And Seaton proceeded to give him the treatment commended by even Fitzjames Stephen himself, who believed it was society's right and duty to hate the criminal:

A criminal trial is a substitute for private war and is, and must be, conducted in a spirit of hostility which is often persistent and even passionate . . . A trial of any importance is always more or less of a battle, and one object of the rules of evidence and procedure is to keep such warfare within reasonable bounds.

He considered, however, that 'questions put in cross-examination may be offensive and odious'. And Stephen accepted, as a regrettable necessity, that 'they may be a means of gratifying personal malice of the basest kind, and of deterring witnesses from coming forward to discharge a duty to the public'. They may also deter a man from trying to tell his own story in the witness-box, a situation which Stephen never had to consider. R. E. Seaton was said to pride himself on his 'deadly' cross-examinations. Any witness coming to face him would at once encounter the odiousness and malice identified by Stephen as a part of the game. He had a rectangular shiny face, the squareness of it accentuated by his dingy grey pelmet of a wig; and the downturned semi-circle of his mouth always gave him the appearance of a deeply offended hake. The tone of his questioning in the case of the accused solicitor could best be judged, since his sneering voice cannot be reproduced here, by his own responses (quite needless and improper) to the answers he got:

I see. And that's what you are asking His Lordship and the jury to believe, is it?

Quite. You were merely concerned, in other words, to cover your tracks?

Rather convenient for you, wasn't it, that things should turn out just like that?

You are lying, aren't you?

As a solicitor of the Supreme Court, you are no doubt familiar with the Perjury Act? I mean you know what you are doing?

Something tells me, you know, that you are not *quite* so stupid as this. But just in case I'm mistaken, let me see if I can put it another way.

And this last one, which Seaton had almost patented as a means of humiliating a witness, was fairly widely used, and was always followed by an elaborately thoughtful silence during which he gazed through half-closed eyes at the middle of the ceiling, his lower gill drawn in as though for the admission of a fresh supply of plankton. The whole performance, horrible as it was to watch, always reminded me of Fitzjames Stephen's rather equivocal comments on the trial of Titus Oates, whose perjury had sent many Catholics to their deaths and whom Jeffreys treated 'with brutality', though 'I must not say', added Stephen, 'that I think the sentence upon him too severe'. He got a prolonged flogging and life imprisonment, but after three years he was liberated (by William and Mary) and given a pension for life. As a matter of interest, Stephen regretted that he couldn't have been flogged or tortured to death (*History of the Criminal Law of England*, Macmillan, 1893, vol. 1, p. 412). The voice of Stephen, revered as that of a great lawyer, judge, historian, and legislator, elegantly expresses the hatred with which, according to him, society must always regard the criminal. It found expression, and it still does, in 'the art of cross-examination'.

Astonishing injustice is also frequent in the matter of defendants' costs. An acquitted defendant should never be left to meet the costs of justice except to the extent that he has purposely and needlessly inflated them himself. In particular a man acquitted because the prosecution withdraws its charges should get not only his costs but adequate compensation for having been forced into such a role by a state machine which monopolizes all the power. It was happening every day when I was in the courts and it happens every day now. Far too often, when it happens, the victim has been awaiting trial in prison, sometimes for a year or more. To me the complacency of the public about this, and of Parliament, and in particular of the lawyers (who do at least know what's going on) is endlessly astounding. In 1961, when Penguin Books were prosecuted for publishing D. H. Lawrence's *Lady Chatterley's Lover* and acquitted by an Old Bailey jury, Mr Justice Byrne was asked to award the publishers their costs. 'I make no order as to costs', he said. In other words, let them pay their own. Their costs amounted to £13,000. They had dared to call a number of witnesses, as they were then newly entitled to do, whom His Lordship plainly disapproved of, to speak in defence of a book he plainly thought should never have been published. Let them pay. They were simply unlucky in their judge. How can any man, hand on heart, call that justice?

Fifty years ago it was denied, and it is still denied, that court lists were ever manipulated so as to get a particular case before a particular judge. They were and they still are. Typically, I have known a CID sergeant hurry jubilantly out of No. 1 Court at the Old Bailey, rubbing his hands and telling me through clenched teeth: 'I've worked five years to get that bastard in front of Avory and at last he's got his lot.' Mr Justice Avory had just given a man fifteen years (which he richly deserved) for armed robbery. There are ways of delaying or expediting a trial which have their origin in the means of discovering which judge will be sitting in which court and when. Such little plots often go wrong, possibly more often than they go right. But they should never be allowed to go anywhere.

Yet I believe I can report two advances, or at least the shedding of two pretences. Fifty years ago there was frequent recourse to both plea-bargaining and jury-vetting, and the existence of both was always officially denied. Both practices were so self-evident in operation that I could never see the point of the denials. It was possible not merely for the police to hunt out the potential and likely jurors, but for anyone to do it, including private enquiry agents whose masters fancied a particular type of jury. The jury list (the 'panel'), containing hundreds of names each session, showed all the trades and professions as well as the addresses, and could be seen by anyone with seemingly sufficient reason plus one shilling. Today, through the effective intervention of Lord Hailsham as Lord Chancellor, it shows such a minimum of information that it is not worth anyone's attention. In cases where it is thought necessary by the Director of Public Prosecutions, and he certifies accordingly to the Attorney-General, the police are given the necessary details and off they go on their jury-vetting exercise. I could never see anything wrong either in that or in the even older practice of plea-bargaining. This means the private meeting in the judge's room, both counsel present, as a result of which the defendant is given the chance to shorten his trial by pleading guilty to some modified charge on the understanding that his sentence will be less severe. The courts are a lot more honest about all this today. I wonder if this is because there are so many hundreds of Crown Court judges and recorders today, all of them men and women who have practised at the criminal Bar and seen it all in operation, and who are less disposed to discuss the more common-sense practices of the judiciary in whispers. To me, it all seems sheer gain.

Certainly the lawyers are a lot more frank. I know many who would agree with all that I have written here, and some of them have been good enough to read it through before publication. So it is fair to say, and pleasant to say it, that today's lawyers are on the whole an unjustly maligned lot, and that they (like doctors and others with professional knowledge and skills) give much of their time and assistance in emergency cases without fee, saving much litigation, and are to be found in the vanguard of all law reform movements, working long hours without payment for causes that will profit almost anyone but themselves. During my own involvement with such movements, and with probation committees and prison after-care societies, I have sent so many difficult and penniless clients to my lawyer friends, with problems ineligible for legal aid, that I marvel at their not crossing the road whenever they see me coming. Perhaps they do. They do everything unobtrusively.

As I write this, trial by jury in criminal cases has the appearance of a dying institution. (In civil cases it has been virtually dead since 1949, but it refuses to lie down.) Some historians have noticed this ailing appearance since the year 1215, when the priestly Lateran Council abolished 'trial by ordeal'. And although it has changed in some ways since 1215, the most important changes were delayed until the Juries Act 1974 ensured that I should be among the last few citizens to be called for jury service after having been a policeman. As the law now stands, no such creature can be permitted to serve on a jury, a disability which he now shares with judges, magistrates, barristers and solicitors and their clerks, court officials, coroners, court shorthand writers, prison chaplains, medical officers, probation officers, sentenced criminals, and people who work in forensic science laboratories. If the jury is to sit in Scotland, this list of the unwanted will include lighthouse keepers. It is a list which seems to reflect a determination to reject anyone who can have any possible knowledge of the law and its works, even if he might have got that knowledge by accident. This being so, I have always thought it strange that there is no objection to qualified criminologists (a fast-growing community, many of them not qualified lawyers), who might be thought to know as much about the operation of the criminal law as almost anyone.

At the Old Bailey I took a great interest in juries, who, it seemed to me, could be regarded as the Poor Bloody Infantry of the whole system. They received from the official machine every extreme of treatment between courtesy and irritated contempt. Talking to jurors then,

I became aware of a great gulf between them and the lawyers, sustained by a wilful (and probably high-minded) determination on the part of the lawyers to keep themselves uninformed about what went on in jury rooms, and at the same time (less high-mindedly) to use in the presence of jurors a private or 'learned' language which would keep jurors in their place, a not-in-front-of-the-jurors dialect. A surprisingly high proportion of jurors resented being there at all: it surprised me, that is to say, because I always found in private conversation away from the Old Bailey that everyone seemed to be longing for a jury summons and never getting one. No doubt the actual experience involved far too much hanging about in waiting-rooms and corridors for days on end, without being called to serve on a trial. Most of the ushers and jury bailiffs were considerate, indeed almost protective, while some were petty tyrants enjoying an authority which, in the rather awesome atmosphere of the place, no juror quite dared to challenge—I often wished they would. All the ushers operated a code of unwritten rules for the conduct of jurors in waiting, which survived through the generations only because no one dared expose their kindergarten principles by committing them to paper. These I suppose took the place, in those days, of any kind of useful instruction for the several hundred assembled ratepayers as to their duties, obligations, and standards of behaviour.

For unlike the grand jurors, abolished without loss in 1934, who always had a long lecture from the recorder before they began their superfluous duties, these jurors got no instruction whatsoever in these matters. After the first day of each session, perhaps I should say after the first few hours, a waiting juror would furtively produce his morning newspaper. Others, observing after a time that nothing had happened to him, did the same. Magazines came out, paperbacks, library books, knitting. But once a waiting jury was seated in court, in the place reserved for waiting jurors who were next on the list for a trial, none of this was allowed. And here the restraint must have seemed harsher, because they were seated behind a huge dock (built to

contain about a dozen prisoners at a time), could neither
hear nor see anything, and were not allowed to talk. It may
well be that a reading or knitting juror is nowhere
condemned in the canon of English law, but the control
of jurymen has a Common Law of its own. A knitting juror
would suddenly find, if the knitting was spotted by an
usher, that that outraged official was bearing down upon
her in fiercely whispered reproof. I have even seen the
knitting impounded. I once found one of my constables
directing a lady to put away her crochet, and told him
quietly to leave all that kind of thing to the ushers. But
there is perhaps a symbolic hostility between knitting and
the course of justice, if the latter is to be seen as an
unravelling.

There was at that time a large waiting-room for Old
Bailey jurors, a stone-flagged echoing hall of about tennis-
court size, equipped with scores of movable oak benches.
This was at times so crowded that an usher was unable
to see all that was going on. I remember going in there late
one afternoon in search of an usher who had a message
for me, and as I went in I saw from the corner of my eye
two pairs of seated men facing each other on a couple of
forms. Between them was another form on which cards
were set out for a game of solo whist. The fact that I was
in uniform probably lent speed to the concerted movement
that got all the cards out of sight in little more than a
second (the players had obviously done it before). The next
day the same usher told me, in the kind of voice one would
normally use in reporting the murder and dismemberment
of a small child, that he had found four of his jurors actually
playing bridge. I told him it was solo. But I have since
discovered that in some jury waiting-rooms today there
are solo schools wherever you look.

Such are the changes that have occurred. And twenty
years later, ten years after leaving the police service, I
received a jury summons myself. Why me, I thought? Had
there been any discussion, at some suitable level, of my
eligibility? There had not. At the sheriff's office, the source
of this summons, no one knew my age, or whether I was

a nun, a pilot licensed by the Elder Brethren of the Corporation of Trinity House of Deptford Strond, a dentist, or the keeper of a lunatic asylum. None of these can be jurors, however willing. Nor, of course, did they know I had been in the police service, though at that time such a past would not have disqualified me. The small blue document told me that I was 'to be of a jury to try between our Sovereign Lady the Queen and the Several Defendants and Prisoners to be at the Bar', at what was then known as the Quarter Sessions of the Peace for the County of London and is now the Inner London Crown Court (with an enlarged jurisdiction). 'Whereof fail not,' grimly concluded the small blue document, 'as you will answer the contrary at your peril.' I can't remember now what the peril would have been, but today it would be £400.

At 9.15 a.m. on the appointed day I stood with about 200 others in a court room which had begun life as a small swimming-bath. The County of London Sessions were then being held in the rather hastily converted municipal swimming-baths at Seymour Street, Marylebone, while their bomb-damaged home at Southwark was being rebuilt. We had been herded into this room, which was too small for us, so that we could be addressed by the Clerk of the Peace, no less. After about ten minutes he arrived, and I was astonished and delighted to recognize in his large wigged-and-gowned figure the person of Mr Leo Burgess, whom I had known many years earlier at the Old Bailey, where he had been one of the 'learned clerks' in the Public Office. He was a universally popular man. He said good morning and told us something of the duties that lay before us. Then we were marshalled into groups of fourteen (two extra in each group to allow for casualties) and given a date on which to come back and start work; a great improvement, I thought, on the old business of hanging about for days. But on the way out I met Mr Burgess. 'What on earth are *you* doing here?', he said, and the words sounded much more affable than they look. I told him I was one of his jurors. He looked incredulous, and then 'Over my dead body', he said hospitably. 'You're a cop,

or you have been, and that disqualifies you.' Not as the
law stood, I said with what I hoped was suitable diffidence.
(After all, he ought to know what kind of jurors he was
legally entitled to spurn.)

He knew about my *New Statesman* scribblings. 'I
suppose,' he said, 'if I turf you out you'll go and make a
great fuss in the old Staggers.' He would look into it, and if
I *were* disqualified he would see that I was notified in time
to save me a futile second journey to court. No notification
came, and it was to be another ten years (1974) before a
Juries Act saw to it that no one like me disfigured jury-
boxes any more.

My jury, with whom I was to serve for three weeks and
try about fifteen cases, included three women: one of them
sharp, cynical, suspicious of the whole world, and very
annoyed at being there at all, and the other two comfortable
Mrs Mopp types, rather bewildered about everything but
determined that, from our second day onwards, we should
all have cups of tea when we retired to consider our
verdicts. This they ensured by bringing, in turns, shopping
bags containing (in addition to their knitting) a huge
Thermos jug of hot tea, a pint of milk, a cocoa-tin full of
sugar, and some mugs and spoons. By the fourth day all
the men were coming with buns and biscuits. It was a great
surprise to me that we seemed to be expected to retire for
consideration of our verdicts — at the Old Bailey most juries
were strongly influenced against retiring ('turn to each
other, members of the jury, and consider your verdict');
and the cases we were trying were mostly trivial affairs
that ought to have been dealt with by magistrates.

I didn't tell my fellow-jurors about my police experience,
sensing that the disclosure probably wouldn't go down very
well. But once or twice I was able to supply the answer
to a question that was bothering some of them, and I
suspect that they put this down to some supposed
experience as a court reporter — they knew that I was a
journalist. But they should have needed no such aid from
me, or from any other chance fellow-juror. They should
have had a booklet telling them why they were there, how

they had been chosen, what they couldn't do, why they would have to sit silent and useless when a prisoner pleaded guilty, why they would have nothing to do with the sentences passed on the guilty, what expenses they could claim, what to do if they found themselves unable to agree on a verdict, and how to keep awake after a pub lunch while listening to a two-hour speech about the theft of a bottle of Scotch (which my jury actually did). Some courts, I believe, now supply some such booklet. But it seems an odd thing to leave to local option.

For the first day my colleagues were all attention: interested, anxious, rather sceptical and, above all, worried about the inaudibility of witnesses. There was one nervous lady, a witness for the Crown in a case of employment insurance fraud, whom none of us could hear. 'You *will* speak up, won't you?', she was constantly urged by prosecuting counsel. 'It's essential, you see, that My Lord and the jury should hear what you are saying.' 'Yes', she said timidly each time, and otherwise took absolutely no notice. I thought it was a bit more essential for us to hear than for His Lordship, who, after all, had read the depositions before the case started. When we were at lunch in our chosen pub, recklessly ingesting steak-and-kidney pudding and other soporific fare, our foreman asked me if I could hear the poor woman's evidence. 'Not a word', I said. 'Neither can I,' he admitted, 'so what the hell's the use of that? What do I do? Pass a note to the judge?' We decided that it was the only thing to do, and on our return he gave the court usher a note accordingly. 'Oh dear', said the judge (it was Mr Henry Elam, whom, by another strange chance, I had known when he was a junior clerk in the offices of the Corporation of London at the Guildhall, my former bailiwick; but of course he didn't remember me). 'Are you saying you've heard nothing this witness has said?' The foreman said yes, and we all nodded our heads. Mr Elam said he wished we had said so before, and our foreman, greatly daring now that the ice round the seat of justice seemed to be broken, made two observations that seemed to me unanswerable. First, we had all been very much discouraged about interrupting the proceedings or addressing the judge, even on bits of paper. Secondly, we had all supposed that the witness was audible to everyone else, and would anyway yield sooner or later to the entreaties of counsel to speak up.

Judge and counsel went into a concerned huddle, at the end of which both counsel agreed that the shorthand-writer should 'read back' the whole of the poor lady's evidence. (This has always seemed to me, by the way, as a shorthand-writer of sorts myself, a prodigious feat which the court shorthand-writers can always perform with unvarying and almost insolent ease.) After which, both counsel repeated loudly every answer they got from the witnesses they were questioning — a course which might be worth adopting universally, if only you could be sure of hearing the questions as well.

Of the three ladies on our jury, one would, I think, have liked to be foreman and tell us how to comport ourselves (the foreman was chosen, in fact, by the usher, seemingly because he wore a smart pin-stripe suit and a bow-tie; and a very good foreman he was). The other two ladies, having poured out the Thermos tea, got out their knitting and said they would 'leave it all to us'. One of them said many times that she thought these things were 'not for the likes of us', by which I think she meant all of us. There were three men who wanted to acquit everybody and were obviously unhappy each time they were overborne. They displayed what was to me a quite unexpected veneration for the judge's many references to 'reasonable doubt'. They seemed to feel, though I'm sure that one of them led the others in this, that there could never be a contested case that was free from reasonable doubt. There had been a run of cases in which juries had convicted and then, sometimes years later, another man already in prison had confessed to the crime, the confession being checked by the police and verified. I believe that, before the law of England was changed (in 1967) to allow 'majority verdicts' as in Scotland, there were in effect thousands of majority verdicts reflecting the uneasy complicity of timid or bewildered jurors whose doubts might have been well founded. Yet once you admit the principle of majority verdicts you are accepting the certainty of convicting *in spite of reasonable doubt*. In any ten-to-two-verdict, the two dissentients might be the only two on the jury with any sense.

Of course it is the experience of those who have served on a criminal jury, as of those who have watched criminal juries in operation (and I now belong to both classes), that every jury gets tougher as it gains experience. Towards the end of every session of a court the proportion of convictions goes up. On my jury, there were no awkward characters, no idiots, and no dictators, and all were likeable people. As an assembly designed to effect random representation of the community, they must have been among the last of their kind. Representation of that nature has not, in practice, been achieved by the admission of eighteen-year-olds and the abolition of the property qualification. These provisions of the Juries Act 1974 were expected to produce right-across-the-board juries, but two developments, both of them foreseen by critics of the Act when it first came before Parliament, have frustrated all such intentions. First, there has been a higher proportion of teenagers serving on juries than could have been foretold, due probably to the likelihood that older people are better supplied with excuses and quicker at using them. Secondly, there has been a remarkable revival of both jury-vetting and the exercise of the right of challenge.

Jury-vetting has lately been officially disparaged, as something that should never be allowed to happen, a violation of the whole historical concept of random selection. (To my knowledge, it was going on in the early 1930s on quite a large scale, but it may have been without the knowledge of the authorities. I have always supposed that their consent was tacit, and liable to instant disavowal in emergencies.) In 1980, in a case known as *R. v. Sheffield Crown Court, ex parte Brownlow*, Lord Denning described it as unconstitutional, and Lords Shaw and Brandon had serious doubts as to whether it should be allowed at all.

But they all thought that if the prosecution were allowed to do it 'in certain categories of cases', which really meant spy trials and similar security matters, then it would hardly seem just that the defence should not be allowed to do it in any kind of case. But in the same year the Court of Appeal in *R*. v. *Mason* said, in effect, that it was all right (and 'a long-standing custom') if the police did it, for example in supplying counsel with details of criminal convictions against embryo jurors, but that the judges were not making any pronouncement about the desirability of making any other kind of enquiries about jurors. And although Home Secretaries and law officers will always deny that it goes on except, regrettably, in rare security cases, it will go on until it is prohibited by statute. After which it will be done with much greater stealth.

The challenging of jurors is certainly an old-established right, and has now been whittled down until, by the Juries Act of 1974, a defendant may challenge no more than three prospective jurors without giving any reason. Where there are half a dozen youthful prisoners in the dock, this means that eighteen jurors can be turned away on no better ground than that (perhaps because they are soberly dressed) they look likely to have a prejudice against youthful prisoners in the dock, or that they look too hard-boiled or not stupid enough. By this means, the law of averages can be enabled to produce a jury of possible teenage sympathizers. Similarly, where the case to be tried is an allegation of involved commercial fraud, three teenagers or simians per prisoner can be got rid of. It is sometimes said that a dockful of prisoners could thus exhaust the entire jury list and end with no one to try them. But this would have one of two certain consequences, neither attractive as seen from the dock. Either the case would be put back for trial at some future session, or the court would proceed to try each prisoner separately. They *might* get both— adjournment *and* separate trials.

After his third 'peremptory' challenge, as the law calls it, a prisoner can go on challenging jurors for stated reasons, all of which can be pondered by the judge and are most likely to be disallowed. But if a prisoner discovered a formula which did indeed wrong-suit all the jurors ready to try him, so that the judge had to allow the lot, the prisoner would have achieved two distinctions: first, a remand (or remands) in custody while a fresh jury, or a series of fresh juries, was assembled to try him, and secondly a secure place in the legal text-books. But in the process he would have become famous in a way that would not help his case.

I find that I'm against the continuance of 'challenge without cause'. It belongs to the days when, if a prisoner knew something discreditable about a member of the gentry, he would be better advised to keep his mouth shut than to state it in open court. Nowadays not many prisoners and jurors know and recognize each other, while a vastly increased proportion of jurors must feel, as they survey the man in the dock, 'There but for the grace . . .'. If prisoners had to state their objections in all cases, the law could build up a useful library of costume, deportment and hairstyle, social preferences, and personality disorders which, at least as seen from the dock, stamped the unsuitable juror. But I am also against the abolition of jury-vetting, which I think has become more desirable, not less, since the 1974 Juries Act so enormously expanded the catchment area.

And having thus confidently stated what I'm against in the matter of jury service, let me state briefly that I am not against jury service. I want to see juries selected as if they mattered, as if the trial of an accused man bore no resemblance to the roulette wheel or bran-tub, and as if the deliberations of a jury at the end of a trial were not some shameful secret, guarded by severe penalties (recently made specific and increased). My jury would comprise a judge and two or possibly four assessors. The assessors would not be practising lawyers, but they would have law degrees. They could be barristers or solicitors. They would be chosen by a council — an electoral college, some would like to call it — on which would be representatives of bodies like the Consumers' Association, the Office of Fair Trading, the TUC, the National Council for Civil Liberties, NACRO, the Law Commission, and the Association of Chambers of Commerce. They would be elected for three years, could stand for re-election, and would be removable from office by resolution of the council. Their verdicts (counting the judge as an equal) would be by majority, and could be challenged, as could their sentences, in the Court of Appeal. *They would give written reasons for all their decisions.* And the whole of their proceedings would be tape recorded. I shall not live to see this happen. But when it does happen, let no one exhume me as a prophet, for it all started in 1215 and there have been thousands of us.

But before I end these Old Bailey reminiscences I want to leave a brief elegiac reflection about the grand jury, abolished in 1933. It had long been an obsolete institution. It was a useless survival from the hundred, which in the tenth century was a division of a county. (When the Danes came they called it a wapentake.) There are several accounts of its etymology, all bearing the appearance of inspired guesses, but the most plausible seems to be the one based on the 'hundred best families' in a geographical division, headed by a high constable or hundredor, and having its own court of law administered by a steward. Only two such stewardships still pretend to be alive, that of the Chiltern Hundreds and that of the Manor of Northstead (a manor being a subdivision of a hundred). Their office-holders, who have absolutely no valid functions left, are always moving over to make room for the latest Member of Parliament who would like to resign his seat if only he could. In applying for one of these stewardships an MP is 'seeking an office of profit under the Crown', which as an MP he is debarred from holding. So, without waiting for an election, he stops being an MP, and becomes a paid steward until some other MP wants to do likewise. No one seems to know why an MP can't simply be allowed to resign, the accepted reason being that it has never been done. This little custom has now been given statutory authority, and the Chiltern Hundreds and the Manor of Northstead their special status, by the House of Commons Disqualification Act 1957.

But the hundred, the best families, were the people from whom the grand jury was drawn. They were carriage people. When I saw them in operation they came to the Old Bailey in Rolls Royces, Bentleys, Daimlers, Darracqs, Lanchesters, and Hispano-Suizas. There were twenty-three on a grand jury, so that they could always reach a majority vote. Their job, always completed on the opening day of each session and usually by lunch-time, was to decide which of the cases set down for trial by the ordinary juries were really matters that ought to be tried at all. It didn't matter that the injured party, if any, and the police, and the prosecuting solicitor, and the magistrates in the court below, and the barrister briefed, and perhaps the entire population of Great Britain, thought the case ought at least to be tried. If the grand jury, which heard only the prosecutor's side of the case, decided that the defendant had no case to answer, they wrote on the indictment the words 'NO BILL'. If they thought he had, they wrote 'TRUE BILL'. They were frequently wrong both ways. But if they wrongly said 'NO BILL', the Crown could always have another go at the next session, and usually did, successfully. When a petty jury, on the other hand, the one which heard all the evidence, said 'NOT GUILTY' that was the end of it, even if the acquitted man then perversely shouted from the dock that they were wrong.

On the opening day of each session the grand jury would assemble in Court No. 2 to be 'charged' by the senior 'resident' judge, the Recorder of London. 'Charging' them meant telling them about any special features of the 'bills of indictment' they would be looking at, and informing them that when a defendant was known to be pleading guilty they were bound to say 'TRUE BILL'. In my time the Recorder was Sir Ernest Wild, who made his charge to the grand jury the occasion for a wide-ranging socio-political commentary, carefully larded with phrases that would excite news editors. If Sir Ernest were still with us and charging grand juries today, he would be heard on surrogate motherhood, the pill, football hooliganism, inflation, rock music, and the Channel Tunnel. At the end of which, he would nod and smile at the grand jurors and send them off to their special room to get on with their totally superfluous job. And the grand jury bailiff would motion to them all that they were to follow him thither.

The grand jury bailiff, Mr Edmonds, was a rotund and bustling little man in a gown, with a totally bald head which had a bump on the top. He would already have been through a Court No. 1 ceremony in which the grand jurors were empanelled. Encouraged by their cries of 'Here!', the Clerk of the Court (Mr Wilfrid Nops) would go on calling their names until suddenly there came no such answering cry. Mr Nops would try again twice, and then — 'County of London Officer, did you summon Benjamin Robert Bloggs?' Mr Edmonds would say loudly and indignantly 'I did, Sir, and I have no knowledge why he is not here.' And Mr Nops would intone 'Benjamin Robert Bloggs — come forth, answer to your name, and save the fine of 200 shillings at issue.' No Bloggs. 'Fined 200 shillings', Mr Nops would say impassively and the process would continue.

When in 1933 all this came to an end, there was no visible consequence apart from a considerable saving of money, the welcome acquisition of an extra court room for real trials, and a few letters to *The Times* calling attention to the way in which everything good and sacred was being scrapped by the mad government of Mr J. Ramsay MacDonald.

But the petty jury, the trial jury, although a dying institution, survived. As I have said, it has been dying since 1215, and I perceive now that it will probably outlast me. But it survives because those of our legislators who are interested in law reform do not themselves serve on juries, and because no one who doesn't serve on a jury can have much idea of what really goes on in jury rooms. Since 1981 it has been unlawful (a 'contempt of court') merely to ask a juror what went on; and the penalty for asking, or for publishing the reply you get, is two years' imprisonment. Many people, and they presumably include our legislators, see this as an overdue strengthening of the jury system. Others, a lonely minority to which I firmly belong, see it as a hasty drawing of blinds to keep out the truth for a little longer.

But from 1935 onwards I was established, in the intervals between the monthly Old Bailey sessions (they don't get any intervals now) at City Police headquarters as a kind of one-man scrivener's department, where I wrote other people's letters, memoranda, and protocols rather like the village scribe under the palm-tree. Indeed I find the simile the more apt when I consider the village scribe's chances of getting a coconut on his head. Before long it became known as the Legal Department (and, fifty years later after a succession of incumbents, it still is), though this could have been understood to mean no more than that its activities were not perceptibly illegal. Professor C. N. Parkinson, who had just promulgated his vital law of economics that work expands to fill the time allotted to it, would have been happy to adopt my new little job as his working model. Its importance in my story is that it not merely helped to satisfy my urge to write, but it also nourished a strictly private opinion, subsequently much dented, that I was rather good at it.

And in this context, the decade had begun for me with a sad event, the death of the dear old *Daily News*, the first national daily paper to which I had ever contributed. It was swallowed up by the much less exciting *Daily Chronicle* — or perhaps it did the swallowing, I never really knew. Let's say that they fell into each other's arms and produced the *News Chronicle*, a paper which lasted exactly thirty years and for which, throughout those years but mostly in its last fifteen (when I was out of the police service), I was a fairly regular feature writer. It was then that I first met Robert Lynd, resident *Daily News* (and then *News Chronicle*) critic and essayist and a man whose soft-spoken Irish mannerisms would, as they say, charm the birds out of the trees. Coupled with his droll literary style and comic percipience ('you can't couple three things', he would have told me), this went far to support my private estimation that most of our best writers have come from Ireland. It was he who told me, standing on the corner of Bouverie Street and Tudor Street as he waited for a taxi (he was bent nearly double with some spinal deformity and looked up at me sideways), that whenever I stopped writing for the day, or was proposing to stop for any period longer than an hour, I should stop in mid-paragraph, or even in mid-sentence, and make a marginal note to indicate what I had been going to say. It was only thus, he said, that you could achieve continuity without tears—it was a complete answer to 'writer's block'. I don't recall ever having writer's block, but this may be because I have thenceforth followed his advice. I'm not really sure that he did it himself.

An exactly concurrent thirty-year period, beginning and ending with the *News Chronicle*, was Kingsley Martin's editorship of the *New Statesman*. He was to become a figure of much importance to me, giving a personal dimension to the journal I had been reading on and off since 1917. His predecessor as editor, Clifford Sharp, seemed never to have stamped his personality on the paper, or gathered round him a team of writers with the loyalty and collective brilliance of Kingsley's chosen men and women. I didn't meet him until 1936, though I had been sending him occasional pieces for a year or two before that. But his influence on my thinking during the thirties, even if (as his critics always said) he was a mere conductor for the conclusions of others—Bernard Shaw, Maynard Keynes, Desmond MacCarthy, G. D. H. Cole, H. N. Brailsford, and Harold Laski—was certainly profound. And Brailsford alone would have merited the weekly sixpence which I still found sometimes hard to come by. It was often said of Kingsley that his grasp of current affairs was quick-witted and absorptive rather than profoundly original, and that in current controversy he was too often 'the prey of the last speaker'. Which meant that he could change his mind—and his paper—overnight or during a hurried lunch. It may have been true, but it seemed to me to give him the edge over those who could never change their minds about anything; and I remember thinking sometimes that he could have edited something like *The Economist, Time and Tide*, or the *Spectator* without changing his habits of thought, administering weekly shocks to his editorial staff and contributors and assuring them that only thus would the truth prevail. What he was a prey to, I now believe, was his own honest realization that the truth about anything was always many-sided, that evasion and prevarication and downright lying were rife in the councils of the nations and the newspapers which reported them to the people, and that most partisan anger (including his own) was accordingly synthetic, self-deluding, and rather sad.

I therefore had the feeling that it was through a window of inferior and distorting glass, so to speak, that I saw the rise of Italian Fascism, the emergence of Hitler's maniacal Germany, the Spanish Civil War (in relation to which absolutely everyone was lying from the beginning), the Abdication crisis, the German reoccupation of the Rhineland, and the agonizing sell-out at Munich in 1938. Among my colleagues in the police service there were at that time half a dozen at the most, anyway among those I could claim to know closely, who privately opposed official thinking on all these matters. They were wise to do it privately, in the current atmosphere of growing warmindedness and the almost reluctantly patriotic fervour provoked by the ever more frenetic noises from Germany. Warmindedness was the more depressing for those who, like myself, were at the immediate receiving end of a steadily growing torrent of government circulars, from about the middle of 1936 onwards. These were concerned with air raid precautions, civilian evacuation, the strengthening of police buildings with timber and sandbags (our office windows were in due course completely blocked up with these, and had to be partly unblocked again so that we could breathe without giving each other mouth-to-mouth resuscitation; and for some weeks they added to the population of our office by incubating myriads of sand-dwelling insects which hopped about on our papers), and the way to deal with incendiary bombs.

I remember a Home Office-inspired lecturer, a Mr Bayes Copeman, who had been fighting in one of the International Brigades in Spain and seemed a bit surprised at Whitehall's approval, talking to 100 of us in Gresham College about what was in store for us. He showed us (with pictures) how to improvise stretchers, what to do with partly consumed victims of chemical warfare, and (we had to assume) how to lay out rows of dead schoolchildren, as he had had to do in Barcelona after air raids. We thought much about the change of anxieties at the Home Office, which could now require us to listen to a man whom, a few months before, they would have anathematized as a murderous crypto-communist. Some of us knew that the 'gilded youth' of English life and letters had died fighting alongside him. Stephen Spender, who had come back alive, had told Harold Nicolson, 'They go out there with a deep faith in communism, and in a few weeks they lose all their faith and illusions. But they have to stay and be butchered for a cause they do not believe in. Only some 40 per cent survive.' (Harold Nicolson, *Diaries and Letters: 1930–1939*, Collins, p. 321.) Then we were lectured by our own colleagues who had been away on courses of instruction about poison gas, thermite bombs, and the mass burial of air raid casualties — millions of papier-mâché coffins were being made in anticipation of the holocaust which never came. And in my rapidly growing Legal Department I was required to collate, classify, paraphrase, and in due course promulgate in 'Police Orders' such a mass of written instructions for the rank and file as none of them could ever have had time to read. Their anxiety and bewilderment must have been mutually sustaining. I know mine were, and I was supposed to be sitting at the nerve-centre, scribbling and typing away like an oracle in a hurry. I believe that my sanity survived this period, if it did, because at such times I'm always able to imagine that it is all happening to someone else, who will tell me the story of it at some quieter moment. Sanity seemed, in any case, a distant prospect when we were hearing daily of the merciless and bestial persecution of German Jewry, listening to the mad screams of Hitler's frenzied audiences on our radio sets at home, and trying to accustom our eyes to the twilight of civilization.

To my surprise, I find that many people have forgotten that the huge operation of 'evacuating' the children from the big towns had begun in January 1939. But between 1 June and the outbreak of war on 3 September nearly four million people had been moved, or had moved themselves, from areas of supposed maximum danger to areas of supposed minimum, both suppositions proving in many cases to be quite unfounded. Indeed among people now old enough to have adult memories of Hitler's war, it is astonishing to find how confused those memories are. For at least nine months before the war began, children were everywhere being moved to country villages or to the smaller towns. And yet, as I recall clearly, people were telling each other that there would be no war, that this was all part of the preparedness which would fend it off. In this they were encouraged no doubt by voices like that of the *Daily Express*, which throughout that time proclaimed on its front page that 'There Will Be No War This Year, Or Next Year Either.' I want to end this chapter by recalling two such lapses in the public memory which, placed incongruously side by side, show that the general capacity to forget is unselective, widespread, and sometimes merciful.

By June 1940 there were few knowledgeable people who saw any prospect for Britain but utter defeat. Poland, Belgium, Norway, and Denmark were all occupied by the German armies. A huge British Army had just been evacuated from Dunkirk, with the loss of all its equipment, armoured vehicles, guns, supply trucks, everything. France had capitulated. The Germans were in Paris. If ever a nation had been thrilled and rallied by the voice of one lion-hearted man, it was when Churchill told the House of Commons on 4 June:

We shall go on to the end. We shall fight in France. We shall fight on the seas and oceans. We shall fight with growing confidence and growing strength in the air. We shall defend our island whatever the cost may be. We shall fight on the beaches. We shall fight on the landing grounds. We shall fight in the fields and in the streets. We shall fight in the hills. We shall never surrender . . . Let us therefore brace ourselves to our duties; and bear ourselves that if the British Empire and its Commonwealth last for a thousand years, men will still say 'This was their finest hour.'

I vividly remember the effect, the visible and totally unfamiliar effect, of those words as I watched people taking them in. They put courage into the most craven, strength of will into the most flaccid. Cynics and sophisticates, caught off guard, gulped with pride. There was something in the air that no one had ever known before, an atmosphere in the streets, trains, buses, pubs, restaurants, offices. Men who, to my knowledge, had always detested each other were united in a surge of righteousness that they barely understood, even if they later came to see it as self-preservation disguised as brotherhood. I have always enjoyed reading verse, and (when strictly alone) reading it aloud. There have always been some passages in which my voice fails completely, fading away in defeat; and this is one of them. I suppose that most people who heard will never forget it (it was specially rerecorded for broadcasting to the nation by Norman Shelley doing his Churchill voice, a process in which it lost nothing in dramatic colour).

And yet by contrast I cannot find anyone who remembers a rather spine-chilling public warning put out by 'the Ministry of Information in co-operation with the War Office and the Ministry of Home Security', headed 'IF THE INVADER COMES', and dispatched to millions of homes in Great Britain (14,300,000 copies were printed). I have a copy in front of me now.

The Germans intend to invade Great Britain. If they do so, they will be driven out by our Navy, our Army and our Air Force. Yet the ordinary men and women of the civilian population will also have their part to play. Hitler's invasions of Poland, Holland and Belgium were greatly helped by the fact that the civilian population was taken by surprise. YOU MUST NOT BE TAKEN BY SURPRISE . . .

If people ran away instead of 'staying put', it went on, they would be machine-gunned from the air. 'You will also block the roads by which our own armies will advance to turn the Germans out.' The Germans would spread rumours to create panic. Managers of factories and shops were enjoined to 'organise some system now by which a sudden attack can be resisted'.

It seems to have had two authors. Two men, that is to say, claim to have written it, though in each case the claim might more aptly be called an uneasy confession. In 1940 Sir Kenneth Clark (later Lord Clark), who was Controller of Home Publicity at the Ministry of Information, was instructed to set up a body called the Home Morale Emergency Committee. One of its members was Harold Nicolson. In his autobiography, *The Other Half* (Murray, 1977), Sir Kenneth Clark writes (p. 19):

The Government had decided to circulate to every house in the country a document entitled IF THE INVADER COMES. I thought it was an unwise decision . . . Its very existence would put into people's heads the idea that the invader *was* coming. I wrote this useless document and it was duly circulated to many millions of homes.

But Harold Nicolson, in his war diaries, says that it was he who wrote that desperate document, which should have been so frightening but which no one remembers. 'It is not an honour that I would keenly contest,' says Sir Kenneth Clark, 'but as a matter of fact, I wrote it.' I suppose it might be possible for a failing memory, if it rather wanted to fail, to draw assistance from embarrassment. But how could *anyone* forget the purport and language of such a thing?

It may be that I remember it because I saw some parcels of these messages of controlled panic stacked in our City ARP office — the leaflets were to be delivered by hand, not by post. The bundles had been piled, temporarily and untidily, in an ill-chosen corner near a much-used door, and someone accidentally sent them spinning across the floor. Two parcels burst open, and anyone with a fanciful mind could have seen it as an omen.

But another lot of parcels that burst open figure in an even stranger episode in the City of London's wartime experiences. This concerns the Germans' famous attempt to ruin our paper currency by flooding our money market with forged Bank of England fivers. Vast quantities of perfect forgeries, printed by our industrious enemies and ready for feeding into the British economy, had fallen into British hands and had to be disposed of. Many of them were found by the Allies in 1945 at the liberated Sachsenhausen Concentration Camp, where they had been printed by trained prisoners in conditions which, for the Nazis, provided absolute secrecy with instant death as its readily used safeguard. As late as 1959, huge quantities were found buried in a small lake at Toplitz in the Austrian Alps. Mr Yasha Beresiner, editor of the *International Banknote Society's Journal*, says in his *Collector's Guide to Paper Money* (London, 1977) that at Sachsenhausen 300 prisoners falsified £130,000,000 worth of notes and were then put to death at Ebensee. When the recovered notes were brought to England, hired lorries with specially picked drivers were loaded with them in the Bullion Yard in Lothbury at the rear of the Bank of England, and the City Police were required to find an armed escort to take them to Battersea Power Station for burning. Each lorry accordingly carried two City policemen, one of whom carried a Webley Scott .32 automatic pistol and eight cartridges. Why this was thought better than soldiers with automatic weapons I never discovered, but it was deemed a sufficient armed guard for a vanload probably worth a million—to anyone able to get rid of the notes with sufficient speed. One of the men thus detailed was Sergeant Robert Shiers, an old friend of mine who vividly remembers the episode. He is one of those highly unusual and probably dangerous people who can score endless successions of bull's-eyes with a Webley Scott automatic, and was always winning medals at it.

When they got to Battersea, the packaging proved to be so tight that the parcels simply would not burn. Placed on the rollers that fed the furnaces, they travelled to the end,

dropped off, and lay in the flames unconsumed, a lesson
to all householders on how not to light fires. So they had
to be recovered, cut open, and sent on the same journey
with their stays loosened. I suppose the possibility of some
such mishap, with its enhanced opportunities for liberating
a few of the condemned fivers, may account for the use
of armed civilian police rather than soldiers. The millions
of notes for destruction necessitated many to-and-fro
journeys from the Bank of England to Battersea.

It is through such fortuitous happenings that I remember
matters of widely varying importance which, equally, my
contemporaries seem to forget. Ask any man, for example,
when it was that Englishmen stopped wearing hats. He
won't know, unless he comes of ancestral hatters. From
my babyhood in 1902 until 1938 a bareheaded man in a
London street was an oddity. Such creatures were
sometimes to be seen, and in my circles they were known
as 'the no 'at brigade'. In any photograph of a mass meeting
of men — a football crowd, even a horde of the poorest
children — every male head was covered, usually with a
flat cap. Straw boaters, which you could get for three
shillings and sixpence, took over in the spring, and in
October these were cleaned with 'salts of lemon', pushed
into brown paper bags, and put away to hibernate. Then
came the trilby, which started its career among the upper
middle class and worked its way down. It took its name
from George du Maurier's heroine (more memorable for
her bare feet, which rather confused the derivation with
the Yorkshire name for a pig's trotter: when I was a boy
a slovenly walker would be told to 'pick up yer trilbies').
And after the trilby, almost suddenly, nothing.

At police headquarters we had a man named George
Clarke, a slightly eccentric but very knowledgeable chap,
who never wore a hat. Indeed he had a huge shock of
unkempt (or relatively kempt) hair which was thirty years
ahead of the fashion and would have made it very difficult
to keep a hat on. We also had a Commissioner of Police
whose self-esteem, which was large, needed continual
sustenance in the form of sycophantic gestures and

forelock-tugging. If, being in uniform, you passed him in the street without saluting, it was as if an untouchable had sat down on a brahmin's breakfast. Once back in the office, he would actually send for disciplinary forms, report such defaulters to himself, solemnly adjudicate, and impose a penalty. One day in about June 1939 (I remember the date because I had just had to relinquish my interesting Old Bailey job for war duties, and Clarke was working for me) the Commissioner passed Nobby on his way into the office, and Nobby, having no hat to raise, gave him an ultra-smart eyes-right. Once in his office the Commissioner sent for me. Why did this man Clarke not wear a hat, he demanded crossly? I didn't know. Some people didn't, perhaps a growing number. Had he got some scalp trouble? What sort of man was he? Was his work satisfactory? I could see the way this was moving. Oh yes, he was most valuable, experienced, intelligent, reliable, etc. The Commissioner bit his lower lip, which, I have always understood, is what people bite when frustrated. 'Very well', he said at last. 'He certainly does a very smart eyes-right, I will say that.' The 'no 'at Brigade', through a careless defect in the disciplinary regulations, had received official recognition. Social anthropologists should note this at once, for it has never before been revealed. Before the end of the war, hardly anyone was wearing a hat, and Nobby Clarke would have been inconspicuous. It may, of course, have been a national gesture of liberation from the Battle Bowler, worn for nearly six years by so many millions.

But before leaving these disjointed wartime recollections I want to record an episode which, though I didn't realize it at the time, would powerfully influence my feelings about refugees and persecuted minorities, the problem to which Hitler and his maniacal inhumanity had given a horrifying and bewildering dimension. I had become friendly with Allen Herbert (he was in fact a cousin of my first wife's), a chartered accountant who was secretary to Peugeot Motors (England) Ltd. and, accordingly, was an authority on the devious methods of the motor trade—

methods which, among other things, seemed to entail day-by-day insecurity for all its employees at managerial level. In 1937 the parent company was 'reorganized' and he lost his job. For a few years he then tried to make a living as a 'business consultant', pretending to all his friends that the fates had at last manoeuvred him into his true *métier* (but not deceiving me, for I knew him to be a man of great and varied talent who, in a perfectly ordered world, would have been the head of an Oxbridge college). He proved to be almost incapacitated by worry about his insecurity; and one day shortly before the war, when I was on duty at the Old Bailey, I had a telephone call from his wife Betty to say that he had just had a heart attack and died. He was leaving his Chiswick house as usual in the morning for his day's business, and between his front door and his garage he sank down and died. Betty knew few people in the neighbourhood, where they were new arrivals, and I hurried over to do what I could to help. She was left with two boys, aged eight and six, and to them I became a kind of unofficial guardian *ad litem*. The fact that Betty Herbert was a highly civilized woman, warm-hearted, socially concerned and affectionate, is sadly relevant to the rest of this story. So is the fact that she believed Allen's misfortune and his death to have been brought about by 'Jewish influences' in the Peugeot Company (of which I know nothing).

In December 1942, deeply immersed at police headquarters in official wartime correspondence, I had accidentally come across a report from Leconfield House, the London Civil Defence Headquarters, from which it was apparent that there had arisen an undreamed-of opportunity to rescue large numbers of potential victims of the Nazi blood-hunt. Neutral merchant ships were coming out of Lisbon Harbour with empty holds, and their owners had expressed their readiness to bring out a regular flow of refugee women and children. It had been learned by the Portuguese and Swedish governments that the German occupying forces in France might not oppose the escape of a certain number of their victims across the

Pyrenees to Lisbon. It would be possible for such a rescue operation to be mounted, or at least effectively encouraged, by the British government.

I turned it over in my mind for two months, trying meanwhile to discover whether anything was being done. In certain exalted quarters I was given to understand that I should do better to mind my own business, but I was unable to see what 'doing better' could mean.

It seemed to me, presumptuously no doubt, that here was a piece of information which was destined to go to waste for the lack of someone to light a fuse . . . Eventually I composed a letter for dispatch to fifty of my long-suffering friends (it was typed for me, with unexpected complicity, by the Commissioner's private secretary), begging them to urge upon their MPs that they must try to get the Government interested in this life-and-death enterprise. In case they might feel uncertain about the suitable wording of such a letter I enclosed a cyclostyled copy of what I thought was an appropriate plea. I still have copies of these letters, and I must say they seem pretty naïve to me now. But they may have had the right simplicity to carry conviction. Their recipients all did what I asked, and I think most of them used the suggested formula. And they nearly all got encouraging replies from their MPs, who included Sir Alfred Salter, Sir Francis Fremantle, Duncan Sandys, Nigel Colman, and Sir Leonard Lyle. Sir Alfred Salter pointed out that even if the plan were taken up we should not, in the nature of things, get to know anything more about it until the war was over. This we all accepted, and all felt, I believe, that we had made some sort of desperate attempt.

But not Betty Herbert, who would have nothing to do with it. I have her letter before me now, dated 22 February 1943:

I would not have believed it possible that I would hesitate to do anything you asked of me, and yet this letter to my M.P. remains unposted. Finishing the war is the surest way of rescuing Hitler's victims (among whom we must not forget to count our own men, many of whom have been languishing in prison camps since Dunkirk and before, and the British women and children in the hands of the Japs). The war must be won at the earliest possible moment in order to free our own as well as the European victims, we must not allow ourselves to be sidetracked. I think we would be playing into Hitler's hands if we diverted even a part of our war energy. By war energy I mean using precious ships to transport refugees, among whom incidentally would be many spies, and also taking on the feeding of extra mouths when already we are using our food reserves. It is very terrible to picture the sufferings of his victims, especially the poor children; but offering asylum to those who can escape does not seem to me to be the answer. Winning the war at the earliest possible moment is the real answer.

I am not anti-Semitic—I even admire the Jews in some ways. I admire their family life and the way they help each other so that no Jews are ever poor. I even have a Scots admiration for their business acumen. I won't repeat the hackneyed phrase that we have too many Jews in this country already, but I confess it does make me sick to see so many Jews of military age still in civilian clothes, crowding into the best seats in the West End shows and restaurants. It is a well known fact among the doctors who attend medical boards that Jews, generally speaking, will go to any length to evade military service. Now if the Jews are really worried about their fellow men being persecuted by Hitler, why don't they join in the fight and help to get them rescued as soon as possible?

A few days later she telephoned me. What she had not told me in the letter, she said, was that since Allen's death she had not felt she could ever again support any enterprise that would help the Jews. But I hadn't mentioned the Jews, I said. 'No, but it was Jews you meant.' Did I? Even if I did, suppose she saw a trainload of Jews on their way to Belsen or Auschwitz, would she still feel the same? 'You are accusing me of lacking imagination', she said. 'I'm talking about what is practicable.'

Every time I saw Betty after that, every time I thought of her, I remembered the universal phrase 'I am not anti-Semitic but—'. She was not anti-Semitic but the sight of Jews at West End shows and restaurants and the thought of Jews evading military service enabled her to accept the

Holocaust, or at least to endure it vicariously. It was incredible to me, and inexpressibly sad. I am quite certain that if she could have seen a trainload of people on their way to an extermination camp she would have thrown her life away in an effort to save them. But even when I had made her understand that my proposal would not entail 'using precious ships' in a way that 'diverted our war energy', that the ships were neutral and coming to Britain anyway, she began talking again about the Jews.

But we remained good friends. She died soon after the war, still only in her mid fifties. She had shown me that anti-Semitism, once it has been articulated, is as incurable as colour-blindness; and that it can supply the irrational solace of hate for the minds of educated people who feel the need of it but don't even know what a Jew is.

CHAPTER SIX

I HAVE tried to describe elsewhere the metamorphic experience of becoming, in 1946, a salaried journalist after so many years as a policeman who merely scribbled for the public prints in his spare time. Among the depressingly few periodicals which had been accepting my material, none had seemed so inherently unlikely as the *New Statesman*, where I was now to become a staff writer; and in none had it seemed so important to remain impenetrably anonymous. The pen-name C. H. Rolph, whatever cover it may have afforded for a year or two, was soon deceiving no one. And sitting in a police office while one wrote pieces for the *New Statesman* was a bit like writing in praise of blood sports while employed by the RSPCA. I had often reminded myself that you couldn't expect a 'journal of protest' to compose hymns of praise about the police, but it was the special role of the police to attract flying bricks whatever the politics of the government in power. The most you could look for was a temporary lull in the flight of bricks during the few weeks of a changeover from left to right (or vice versa); after which they came with renewed volume from a slightly different direction, the difference growing slighter, it seemed to me, with each change of government.

But a similar transition had been made in the field of broadcasting. In 1944 the Army Bureau of Current Affairs had asked my Commissioner if I could do some talks to garrison units and bored troops on stand-by duty at gun-sites and barrage balloon depots. He seemed unexpectedly keen on the idea. For a time there had to be, on each occasion, a letter from the OC Unit and a formal reply that Chief Inspector Hewitt would be available and had been 'detailed'. Gradually it became less and less formal, until it was a mere phone call the day before, and hardly anyone knew when and where I was lecturing and what about.

From this developed a connection with the BBC's Forces
Educational Network, and a gradual absorption into the
pool of regular broadcasters, doing talks which were
sometimes police-approved and sometimes not. These
grew so numerous that in the end no one was bothering
about specific police approval. Either in my lunch-time or
after office hours I hurried along to Broadcasting House
or Bush House and recorded talks about current events for
programmes like *Radio Newsreel* (still going strong but
now only in the World Service, and still after forty years
using its own stately military march theme as signature
tune), *Woman's Hour*, and *Current Affairs for Schools*. I
made the agreeable acquaintance of dozens of 'talks
producers', whose job at that time was distinguished by
great patience and—I used to think—a dedication worthy
of some vital cause, each one an impresario. A few years
earlier it had been very largely a jobs-for-the-boys kind of
billet, a means of getting people like Guy Burgess and
George Orwell on to the BBC payroll until they could be
found more suitable appointments. After that period 'talks
producing' became the perfunctory and strangely
ineffectual function it is today.

But at the time I am speaking of its practitioners were
people like Robin Day, George Steedman, Patrick Harvey,
Joan Yorke, Madge Hart, Joanna Scott-Moncrieff (who
became editor of *Woman's Hour*), and Peter Dunne. There
was Douglas Muggeridge, endlessly asked whether he was
related to you-know-who, endlessly amiable in saying
'uncle'; Jack Ashley, the good-natured Lancastrian trade
union man who became President of the Cambridge Union
and eventually Labour MP for Stoke-on-Trent South,
completely and tragically lost his hearing, and then
demonstrated that you can be an even better MP when you
can no longer hear what the others are shouting. (A friend
of Jack Ashley's lately informed me that he has become
highly efficient at lip-reading but even more skilful at
interpreting the veins standing out in a speaker's neck.)
There was Philip French, now one of our leading literary
and film critics; and Michael Gill, the producer of such

'epic' television undertakings as Lord Clark's *Civilization* and David Attenborough's zoological programmes. 'Talks producing' for the BBC has been the ante-room to literary and dramatic success for a host of good writers—I wonder why?

I see it as a job which has been left to die of inanition, just as the BBC's one-time concern about pronunciation, syntax, and cliché has withered under the blight that is killing off the most beautiful language ever evolved. It's a skill of the forties and fifties which has not been handed on. At that time no talks producer who valued his job would have tolerated the awful quality of (for example) the phoned-in reports which now pass without complaint, so far as I know, from anyone; or the strange habit, where there is neither background noise nor music to make speech more difficult to listen to, of improvising noises or moving the microphone around until you can pick some up.

Francis ('Jack') Dillon, a name to conjure with among BBC producers, told me once 'Don't gasp like that between your sentences, bloody great gulps for air before you start the next one. Like some walrus. Natural? Not unless you've got asthma. Ghastly noise. Look, immediately you've got to a pause and you're not actually talking, start breathing in, *slowly and quietly*—don't let the mike pick it up at all. Quite easy, but don't forget about it, practise it all the time. Otherwise you get people listening for the gasps; they lose interest in what's between them.' Today, using microphones that pick up the slightest sound, speakers (including the professionals) gasp without restraint and even *begin* their talks with a preparatory gasp. Everyone gulps and gasps, starting every sentence as if about to impart something really stop-press, some exciting afterthought. With no producer to put a stop to it, gasping will come back even when you imagine you have kicked the habit.

Somebody took a recording of a *Letter From London* that I did in the BBC World Service in 1975, the 'producer' of which I will not name. It sounds as if each sentence is

ushered in by someone giving me a tremendous kick in
the backside. I had absolutely no idea that I was doing it,
but no one told me. I can remember Clifford Smith, a
Canadian now reporting for the BBC from Brussels and the
EEC, asking me at Bush House very firmly not to say
'pleece' for 'police' (which, hand on heart, I swear I wasn't
doing), and saying that he preferred '*ac*umen' to '*ac*umen'.
Today, who would bother? There is a new indifference,
masquerading as folksy archaism and dialect-preservation,
which allows people to say 'seckertary' for 'secretary',
'ecksetera' for 'etc.' (I hear this at least once a day), 'dahta'
for 'data', 'deteriate' for 'deteriorate', 'dysect' for 'dissect',
'Febyouary' for 'February', 'grievious' for 'grievous',
'irrevalent' for 'irrelevant', 'longtitude' for 'longitude',
'reconise' for 'recognise'. We can't blame all this on dear
Dr Burchfield, who from his cloistered lexicography unit
pops out occasionally for air and, before disappearing again
to get on with his next *OED* Supplement, advises us all
once more to acknowledge the futility of opposing linguistic
change. He at least will never admit 'longtitude' to the
Oxford English Dictionary merely because it is what such
a lot of us say. Or if he does, I shall never again refer to
him in the public prints.

I had one special piece of advice from Jack Dillon which
I sometimes think no one else has ever heard—no one
follows it. 'When you interview politicians and trade union
leaders and publicists of that kind,' he said, 'most of them
will guess that your third or fourth question is going to
be their last one. So they'll finish off their answer to that
one with what they hope is a good pay-off line. That comes
over as a kind of brush-off. And it means that they're less
concerned with what they are saying than with how it's
going to sound. So never let them see the last question
coming. Watch the whites of their eyes. About half way
through your allotted time, begin each question with
something like "And then, Mr Smith, before we move on
to something else . . ."—it doesn't matter if he then goes
on for so long that you never get to something else.
Otherwise they will always sound like Peter Sellers being

a shop steward or Dave Allen pronouncing a benediction. You've got control of the mike, keep control of the interview — it's up to you, not him, to decide when to put in the full stop.'

I ought to be kinder about BBC producers because, after the ending of my first marriage in 1947, I became the rather astonished husband of one. I have told elsewhere the story of my marriage to Jenifer Wayne, and of its mixed consequences for the two women who have brought themselves to try me as a husband (in *Living Twice*, Gollancz, 1974). And in the same book I have said as much as I want to record about Audrey, my first wife. The story is sad, the facts irreversible, and the requirements of objective fairness too much for me. Moreover I know that she would simply hate any further public reference to it . . . Both she and Jenifer have died in the past four years, Jenifer in 1982 at a time of life when her highly individual mind, so bright and sensitive and *young*, had so much more to give.

But I do want to record that as a result of Jenifer's long final illness, during which I must have set up new records of ineptitude in nursing, she and I found ourselves after thirty-five years of happy marriage discovering new affinities. We started from the shared discovery that, despite John Donne and his 'No man is an island', everyone has an utterly private self, an innermost core of being, which resists all fusion. It is sacred to its host, inaccessible to everyone — be he doctor, priest, wife or husband, lifetime friend, or dearest lover. And it is only those who will recognize this, abandoning any will-o'-the-wisp pursuit of total intimacy, who will ever get within sight (so to speak) of another person's little fortress of privacy. I've called this a discovery as between Jenifer and myself, but rather than that it was a recognition, a long-delayed acceptance, of the disturbing truth that we had never really *understood* each other. It involved the admission that we never would understand each other; not because we were in any recognized way incompatible, which we were not, but because no two persons can ever fully understand each other. She and I came to realize that the Delphic injunction 'Know thyself' could not be fulfilled in solitude, and it meant surely the beginning of knowing anyone else; self-knowledge increased enormously through the effort to know another. For years and years we had been kept from it by our separate, scribbling lives.

From that moment we became daily closer to each other, reaching a mental intimacy I had never before thought possible. I am not sure that I should ever have thought it desirable. It was an astonishing experience; and when she was taken from me it was seeming bright with further promise. In some ways it was almost as ecstatic as adolescent first love. It was not until a year after her death that I discovered how little relative progress I had made. I had to go through her private papers, a duty long deferred. I came across a cardboard carton full of her poems and snatches of verse. There were hundreds of them. Some were sketches and experiments not proceeded with. Some were much-altered 'work-outs' for poems already published (Jenifer Wayne, *The Shadows*, Secker and Warburg, 1959). But most of them I had never seen, and they revealed to me a person I had never known and should never have got to know in an eternity of trying. If this experience means anything, it has a message (not now of much consolation to me) which I diffidently pass on to others. If you think you know your closest friend, your wife, husband, or whomsoever, think again; and try again. You will never succeed, but the effort will be its own inconceivable reward. And it's fun.

I know that Jenifer was esteemed among the best features-and-drama producers in Laurence Gilliam's famous team, which then included Louis MacNeice, D. G. Bridson, Jack Dillon, Rayner Heppenstall and W. R. Rodgers. I never witnessed drama production of a more intelligent and sensitive nature, and I noticed from the beginning (for example) that she understood as few people do the dramatic value of the pause, the need in directing dialogue to allow time in which a remark can sink in and be understood before the reply can seem natural. I have thought for a long time that it is something experienced actors appreciate far more than most producers do.

As the war was ending, Jenifer was writing and producing a long weekly series of feature programmes called *This is the Law*. Her retained legal adviser was Mr T. R. Fitzwalter Butler, Recorder of Newark and editor-in-chief of that holy bible of practice at the Bar, *Archbold's Criminal Pleadings, Evidence and Practice*. Technical advisers to the BBC are many and various, but I doubt that any was better chosen, more involved, more careful, more theatre-minded or more generally 'part of the show' than Fitzy, as she privately called him. (He was 'Theo' to his friends, and in later years I came to know him on committees — a man of grave courtesy and startlingly irreverent wit.) He would never allow his name to be published in connection with the programmes — lawyers are less shy today — and even when a collection of them came out in book form in 1948 she thanked him in a preface for the 'patient advice of a barrister-at-law'.

She had an acute ear for dialogue, and it was the more arresting at the time because so many radio plays, particularly long-running popular serials, were in this respect surprisingly pedestrian, having much of the quality (without the poignance) of a school pantomime written by 10-year-olds. The narrator of all the *This is the Law* programmes was James MacKechnie, who did the job *con amore*; and the BBC then had a repertory company from which Jenifer drew nearly all her players. They were a happy lot, loved the programmes, and thoroughly enjoyed themselves. It is shocking now to realize how many of that team have died in these thirty-five years, but among those who happily survive I salute Marjorie Westbury, Preston Lockwood, Derek Guyler, and Lockwood West. I know that Jenifer's favourite 'female leads' were Gladys Young and Mary O'Farrell, secret competitors in an undeclared contest for the title of Queen of Radio Drama. Both had long stage experience in multitudes of parts, and both would understand from one reading of a script what was required of them. They must have been a joy to any producer; as were Norman Shelley, Carleton Hobbs (I still think no one reads verse so beautifully as 'Hobbo'), Duncan McIntyre, Ernest Jay, and Betty Hardy. I cherish the inscribed silver tankard which they all presented to Jenifer when, as all good things must, *This is the Law* came to an end.

And I'm taking leave at this point to indulge myself, and honour her memory, by including three appreciations of her work — two in radio and one in television. The first is by C. Gordon Glover, introducing a week's wartime radio programmes in the *Radio Times* of 16 October 1942:

THE STUFF OF RADIO

Since one cannot hear all the programmes all the time, one is sometimes beaten to it by a contemporary. In this case Mr Tom Harrisson of *The Observer* who, a week or two back, let out a burst of praise for Miss Jenifer Wayne, one of whose programmes I chanced to hear for the first time on the very day that he burst. Needless to say, Miss Wayne gets my appreciation here and now, with or without Tom Harrisson. The programmes? Modestly proclaimed little quarter-hours at 7.45 on Sunday evenings on 'little-known industries'. The one I first heard was about flax, and within the first minute I knew that here was the work of a thorough radio professional. None of your linking narrations, 'now tell me Mr Fetlocks', hollow sniggers, and 'how interestings'. Just straightforward architecture in sound, which, when it is on the grander scale, as will be the case on Friday with Miss Wayne's programme on Salisbury Plain, should be highly impressive.

Jenifer Wayne herself is a dark, modest person of twenty-five whose work so far — she has been with the BBC just over a year — has been confined chiefly to the Overseas Service. She is an Oxford graduate and a schoolteacher. And that's about all. Though how on earth you are able to slip from a high-school classroom straight into broadcasting in this highly competent fashion beats me. Some people take years to be half as good.

The second is Walter Allen in the *New Statesman* of 4 September 1948, writing as William Salter, the name he temporarily assumed when he was its radio critic — he became its literary editor in 1960:

RADIO NOTES

What a good writer Miss Jenifer Wayne is! It would be difficult to imagine a better programme of its kind than *A Week in Chalet Land*, an examination, in terms of the dramatic feature, of holiday camps and their social implications. It made most recent examples of radio feature journalism appear by comparison crude and ham-handed. I do not think I have ever heard actuality recordings used with more brilliant effect than in this programme; together with the sheer ability of the writing they made one feel for a few horrifying minutes — horrifying to a shrinking introvert — that one really was at a holiday camp being assailed by ho-de-ho's and chivvied ever so gently by loud-speakered instructions into mass recreation in hygienic surroundings. It was a programme packed with factual information; we were given budgets of typical families attending holiday camps; we learnt that 50 per cent of all holiday campers refuse to be chivvied and go their own ways. The manner in which Miss Wayne handled her material was especially impressive. The case for the holiday camp was most persuasively put through the experience of a working man and his wife — a daily nappy-washing service, nurseries for the children, an evening patrol to listen for crying babies: these alone are powerful arguments for organised holidays — and the principles by which the camp is run were stated reasonably enough by those responsible for its management. And it was surely brilliant of Miss Wayne to put the case against in the mouth of a particularly snooty young intellectual. But what gave the programme its solidity and its sincerity is the fact that Miss Wayne thinks always in terms of human beings. One feels always, listening to her features, that she likes people. And her characters, the working man and his wife, the lonely Scots youth, the middle-aged widow, were flesh-and-blood, real men and women whose problems she understood. It was precisely this sympathy which made her implied criticism of the holiday camp as a social institution so effective. It would be fascinating, too, to see what kind of a novel or stage play she could write, for she alone of our best radio-writers is a product wholly of broadcasting.

And the third one, also from Walter Allen, was in the *New Statesman* of 25 September 1954 and greeted her first television programme:

Take, to begin with, a programme specially written for T.V., Miss Jenifer Wayne's documentary *Can I Have a Lawyer?*.

Miss Wayne is, I suppose, one of the half-dozen best writers of
radio features, and this was her first television programme. It
was most successful; indeed I believe it was as good as any
television documentary I have seen. Part of its success came from
qualities we are familiar with from Miss Wayne's work in sound
broadcasting, her lightness of touch, her warm, relishing
approach to human foibles and her ability to create with a
minimum number of strokes characters that convince by their
truth to observation. *Can I Have a Lawyer?* was excellent
entertainment. The scenes in the East End Legal Advice Centre
between client and client, and client and lawyer, could scarcely
have been more happily human. But there was more than this,
for what emerged in the end was a balanced criticism of the
inadequacies of the Legal Aid and Advice Act of 1949. No
doubt these are perfectly well known to lawyers, but they are
not to people who seek their help under the Act; and in this
programme, which was admirably acted and admirably produced
by Miss Caryl Doncaster, Miss Wayne was doing what should
be one of the main jobs of television documentaries, to expose
the insufficiencies of the public and social services to the eye
of criticism.

When Mary O'Farrell heard that Jenifer and I were to
spend our honeymoon in Dublin (it was 1947 and we
wanted to get away from the rationing of food and clothing
without going 'abroad'), she said we simply must visit her
friends at Malahide Castle. She would write at once and
tell them we were coming. Malahide Castle? Oh, Lord
Talbot de Malahide — he had married a friend of hers, a young
actress — marvellous couple. We had found it difficult to
suppose they would much want to see us, and our Dublin
fortnight had only one more day to run, when we suddenly
remembered our promise. Our phone call was received
with a courtesy it didn't deserve at such short notice, and
the next afternoon we went on the bus to the gates of
Malahide Castle, ancestral seat of Baron Talbot, Hereditary
Lord Admiral of Malahide and Adjacent Seas. It was twenty
miles out of Dublin, a beauty spot with a fine view of the
Dublin and Wicklow Mountains across the Fingal Plain.

Sitting on the extreme edges of ribbon-backed Chippendale chairs and wondering if Mr Chippendale had

really meant them to be sat on, in a huge and beautiful drawing-room, we were given tiny triangular brown sandwiches on porcelain plates we almost feared to touch, and tea to drink from wafer-thin fairy cups. As soon as the rather infirm and taciturn Lord Talbot had decided that Jenifer and his wife were fully engaged in womanly talk, he beckoned me into an adjoining room, which turned out to be his library. There he opened a large elm chest to display, proudly, that it was packed to the top with bundles of letters and papers tied in tape. He opened one bundle and handed it to me. The edges were yellow, the ink had faded into brown, and here and there on the pages I saw the names Boswell and Auchinleck. Watching my face, he told me that he was the great-great-grandson and only male descendant of dear old James Boswell, the diarist and biographer of Samuel Johnson. I knew then that I was looking at a literary gold-mine.

He told me sadly that it had all got to be sold, to help pay for the upkeep of Malahide. Much had been sold already—I was looking at a mere remnant. I reflected, but didn't say, that if I were in his position I would have the money rather than the letters, which would now be published anyway for all to read and which I would gladly share with the world. But he seemed inconsolable. I learned a year later that the whole lot—there must have been hundreds of bundles—had gone to an American university.

Now, among my wedding presents there had been a book token, which I had already exchanged in a Sackville Street bookshop for a copy of Wyndham Lewis's book *The Hooded Hawk, or The Case of Mr Boswell* (Eyre and Spottiswoode, 1946). On the boat home from Dublin to Liverpool I pulled this out and started reading, knowing vaguely that the hooded hawk was the Boswell family crest. It's a glorious, heart-warming, aggressive defence of Boswell against all his moral critics and eager diminishers from Macaulay and Carlyle to Hume and Walpole. Three years later there appeared *Boswell's London Journal 1762-1763*, in which the publishers tell the whole amazing story of the piecemeal discovery and rescue of Boswell papers from imminent destruction in a variety of circumstances, where their identity had been realized in a series of last-minute miracles.

At about this time I received what seemed to me an extraordinary offer of cloak-and-dagger employment. I had become friendly with David Kessler, then business manager of the *Jewish Chronicle*, and occasionally wrote pieces for that excellent paper, mainly book reviews — I think it began in the early fifties when I was asked to write two articles about the police and the fascists. (There was a widespread belief then that the police were pro-fascist, though I never saw any sign of it, even among the least intelligent of them. I find that the belief still exists, but then so does a belief in the Protocols of the Elders of Zion. There is also a Flat Earth Society.) I have always felt warmly pro-Jewish, even though one of the private perplexities I have had to give up is the real meaning of the word 'Jew'. I believe I can trace my feelings back to a time when I was a kind of self-appointed guardian of a small Jewish boy at school who was much persecuted, for no other reason than that he was a Jew (see *London Particulars*, OUP, 1980, p. 87). I won't retell the story here, but since that time I have hated anti-Semitism and 'Jew-baiting' with an intensity that sometimes startles even myself. It is true hatred, allowing no scope whatsoever for possible redemption and forgiveness, and sustained by the inescapable nightmare of the German Holocaust, the point at which we all perceive the uselessness of language. I realized the potency of this poison when Victor Gollancz, my own publisher, put forward his famous, daring, and utterly genuine plea that we must now attempt to 'understand' what had happened in Germany and seek ways to live with a nation which had recovered from its hideous madness. Arthur Koestler had told me how he hated Gollancz with all his heart and soul ('I *loathed* Victor'); and I, trying now and again to defend some members of Arthur's demonology, could find no word to say about Victor Gollancz, the Jew who forgave for what he had not endured. I have, in short, hated anti-Semitism more than the average anti-Semite hates his Jews, and I like to think that I have done my hating more intelligently; but of that I am far from sure.

David Kessler used to come to an informal weekly lunch party, mainly of *New Statesman* supporters or haters, which in my time met at a sequence of pubs and cafés in the Holborn area. Its geographical centre, I suppose, was the *New Statesman* office at the corner of Lincoln's Inn Fields and Great Turnstile; and its *primus inter pares*, without whom it might well have faded away, was John Roberts, the business manager of the *New Statesman*. (In every big city in every country I have visited there are many of these little lunch-time sodalities, all with some kind of common denominator, and all with unspoken rules about membership and admission. And an interesting though difficult study could be made of their social and often political importance.) David Kessler, nearly always the last to arrive, was the one who then insisted on ordering drinks for everybody. One day he told me that the Board of Deputies of British Jews was looking for someone who would be willing, able, and suitable to become a member of the British Union of Fascists as an 'undercover agent' for the Board of Deputies. He made it fairly plain, not only that he thought I might be suitable, but also that he had mentioned my name in such a context to Mr Sidney Salamon, the President of the board. If I was interested, could he leave me to get in touch with the board? The payment would probably be very good indeed. David was cautiously non-committal about what it might entail. It would be much better if I got that direct from Sidney Salamon.

I believe I would have done anything, at that time, to hinder or frustrate the poisonous activities of the BUF. I made an appointment with Mr Salamon and went to see him at the offices of the Board of Deputies of British Jews in Woburn House, Upper Woburn Place. I was shown into an office where Mr Salamon introduced himself, and then presented me to the Chief Rabbi (whose presence I suspect was not pre-arranged) and a young secretary. After a few sounding-out preliminaries he asked if I would be willing to ingratiate myself with the Fascists, set about becoming a member of their unholy movement, and then provide him with reports, say monthly at first and more frequently whenever events seemed to call for it, about the BUF's movements, plans, intentions, members, and any other particulars I might think useful to a defensive Jewish community.

After the unspeakable evil of the German death camps, to say nothing of the years of public humiliation, degradation, and torture inflicted on Jews in Germany, Russia, Poland, and indeed half the countries of the world, I simply couldn't understand how anyone could identify himself with Fascism or any other Jew-hating ideology. I knew three men who were members of the BUF, and loathed them all. One of them, the truly thick-necked and moronic one, whose face always looked to me as if it had been built by arranging frozen offal around the skull of *Homo Neanderthalensis*, was a former policeman sacked for attempting to rape an early-morning office cleaner. The two others I had met at pub billiard matches: one a bus driver and the other, when I knew him, unemployed and I should think unemployable. The trouble about them all was that they knew me, and that the total BUF membership was so small that my meeting them inside the movement was almost a statistical certainty. My 'cover' might not therefore last as much as a couple of days.

None the less I was so anxious to do *something* expiatory about the fate of German Jewry that I decided at first to make no mention of these three men in talking to Sidney Salamon. And then suddenly he said: 'I suppose you're not *known* to anyone in the BUF, are you? That would be fatal to the whole idea, of course.' And I have to confess that I equivocated, telling myself that these three creatures *might* have left the movement, or might have been kicked out as too unpleasant even for that septic company. I pretended to myself that I needed time to think, though in fact I needed nothing of the sort. The interview ended with my asking him if I could have two days to think it over. In fact it took less than two minutes to discover that in the comradely presence of these anti-Semitic thugs I should probably be physically sick and have to explain why. I couldn't present even the clumsiest façade of Fascist sympathy, and would be recognized and denounced at once.

CHAPTER SEVEN

THERE was another unforeseen consequence of slithering, perhaps you could call it backing, into the world of literature and the arts at the end of a police career. Career? Strange word for such a circumscribed and disillusioning job. As a noun it used to mean 'race-track'. As a verb, it still means 'go swiftly or wildly' (*OED*) or 'rush in an uncontrolled way' (*Collins*). That's not what I did or, I think, what anyone does in the police service. Still, we all talk about a career in the Church, medicine, the law, or funeral directing, in all of which an individual is assumed to be concerned with a care for people at different crises in their lives. They don't seem to me wild or uncontrolled. Anyway, once into the world of professional writing and other creative toil, I met more and more actors, producers, film people, agents (literary and theatrical), publishers, editors, and a great number of those nondescript figures who haunt the fringes of 'literary London', liked by everyone, employed by none, often mysteriously able (and pathetically encouraged) to stand a round of drinks, and accepted without enquiry or curiosity by everyone but me. From somewhere in this heady mixture of loosely linked creatures I was recommended to Metro-Goldwyn-Mayer as an authority on the Old Bailey, on police routine, and (more recklessly) on the criminal law. Within a fortnight I found myself at Elstree Studios at 7 one spring morning, retained at £10 a day (paid in cash) as a Technical Advisor, the final 'r' being stressed in a way that sounded satisfactorily real and transatlantic. I was now to meet a lot of film-world personalities. I think I should have said 'observe' rather than 'meet', for I had little direct contact with them and would have had no idea what kind of things you *say* to international film stars and how best to avoid boring them. This, none the less, has to be one of my two name-dropping chapters.

I was taken to a vast studio, the size of a football pitch, and allotted one of those directors' chairs which usually have some illustrious name stencilled on their canvas backs. Nothing was stencilled on mine. But I soon discovered that I was expected to sit on it, not move it about, and thus be easy to find when wanted. On the first day, having taken in the enormousness of the place, its high-up temporary wooden galleries (or catwalks) equipped with lights, cameras, and hurrying technicians dwarfed by distance, I eventually opened a newspaper and began to read. I think it must have been 1951, because what I read was an account of Gerald Barry's plans for the centenary of the 1851 Great Exhibition, plans for an exciting peacetime aesthetic jamboree on the south bank of the river Thames at Waterloo. Hugh Casson was to look after the architecture — the crux of the whole 1951 Festival of Britain. In due course I was to come to know both these extraordinary men, Gerald Barry as editor of the *News Chronicle* (as well as a director of the *New Statesman*), and Hugh Casson because he became my chairman on the Koestler Award Trust — of which more later. I remember too that I had brought with me a review copy of Nicholas Monsarrat's *The Cruel Sea*; not that I was reviewing it, more probably because somebody who was had passed it on to me. It must have been published at about that time, and I discovered it to be the kind of book in which you could become totally immersed in any kind of surroundings, even on the perimeter of a huge indoor film set whereon everything seemed, all the time, to be going wrong.

Suddenly a short and self-confident-looking man, with greying hair and a broad bony face, came to one of the empty chairs about ten feet away from me, flopped into it, and sat looking at the floor. There must have been something about him to extract me from my reading, which none of the other bustling figures had done. I knew at once that it was Spencer Tracy, who had been among my Top Ten film actors for years. (He also looked at times like a smaller and stockier version of my father, the likeness occasionally so striking that it could be quite a shock.) He looked totally detached from his surroundings, and when a young woman in bright blue slacks and huge black sun-glasses brought him what looked like a tomato juice, pulled a little table closer to him, and put the drinks on it, he gave absolutely no sign of having noticed her, what she was doing, or where she went after doing it.

An hour or two later I was shown to the cafeteria where I was to get my lunch. And there he sat, at a table by himself, obviously not one of those who line up (or are allowed to line up) with trays at self-service counters. Then the same young woman appeared with a tray of food, sat down with him, and set out the meal. So far as I could observe, he still said nothing. I remember feeling sad that he should be so indifferent to her attentiveness, and how I then suddenly realized that what he should have done was simply no business of mine, that the whole cameo might have a background reflecting much more credit upon him than upon her (whoever she was), and that I had better mind my own business and get on with *The Cruel Sea*. When at last I looked up again they were just leaving the cafeteria. His jacket was slung over his shoulders with its arms hanging loose, he had one arm pressed tightly round her waist, and they were both laughing loudly . . . I saw him many times in the next few weeks. MGM were filming *Edward My Son*, with Spencer Tracy as the leading man. Leslie Dwyer was there too, looking about the same age then as he does on television today—and it's thirty four years ago. I marvelled at the patience of them all. They would sit or wander or loll about all day, from 7 a.m. until 5 or 6 p.m., smoking cigarettes and endlessly drinking coffee from plastic mugs, waiting (it seemed) for some tiny incident to make it appear that the film-making process had inched its way forward. Three or four times a day there would come, as if from nowhere, a sudden atmosphere of climax. Everyone sprang into ambiguous action at the word of some unseen Master, and a one-minute scene would be shot. But it was nearly always, I thought, the same one

as last time. Try as I would, I could see no difference in
the new version; which must nevertheless have been
different and (I supposed) better.

The producer (director?) was a tiny and swarthy
American dynamo wearing a very tight green cardigan and
plimsolls (or sneakers). I forget his name. At an early stage
I told him that in England the court ushers wore gowns
but not wigs. He yelled at the usher to take that wig off,
and then rounded on me. 'Anyone else wear wigs?' he
demanded. I began telling him about the wig distribution
in English courts of law, and suddenly he was excitedly
beckoning to everyone, waving both arms energetically,
to gather round us and listen. The Oracle was speaking.
Someone asked the Oracle whether the policemen must
keep their helmets on in the courts. Nowhere inside
the building, and certainly not in the court rooms, I
said. 'Get that? Goddit?' shouted the little producer to
everyone. They all looked like people who had got it. But
Spencer Tracy wasn't even there. I supposed that someone
would report all this received wisdom to him. Another
asked whether the solicitors as well as the barristers should
be wearing gowns. No. Oh, but surely they *had* gowns?
He knew an English solicitor with a gown? Yes, they had
gowns and they very occasionally wore them in some
courts where they had a 'right of audience'; but they didn't
at the Old Bailey. 'While we're on it,' said the producer,
'that judge's wig—is that OK?' No, I was going to mention
it. He was wearing a full-bottomed wig, and this he would
do only on the opening day of the session, the ceremonial
day. After that his wig was more like a squiggly little grey
skull-cap with two hanging bows at the back. 'Why does
he change then?' I simply didn't know. It was just
something that had been going on for about 600 years.
Without realizing it, I had found the perfect answer to
satisfy an American.

For another film I had to be at the Dorchester Hotel, Park
Lane, at 6 every morning, to be driven with Peter Lawford
from there to Elstree in a hired car big enough for eight
people. Peter Lawford always looked immaculate whatever

he wore, and always seemed artificially sun-tanned at 6 a.m. I can remember my conversations with him in the car with great exactitude, because every day he just said 'Good morning' without enquiring or (obviously) caring who I was, and went straight off to sleep. The one other memorable remark he made in my presence occurred on the fourth evening, when we had all been told that the next morning, just for once, we were to be in the studio at 6 instead of 7 a.m. (I never did find out why film people choose to start studio work in the small hours. I can understand it with outdoor shooting, when they prefer to put their own people on the streets, but not when they are in studios.) Peter Lawford, it seemed, was notorious for his dislike of getting up early. I disliked it even more, without being notorious. Another actor walked over to him and asked what was happening. 'We godda come back yesterday', he said wearily.

In the same year Elizabeth Taylor was there to play the lovely Lady Rowena in Scott's *Ivanhoe*. I wouldn't have known who she was. She looked about 16 but in fact she was 19, and her almost incredible beauty was startling, even under the added beauty put on by the make-up girls — which, once it was on, had to stay on for the day. I think perhaps she was then the most exquisite creature I have ever seen, and I took every discreet opportunity of making sure that I was not erring in my judgement. I also decided that, in spite of what seemed to me a truly awful script, she was even then a very accomplished actress . . . I have a feeling that *Ivanhoe* would probably defeat any film-maker. It must seem from the book that 'it's got everything' — beauty, adventure, endless Ye Olde business, true love running on paths unsmoothed, Saxons and Normans, Richard I, the Crusades, the great tournament at Ashby-de-la-Zouche where Ivanhoe defeats all the other knights one by one, castles, sieges, even Robin Hood and Friar Tuck. But no one has ever made a good film of it. The one memorable scene from this MGM effort was unscripted, unrehearsed, and unrecorded until now. I want to tell you about it.

Thirty hired horses, with ornate saddle-cloths hanging nearly to the ground, were lined up ready for the Great Tournament, each with a knight in armour on its back. One horse simply would not stand where it was told and wait for the cameras. It kept on prancing out into the arena, always at the precise moment when the scene was being shot. The producer got more and more enraged. 'Put some guy on that animal that can control it', he shouted. The substituted guy was no better than his crestfallen predecessor. Eventually 'Take that goddam beast away!', roared the little man. 'Bring another one in.' There was no other one to bring in. This awful intelligence was delightedly breathed into my ear by the lady who seemed to be in charge of such arrangements, hiring horses and people like me to serve the needs of the cast: it was she who, every evening, paid me out ten much-used pound notes for my day's services to MGM, grinning at me through a kind of booking-office window at the end of a queue. She arranged for the maverick horse to be led in disgrace from the studio, given a knob of sugar or something outside, and then ridden back through a different entrance so that it would seem to be a fresh arrival. The producer accepted it as such. They started again. Silence everybody, please. Four, three, two, one — 'Take Five — Smack' — and another horse began prancing. I thought the producer was going to burst a blood-vessel. At his orders, incoherent and yet self-evident, the second horse was led away, only to be brought back a few minutes later at the end of the row, as if it too were a miraculously produced replacement. It happened four times. Then I slipped out of the arena to see if I was wanted on the other set (which, I suppose, I ought not to have left), and found the studio staff all helpless with laughter. 'Where *does* he suppose they're all coming from?', said the lady who had confided in me before. 'I ordered thirty horses, and thirty horses we've got.' Eventually, I believe (for I couldn't wait about to see) the horses all behaved themselves at the same time, and the *Ivanhoe* epic inched forward.

I felt specially sorry for the extras, the people hired to make up the number, some to wear heavy armour and sit on uncooperative horses. I sat talking to one for many hours, a South African who (he told me) had gained his diploma at the Royal Academy of Dramatic Art, had played in theatre repertory companies all over the world, had been to Hollywood, Nice, and Edinburgh in film work, and now counted himself lucky to have obtained, at the end of a day's queuing outside an agent's offices in the Charing Cross Road, this twelve-weeks' job with MGM. He seemed a well-read man, if you confine that phrase to imaginative literature and all periods of the drama, and he had the larger-than-life charm and courtesy of most 'theatricals' which, however phoney, I have always found heart-warming. But I found that he was a worried man, and he had been seeking an opportunity to confide his worries to me.

Four years earlier, he had stood bail for a man charged at Great Marlborough Street magistrates' court with receiving stolen furniture, rugs, and chinaware. He had signed as a surety for £500. The accused man, a friend of his, had then absconded, gone abroad, and never been brought to trial. He himself was totally unable to pay the £500, which the magistrate had duly declared forfeit. A summons had been served at his lodgings, a summons to show cause why his £500 should not be paid into court. (I forbore to tell him, but he was pretty lucky to get such a summons, for in those days a defaulting surety was often simply arrested and taken off to Brixton Prison.) But he had prudently upped and gone off to new lodgings before the summons arrived. He knew the police would be after him — I got a very vague impression that he was not totally inexperienced in these matters. He even knew that a warrant for his arrest had been issued when the summons had proved ineffective. He had been a hunted man for four years . . . How on earth, I asked him, had the police accepted him as a surety in the first place, when he had neither property nor fixed address? Oh, well, he had told them he was the landlord of the premises. It all seemed a bit slipshod to me, but the police must have satisfied the magistrate that he was a 'sufficient surety', and there he was. What he wanted to hear from me, now that he 'felt he had got to know me', now that he had the sympathy (he seemed to think) of someone with police experience, was whether he could buy back the peace of mind he longed for by scraping together the £500, which he thought he could now borrow. I told him it was a big gamble. He had deceived the police and the court, enabled an offender to escape trial, wasted a lot of expensive police time, etc. The courts were pretty unforgiving about that kind of deception, and about default by sureties; and no magistrate would give the smallest encouragement to any idea that 'standing bail' was something to be lightly undertaken.

I ought to be able to report that he was a picture of contrition, despair, and dawning resolution. He was not. After a few minutes he had cheered up like some Tommy Traddles, and I believe the discussion, which had done him good, ended with my being more worried than he was. In a way, I'm still worried, but still uncertain whether that is because I should have told the police where he was to be found. Which of course I should.

My recollection is that I did culpably little for that £10 a day, even if there were a number of figures on the payroll who seemed to me to be doing culpably less. It may have helped my conscience that I had to get up far too early in the morning. Jenifer and I sadly needed the money at the time, any money we could decently get from anywhere. She was actually ghosting articles for a Harley Street medical man who had a big name in the popular Press, in which he had the status of an agony-column Polonius, though his own writing was far more platitudinous than in any such column you see today — and he knew its shortcomings. I myself came very near to ghosting an autobiography for Jack Hilton the show-biz impresario, in whose world I had taken little real interest. Our weekly political diarist at the *New Statesman* at that time was the Labour MP J. P. W. Mallalieu (Bill Mallalieu to us), incidentally a man who was universally loved; and he must

have been hearing the wolf scratching at his own door at
the time, for he had just promised to ghost the Hilton book
for a sum of money which he simply could not afford to
turn down. Then he got suddenly overwhelmed with
constituency business (I think) and was having second
thoughts. One Monday morning at the *New Statesman*
office (he always came in to put the finishing touches to
his weekly piece on Mondays) he came up to my room and
asked me if I would care to take over the Hilton job if he
put my name forward. Turmoil. I was sorely tempted by
the money, which would have solved all my immediate
problems, but not by the subject. 'If you don't like the
subject you'd much better say no', he said gently. 'I'll think
of someone else. Or I may do it myself later on, if things
get a bit quieter.' I'm certain mine would have been a bad
book. The only ghosting I had ever done was during my
police service, where I had produced articles, reports, and
memoranda for my Commissioner's signature, sometimes
for publication in Commonwealth law or police periodicals.
But there I had no choice, whether I liked the proposed
subject or not.

The filming episode was instructive and funny and
disillusioning, not least in its exposure (to me) of the oral
and visual clichés which cluster round the simple job of
presenting a trial scene. Except in the very best of films
(and even in some of those) witnesses in court, when they
take the oath, say 'So help me God' and then kiss the book,
both little bits of ritual being about a century out of date.
Both prosecuting and defending counsel act their heads off,
as if we were back with Serjeant Buzfuz in *Bardell* v.
Pickwick. An actor who can play a good judge, and still
more a producer who will let him get on with it, are both
rarities. Most men in the role of judge seem anxious to
say something witty, cutting, imperious, or all three, or
to make something otherwise banal sound witty, cutting,
or imperious. Invariably the best actors in a Crown Court
scene are the jury, because they have absolutely nothing
to do, and whatever they look like while doing it can
always pass as typical . . . Perhaps it ought to be recognized,

and at long last accepted even by ancients like myself, that it is no more possible to produce a court scene with verisimilitude than it is to produce a committee meeting which is not stilted, structured, and obviously being acted. But there are producer-proof actors like Anthony Hopkins and Peter Barkworth who *can* do all these things without making them either dull or ridiculous. Why not let all our stage lawyers copy them?

CHAPTER EIGHT

THE fifties had begun with an episode that nothing will ever wipe from my memory. Professor Harold Laski must have had millions of students outside his London University seminars and his public lectures, and for many years I had been among them. Two of his books, *A Grammar of Politics* and *The Communist Manifesto*, had rescued me from the kind of political illiteracy that sustains so many people in the lifelong role of self-confident pundit. Specifically, he prepared my mind (though I should think this would have surprised him) for the salutary experience of reading *The God That Failed*, which Dick Crossman had edited as a final demolition of the communist myth. Laski was, I think, the best lecturer I ever heard. And of course he was a mainstay of the *New Statesman* during my earlier years on its editorial staff. One day early in 1950 I was at a Press conference (or a 'publication party', I forget which) to launch Thor Heyerdahl's book *The Kon-tiki Expedition*, and found myself sipping drinks with a statuesque lady who could have been the original model for *Patriotism in Pale Mauve*. She had such pronounced views about everything that I was seldom called upon to say a word. One of the few words I must have said was 'Laski'. It opened a new floodgate, and what poured forth was pure vitriol. 'I don't often wish people any harm,' she said with the vehemence of people who did, 'but I should be very happy *indeed* to hear tomorrow that that ghastly man had suddenly died.' Of course I had to find out why, and in general it was because Harold Laski had for years been corrupting the young with his septic socialism, and in particular because among the corrupted was a niece of hers at London University. He died suddenly the next day, at the age of 56.

From that time and for the next twenty years, my main source of income was the BBC. I had gradually become known to the producers of various kinds of radio programme — talks, features, documentaries, radio biographies, discussion panels, interviews. I enjoyed them all, and yet never overcame my astonishment (which it was vital to conceal) that I was participating in it all. There were constant difficulties about my *nom de guerre*, difficulties especially for the chairmen of panels or teams, who needed now and again to 'bring me in' by name. 'What are you going to be,' they would ask, 'C. R. Hewitt, C. H. Rolph, Bill Hewitt, Bill Rolph — which is it to be? Make up your mind.' I never got it straight: I had manœuvred my own identity into a hopeless muddle. 'Bill' was a nickname, bestowed originally by Kingsley Martin without, I think, any knowledge that 'Old Bill' had become what Longman's Dictionary (1984) calls 'British slang for the police — perhaps from Old Bill, grousing old soldier in cartoons by Bruce Bairnsfather'. This derivation has always seemed to me more ingenious than plausible, because throughout my police service I never heard or saw the phrase applied to the police, nor did any police officer I have known. Certainly in 1917 the government had decided to exploit the popularity of Bairnsfather's 'Old Bill' (always a bit of a mystery to me) as a vehicle for its wartime propaganda and public instruction. Ministry of Information posters portrayed his bibulous features and walrus moustache surmounted (most unexpectedly) by a special constable's cap, and lending acceptable authority to important messages under the caption 'Old Bill Says . . .'. But I never heard anyone associate that with something the police had said. It was surely that Old Bill had become as real in the public mind as John Bull, Mr Pickwick, Johnny Walker, Mrs Grundy, or Father Christmas, but much more topical and poignant than any of them.

I knew one or two 'old sweats' in my early days who conformed to the Bairnsfather image, but the face was essentially of the Edwardian period, and it went with flat caps and Saturday football crowds. I never met anyone with a knowledge of British catch-phrases and soubriquets who supported the notion that it ever became attached to the British bobby.

However many radio talks you may have done, the fact
that you did them will be of little interest to anyone a week
later unless you used one of the few remaining swear-
words, announced the beginning of World War III, or lost
your place. So among all my *Woman's Hour* and *Radio
Newsreel* talks, one stands out as a catastrophic memory
shared by an embarrassing number of my friends. It was
Woman's Hour in 1956 and the regular presenter of the
programme was the unflappable Marjorie Anderson. At that
time (and it may still be the practice) each contributor to
a *Woman's Hour* programme took his own script and was
allocated his own talks producer—not all of these were
women, by the way. I was to talk about a young Russian
called Nina Ponomareva who, on a visit to England as a
discus-thrower in an athletics meeting, unaccountably
stole some hats in Oxford Street shops. She was caught
and prosecuted, and a police station officer admitted her
to bail. She promptly absconded, and the magistrate at
Great Marlborough Street issued his warrant for her arrest.
The case of Nina and the Five Hats became an international
incident, sustained by angry but predictable Moscow
allegations that the charge against Nina was a frame-up,
the implication being that the NATO powers had been
waiting for a defenceless Russian discus-thrower to go into
a London milliner's shop. It's fair to say that the course
of Soviet justice may have suggested this to the Soviet
mind, for Mr Khrushchev had just been assuring the world
that under the discredited Stalin regime the frame-up had
been systematically used as a means of putting the
politically inconvenient to death. But Nina didn't seem
to be politically inconvenient to anyone. The popular
British newspapers took her up in a big way. She was News,
and her story was exactly the kind of thing I was regularly
invited to comment upon in BBC current affairs items.

My producer, an earnest young woman who was
relatively new to the job, had decided (or had been assured
by someone) that I needn't be rehearsed. I was 'reliable'.
I had four of my own typewritten sheets to read from.
On the air, all went well for a time, each finished page

carefully and noiselessly slid to one side. When I reached page four, it wasn't there. A ghastly silence descended, to be broken by my unprofessionally noisy rustling of papers under the microphone, which must have sounded like a sheep-shearing. My forehead began to feel damp. At the end of about six seconds which felt like six crowded weeks, the resourceful Marjorie Anderson began saying 'That was C. H. Rolph explaining the law about—' just at the moment when I had decided I must ad lib for my remaining two minutes, which I proceeded to do. I don't know how successful this was, but when I got out of the studio and came face to face with my furious producer, who had the missing page in her hand, she cried 'Oh, I'll *never* do that again, never. It's all my fault. We ought to have rehearsed it all.' She was as inconsolable as she was right, and I felt truly sorry for her. Joanna Scott-Moncrieff, the editor, felt sorry for nobody. That kind of thing was just disgraceful and I ought to be ashamed of myself. Well, I was. But I learned afterwards that a typical reaction among listeners was 'Oh yes, they got the tapes mixed up or something; didn't seem to matter.' Except to Joanna, Marjorie Anderson, the poor little talks producer—and me. I never did it again.

Thinking in decades, I realize that it was mostly during the fifties that I had the agreeable experience (I thought it was sheer luck) of recording long radio interviews with many of the writers and other notables who for years had filled prominent places in my private pantheon. In recording them here, I'm unashamedly indulging myself, and trying at the same time to believe that I may be adding useful details here and there to well-known portraits. All the interviews took place in London, my birthplace and livelihood, the city to which the whole world's potential interviewees seem to be drawn. I clearly remember that it was easy to tell which of these eminent people had needed persuasion before agreeing to be interviewed, and were receiving me with some reluctance; and which of them belonged to that vastly preponderant number who will do almost anything to get themselves interviewed on London radio or television. It is the latter kind, I perceive, who have produced and nourished the interviewer of today, who (with admirable exceptions) is concerned to project his own personality rather than to bring out and present that of his victim.

The first one I met, Robert Frost, 'the purest classical poet of America', was of the reluctant kind. He was 78 when I met him. It seemed a great age to me then, and I comported myself almost as though Mr Frost had temporarily nipped back from Elysium to give me an hour's conversation. Today, I would give much to be a mere 78 again. He seemed gentle, simple, kindly, and monitory all at the same time. Many years later I was to read with shocked surprise, in an acerbic article reviewing a long biography by Lawrence Thompson which appeared in the seventies, that 'his treatment of his wife Eleanor and his pathetic son Carol' stamped him as a 'monster' and as a man than whom 'a more hateful human being cannot have lived'. These satanic qualities, when I met him, were skilfully overlaid with a veneer of shyness and seeming simplicity that must have been difficult to sustain. I saw him in his room at the Berkeley Hotel, where nearly all Americans at that time stayed, and which all Americans still call 'the Burkeley'. He looked like a worried farmer with a face 'carved out of native granite', as someone has said, with thick but tightly compressed lips, and with abundant untidy white hair. If you thought you were meeting a Great Man he soon disillusioned you, for he had little belief in great men except as skilful opportunists. He remarked at the outset of our interview, quite probably quoting some compatriot, that no great man ever complains of lack of opportunity.

Having dutifully brushed up my Robert Frost the previous evening, I quoted his own poem *New Hampshire* to him:

No wonder poets have to *seem*
So much more business-like than business men—
Their goods are so much harder to get rid of.

To my dismay, he seemed not to remember this at all. He quietly agreed with it. And then to my richly deserved discomfiture my producer observed that for 'goods' I should have said 'wares'. And Robert Frost approved, not (apparently) because he had written it but because that was what he would have written. He told us that his wife had said, when one of his several New Hampshire farming enterprises had failed: 'Let's go to England and live under thatch'; and he said this kind of romantic impulse was so rare in her that he agreed at once. They came to live in a thatched cottage at Beaconsfield, the little Buckinghamshire town where G. K. Chesterton lived. But they stayed only three years, and he returned to America to find himself famed as a poet.

Raymond Chandler was renting a rather luxurious flat in Eaton Square. When we arrived, he looked white-faced and tired. Drinks were already on the coffee-table. He was businesslike, rather constrained, and artificial, his conversation having few of the sharply turned wisecracks that abound in his books. Those which he did produce sounded uncharacteristic and yet familiar, like his observation that the job of being a writer is the only one in which you can make no money without being ridiculous. (I remember thinking that I wouldn't have minded escaping ridicule as widely as he had.) I made the mistake of asking him whether it was true that he was an Englishman. 'I was born in downtown Chicago', he said with some acerbity. He had lived much in England, and his accent seemed to me like southern English spoken through the nose. He went to Dulwich College, which—I happened to know—was proud to say so. Back in Chicago in his twenties he got immersed in business of various kinds, which he seemed disinclined to talk about. And although from the age of 40 he was writing detective stories for magazines, he didn't publish a novel until he was over 50. This was *The Big Sleep*, and the year of its publication was 1939, 'the year', he said, 'of the Big Wake Up', when people at last began listening to Churchill, though it was very nearly too late to listen to anything. It seemed to me that

most of what he liked about England was in some way
related to Winston Churchill, and he showed us some notes
for a projected biography of his hero which, I suppose, he
never wrote. (I was once assured by David Higham, the
London literary agent, that he had seen more Churchill
biographies, synopses for Churchill biographies, and letters
offering or threatening to write Churchill biographies than
any other kind of project ever put to him.) I recall that my
impression of Raymond Chandler was of an unhappy man
with much to hide from the world, but very much to give
to it. He died, alas, in 1959.

Nicholas Monsarrat was also staying in Eaton Square, and
was then being much interviewed by Press and radio people
(it was the autumn of 1951) because he had just published
his award-winning novel *The Cruel Sea*. He seemed a little
amused at the elaborately clumsy apparatus brought along
by the BBC men—a large green van outside in Eaton
Square, a length of heavy-duty cable from the van through
the second-floor window to where we sat, a box covered
with knobs to stand on the sitting-room floor, headphones
to connect my producer with the mechanics in the big
green van, and much preparatory toing and froing on the
part of everybody. Mr Monsarrat offered us cigars. When
at last all was ready, he talked quickly and fluently, and
with agreeable modesty, about his war experiences as a
naval officer. *The Cruel Sea*, his fourth book, he said,
turned out to be twice as long as he had intended, but he
thought it was likely to be his best book, however many
more he wrote. So far as I know, he wrote at least another
dozen. I am in no doubt that he was glad when we went,
and that he had had more interviewing than he could do
with. He had kept on looking at his watch, not troubling
to be furtive about it; and I remember wondering whether
this was because he wanted us to go, whether he hadn't
yet shaved, and whether the grey stubble on his chin was
the planned beginning of a beard. He was then, I think,
just over 40.

In 1955 I met Georges Simenon. I rather think the BBC
called on me as an afterthought, for I was directed to meet

Miss Dilys Powell of the *Sunday Times* in the entrance lobby of the Savoy Hotel, so that we could interview M. Simenon together. She, I think, was the real interviewer, and I was there as the former 'police chief' (if you were a chief bottle-washer in the police service, the media always called you a 'police chief' when you were out of it) who might be expected to present the great man with one or two criminological questions, or at least behave like a kind of shadow Maigret. With the BBC producer we were conducted to M. Simenon's suite on the second floor overlooking the Thames, where to my surprise he was sitting at a large leather-topped desk. He jumped up as we arrived, a balding, bespectacled and rather rotund figure wearing a dark red velvet smoking-jacket with stains on it. I wondered whether the Savoy Hotel provided leather-topped desks for those who wanted them, or whether he was taking his own around with him. After all, I remembered, there were international pianists who took their own concert grands with them, even in aircraft. I forbore to enquire, constrained by the feeling, as an Englishman, that if a leading hotel, in my own country, could rustle up a leather-topped desk for one of its patrons I ought to know that it could, and not need to be told by some visiting Belgian. It occurred to me that Simenon looked rather like a James Thurber cartoon that had come to life, but in the next moment I realized that nearly everyone does.

The mantelshelf over the fireplace was occupied by an enormously long pipe-rack, or possibly a number of pipe-racks placed end to end. I counted the pipes and there were seventeen, all much used and, so far as I could see, all with heavily reamed bowls and worn-down rims. M. Simenon was much more interested in Miss Powell than he was in me, a preference I found no difficulty in understanding. She, incidentally, was my favourite film critic and still is. I think he might have been a bit nettled if he had known that I found her much more interesting than he was, and that I left him with the feeling that we might have made a better radio feature if he and I had interviewed her. He didn't have much to say. He was the sort of man to whom you do not address questions that can be answered by yes or no. (It is such people who have unconsciously nourished the firmly established interviewing gambits 'To what extent is it true that . . . ?' and 'How angry were you . . . ?' and 'How deep is the public feeling about . . . ?') I can remember, because it is such an odd period, that he told us he wrote each of his books in eleven days. Why eleven, I thought? 'Why eleven?', I asked him. He didn't know. That was how long it took, perhaps because that was what he thought it would take; he had got used to it. And it enabled him to plan the other parts of his life; as to which, I found, he seemed unwilling to say much at that moment, though he has said a very great deal in subsequent lurid autobiography. A marvellous and exciting writer, I thought as I came away, but not a marvellous and exciting man.

Not long after that the BBC sent me to interview Danny Kaye. This again was in a hotel bedroom, I think at the Berkeley. And meeting Danny Kaye, then about 45 but looking more like 30, was an unalloyed pleasure, despite the fact that he spoke all the time as if we were in front of a packed theatre audience. He received me as if we were old friends, and introduced me to a young Indian woman of striking beauty who thereafter sat silent in a corner of the bedroom, wearing a lustrous dark blue sari and watching us with a kind of deferential amusement throughout the interview. He had then been on the stage, he told me, for twenty-five years, in plays as well as in concert parties and night-clubs and Broadway musicals. I asked him if he was Russian. 'I'm American to the funny-bone', he said. 'I was born in Brooklyn and my name is Dan Kominski and I belong all over the world. OK?' A colleague of mine on the *New Statesman*, G. W. Stonier, who reviewed films for us under the unaccountable name of William Whitebait, had recently written about Danny Kaye as 'an inspired chump'. What, he wanted to know, was a chump in England? 'Where I come from,' he said in a tone of mock resentment, 'that's a fall-guy, kind of blockhead.' I said a chump in George Stonier's sense was

a clown, a funny man, and the adjective 'inspired' ought
to have reassured him. 'OK, it does then, OK', he said.
What I did *not* tell him was that George Stonier, when he
first saw Danny Kaye, told us all at the *New Statesman*
weekly lunch that he had just seen an American comedian
who looked exactly like a furtively inquisitive rat, about
whom there was something faintly odious. Those of us who
had seen Danny Kaye urged George to temper his bile for
another couple of weeks and give the man another chance.
George did exactly that, and it gave him time to see *The
Secret Life of Walter Mitty*. I can't recall ever seeing so
complete a reversal of a hasty verdict, but G. W. Stonier was
from that time an almost uncritical devotee of Danny Kaye,
whom he thereafter equated (I thought surprisingly) with
Chaplin, Groucho Marx, and Laurel and Hardy as an enter-
tainer with 'pure comic genius'. To round off the interview
I asked Danny Kaye if he would record for me (and my
children) the cavernous 'quack' he had used in the Hans
Christian Andersen film. 'Most certainly, sir', he said very
loudly. He sucked in his cheeks, swallowed convulsively,
and emitted into the startled microphone a noise such as
any respectable duck would be likely to pretend had come
from somewhere else. He gave us drinks before we left,
and I noticed that he was drinking water. He caught my
eye. 'I always say it's gin and tonic if I'm asked', he said.
'Looks the same? Sure, but it treats me a lot better.'

But when, shortly after that, I recorded a radio interview
with Rosamond Lehmann, I was not at any pains to conceal
my connection with the *New Statesman*. Many years before,
long before I knew anyone on the paper, her first novel
Dusty Answer, which the critics in 1927 had unfairly panned,
was highly praised in the *New Statesman* by Naomi Royde-
Smith. She was normally a severe critic, but she said 'Miss
Lehmann rises to beauty both of conception and of style — a
really fine performance.' There was an office legend, accordingly, that the paper had 'discovered' Rosamond Lehmann.

Some mischievous impulse made me bring up the
question of reviewing in general, to see what she would
say. She got up from the sofa (she was sitting beside me,

and Philip French was in front of us with the recording
apparatus), went to an occasional table, and came back
with a dictionary of quotations and a reference to James
Russell Lowell:

Nature fits all her children with something to do.
He who would write and can't write can simply review.

Truth to tell, I have never accepted this implication, nor
its corollary that if the non-painter or the non-architect
is to discuss a work of art or a building he is to do so only
in terms of praise. But holding other writers' books up to
ridicule and contempt is, significantly, defended most
vigorously by those critics who are habitually cruel for their
own enjoyment. I have known some, and known that that
was what they were doing. I have often wondered whether
it was not the interest and excitement of that 1927 review
in the *New Statesman* which gave Rosamond Lehmann
the impetus that turned her into a major novelist, for she
was known to be sensitive to unkindness. I found her to
be a person of very great charm, and the charm was not
diminished by the obvious faculty of perception which
must have given many of her acquaintances an uneasy
hunch that they might be appearing in her next book. It
was a strong inducement to show her your best side. On
the way home I decided that she was the kind of person
for whom, a few centuries earlier, you would have put on
shining armour, got out a horse, and ridden forth to do
battle with someone.

There was something ordered and leisurely about interviewing people at the behest of the BBC, accompanied,
helped, and organized by a BBC producer—especially one
of the calibre of Philip French. To go out on your own,
making your own appointments and finding your own
transport, was a different matter. You had to call at
Broadcasting House to collect and sign for one of its own
tape recorders, for there was no other machine then on
the market which produced recordings of the quality the
BBC rightly insisted on. (Their standards have fallen

dramatically.) I usually hired a small car for the occasion; and it was this custom, plus the decision to do two such interviews in one afternoon, which provided me with an instructive little adventure. I had arranged to see Ethel Mannin the novelist at 2.30 p.m. and Hesketh Pearson the biographer at 6 p.m. Miss Mannin lived in Burghley Road, Wimbledon, and Mr Pearson at Priory Road, Maida Vale. Driving a hired Austin 1300, I arrived punctually at Miss Mannin's house, slightly surprised (and a more wide-awake person would have been forewarned) to find that not a single parked car was to be seen throughout Burghley Road, which is long and wide. I parked outside her house, she entertained me to tea, and then she proudly showed me round her carefully tended garden, displaying in the process a knowledge of horticulture which confined my side of the conversation to appreciative grunts and whistles. I realized that, as a twice-widowed woman, she was lonely and welcomed the chance to share her much-loved garden with anybody.

I knew her second husband, Reginald Reynolds, who had died in 1958. He was a poet, a Quaker, a close friend of Mahatma Gandhi, and for many years the weekly contributor of a brilliantly satirical topical poem to the *New Statesman*. We talked much about him. As she opened the front door for me to go, we saw at once that my hired car had disappeared. At that moment a police car pulled up on the other side of the road, and a sergeant came across to speak to me. Was I looking for something? My car, I said. It had gone. Ah, I would find that in the police pound. Now why should that be—the road was entirely empty, and I couldn't have been obstructing anyone? Had I not seen the traffic cones placed in the roadway at intervals? What traffic cones? (At that spot, there were none to be seen.) Ah, well, did I not know that this was Wimbledon tennis fortnight, when many such roads were forbidden ground for parking? I'd certainly forgotten about the tennis, and I had come in by a side-turning which was innocent of traffic cones. The sergeant seemed a bit remorseful. 'Tell you what,' he said, 'hop in

and we'll take you to the pound right now.' I said goodbye
to a concerned Miss Mannin and was driven to the pound.
I signed a book for the car, paid my fine, found the ignition
key still in place, and drove off towards Maida Vale and
Hesketh Pearson. Just before Battersea Bridge I decided to
look at a map and make certain about the best route. I
stopped at a convenient place and groped behind me for
my briefcase. What I found myself grasping was a lady's
handbag. I was in the wrong Austin 1300.

All the way back to Wimbledon I prayed that no one had
taken my car and briefcase — and the BBC's tape recorder.
No, the car was still there, contents complete. It was
identical with the one I had taken except for the registration
number, which I had not previously noticed. Without a
word to anyone I drove out of the pound, the two policemen
on duty taking absolutely no interest in me . . . There must
surely be a moral to this tale somewhere; but it's probably
one for the police to draw, rather than for you and me.

Hesketh Pearson was a truly companionable person, a
lanky, gentle-mannered man of about 60 in a very loose
brown pullover and enormous suede shoes; surrounded by
books on shelves that went from floor to ceiling in every
untidy room. He was a perfect example of how commercial
success can be demonstrated as something totally unrelated
to literary success. He had been twenty years on the stage
before he turned to biography, and had worked with
producers like Herbert Beerbohm Tree, Harley Granville-
Barker, Nigel Playfair, and Basil Dean. His biographies of
Wilde, Shaw, Sidney Smith, Dickens, Scott, Tree, Darwin,
Doyle, and many others had earned him little money and a
host of admirers which included me. He was an enchanting
talker, a ready listener, and one of those rare people
(Rosamond Lehmann is another) who send you away
feeling better, happier, taller, and decidedly less pessimistic
than when you arrived.

Rebecca West I went to see because I knew she could,
if she would, talk to me about Kingsley Martin for the
purposes of a biography. 'Come and see me if you like,'
she wrote, 'but be prepared to discover that I didn't like

him. Phone my secretary and come to lunch.' Of course I made much of the notion that if she didn't like him she was just the kind of person I ought to be listening to, implying that most people did. In her comfortable service flat overlooking Kensington Gardens she was looked after by a nubile young secretary who got the lunch, and who was an extremely good cook. I had already met Dame Rebecca when I interviewed her for the BBC in 1957 on the publication of her novel *The Fountain Overflows*. True to her promise, she spent the latter part of the lunch assassinating Kingsley's character with a thoroughness which, I thought, suggested deeper reasons than the ones she was giving me. I knew that Kingsley had regarded himself as something of a ladies' man. I was disposed to credit him with some capacity to gauge his own chances of success, and thought this ought to have guided him in his contacts with Dame Rebecca. They used to meet, or perhaps I should say encounter each other, during weekend parties at H. G. Wells's house at Great Easton in Essex. Kingsley was a poseur, she said, a fake intellectual, a man with no manners, a scribbler who weakly reflected the views of the last person he had lunched with, or on. She would no doubt have adopted every word in Alistair Cooke's bilious little obituary in his book *Six Men* (Penguin, 1977):

Kingsley Martin was one of those ferocious democrats who insist on dominating any open discussion, but I can't be sure now whether it was this trait or his extraordinary, baleful appearance that makes him, forty years later, stand out in my memory like a gorgon at a garden party. He had enormous brown eyes, like hyperthyroid marbles, which rolled across a sallow face that appeared to be in the last stages of hepatitis.

That was written two years after Kingsley's death, and it is like the voice of Rebecca West describing this man who, among many editors, was the best I ever worked for, the most encouraging, percipient, thoughtful, and, in a word, inspiring; and a man who, among many friends, was one of the most warm-hearted in times of difficulty and worry. Alistair Cooke and Rebecca West, for both of whom I have the deepest admiration, must have shared a special gift for seeing the very worst in people, an aptitude which I do not envy them. Kingsley told me in 1958, when I was leaving for America and the *New Statesman* was partly (and I felt a bit reluctantly) financing my trip, that he would have given me an introduction to Alistair Cooke, but that on his own most recent trip to New York he had telephoned Cooke at his Fifth Avenue apartment and that Cooke had refused to see him. I could tell that he was genuinely surprised and hurt about this, but I had to admit to myself that I had little idea why they should meet, and still less why Alistair Cooke should want to meet me, whatever my introduction. In fact I have never fully understood this business of overseas introductions to people who don't necessarily want to see you. But in New York, at Kingsley's insistence (supported by letters he sent on ahead of me) I did go to see Lillian Hellman, Mrs Elinor Gimbel (who owned the New York department store), Arthur Wang the publisher, the editors of the *Nation*, the *New Republic*, and the *Village Voice*, none of whom could have been wildly excited at the prospect of meeting me, but all of whom received me with the hospitality so uniquely American — and with unmistakable evidence of an esteem for Kingsley Martin. I am saying, in fact, that that is why they met me. I could fill pages with the names of men and women, household names, most of them well aware of his failings, to whom the Kingsley Martin of the thirties and forties was a much-respected interpreter of public affairs, a good friend, and a brilliant editor.

But to return to Dame Rebecca West, I asked her whether her dislike of Kingsley was influenced by his cool reception of her book on Yugoslavia, *Black Lamb and Grey Falcon*. Oh, he knew nothing about Yugoslavia, she said. And I now quote from a tape recording which she obligingly made for me. 'I wrote *Black Lamb and Grey Falcon*', she said,

as the result of three periods living in Yugoslavia before the war, each a period of several months in three successive years. It said nothing about Tito or Mihailovich — the war hadn't started. By a curious coincidence Macmillans got enough paper to print it in 1942 on the basis that publishers got paper supplies during the war on a ration according to what they'd been using before the war, and Macmillans had printed *Gone With the Wind*! So when *Black Lamb and Grey Falcon* came along they were able to print it. Otherwise they wouldn't have been. No one had ever written a complete history of Yugoslavia before—that sounds mad but it is actually true. There were books about Bosnia and Croatia and Dalmatia, but there was no book about the whole thing until I wrote that. I sometimes write a book when I've been trying to find one on a particular subject and I discover there isn't one—I did that when I wrote *The Life of St. Augustine*—there wasn't one in English, nothing to show when he was born or how he died.

I asked her how she met Kingsley.

He knew my husband. In 1934 I was living in a luxurious flat in Portman Sqare. Because of the depression we were able to get it in 1931 for £450 a year on a 14-year lease, and we kept it on for some time during the war because my husband was in the Ministry of Economic Warfare. About H. G. Wells, of course, I can't remember any connection with Kingsley except the two words 'silly fellow'. He thought Kingsley was dealing with important issues quite carelessly—he really *awed* me! Whenever you get people who have been much under the influence of the *New Statesman* they've always been spoiled by it. They've always thought that the enemy is not that we don't know how to do things but that there are wicked people who will *prevent* us from doing things—which is true in about 10 per cent of the cases, and in the remaining 90 per cent we haven't found out the way to do it. If you like to say that the Battle of Peterloo was due to wicked men oppressing the poor you can do so, but a very large part of the tragedy of Peterloo was that nobody was *used* to large assemblies and nobody knew how to handle them . . . Kingsley Martin seems to have encouraged an almost spiteful way of looking at any political problem, and I think that's a great pity. Spite is very easy.

There was a coldness [with Kingsley] over Yugoslavia. There was coldness about going into the war. I said to him and Dorothy at a cocktail party 'You've been howling for this war and now you're opposing it—it's very confusing. You didn't even renounce the possibility of war; you aren't even a straightforward pacifist.' He was utterly inconsistent. I was very angry because

a friend of mine who was a conscientious objector and thought
he had been badly treated came to talk to me about it, and I
suggested he should go to see Kingsley Martin. And Kingsley
made so much of it and printed so many lies and embroideries
on the statement, that the man gave up being a CO and joined
the Army!

Then hostility between us grew more and more, but I had a
lot of things to think about, and I didn't worry. I've never *liked*
him. I always thought the *form* of every sentence he wrote was
evasive. And damn it all, he was making a good living out of
it, dealing with frightfully important issues. He was cosier than
Dick Crossman, but there was the same feeling of irresponsibility
about both of them. I think that John Strachey, though he might
well have been ambitious (as were his sister and his wife) *really*
lived for the truth. I think of John with deep respect as a good,
conscientious man who wouldn't have said anything that could
have added to human suffering unnecessarily. There are not
many people I would think that of.

I remember wondering whether Dame Rebecca would
have included herself among them. 'There's a lot too much
hatred in politics,' she went on, 'and Kingsley Martin was
responsible for it.' (What, all of it?) 'When I think of that I
hate him. I also feel that his constant, needling defence of
the Communist Party, while he didn't join it, was *wrong*.
If he felt like that he should have joined it.' (I can actually
recall choking down a reference to the fact that John
Strachey had behaved in precisely the same way.) 'If he saw
it as the only conceivable anti-Fascist defence he was an utter
fool, in the face of the Stalin-Ribbentrop pact. He always had
a soft spot for the Communists — it's like saying you have
a soft spot for the Sermon on the Mount. There's a great
gulf between that and the Communism of Russia and China.'

And finally I asked her whether Kingsley Martin was her
first experience of *New Statesman* editors. 'Clifford Sharp
hated me and I was proud of it', said this advocate of less
hatred in politics. 'He was a *born* fascist — brutal, stupid,
horrible. I wrote for him sometimes, and we had terrible
rows. He was just a tiresome drunk. He was very much
supported by Beatrice Webb — she was the greatest *ass*

there ever was . . . Kingsley Martin had an extraordinary influence on his time', concluded Dame Rebecca, and it was as if he were picking up a little as she thought of his predecessors. I can recall that, as I left her, I was feeling glad she knew nothing about me. Or did she? She seemed to know so much.

It was in 1958 that I recorded a BBC interview with Sir John Gielgud. We met in his dressing-room at the Globe Theatre, where he was playing James Callifer in Graham Greene's new play *The Potting Shed* — and thus, he said, enjoying an agreeable non-Shakespearian interval between Prospero and Cardinal Wolsey. He sat very upright, wearing an elegant dressing-gown and holding a lighted cigarette which I didn't see him once put to his mouth (though I watched closely). When he turned his head to me, his body came round with it; and it was an effective movement, seemingly planned and concerted. He was scrupulously courteous, instant, and fluent in his responses to my questions, and obviously skilled at concealing what he was thinking. He was in fact presenting Sir John Gielgud as Sir John Gielgud and being his own actor-manager. And although he and I were alone it was impossible not to feel that there was present somewhere in that tiny room a Gielgud understudy who, despite his secondary status, was the real John Gielgud I was supposed to be discovering. He told me, and I forget whether or not it was in direct response to a question, that the one part he still wanted to play was Iago; but whether it was because that part specially attracted him or because he happened never to have played it I cannot recall. I remember the whole interview as one that was strangely difficult and yet unforgettably enjoyable.

One thing above all others has tempted me into setting down these recollections of isolated talks with celebrities; and that is the fact that no one ever hears the interviewer's impressions — quite rightly, of course, for he is of little more interest or importance than the camera or the tape recorder. But if camera and tape recorder could keep impressions of a private view, purely subjective memories, might it not be interesting to hear what they thought, the comments they could make? Today we have television producers who are developing a voyeuristic 'fly-on-the-wall' technique by which they can purchase, on our behalf, some of the innermost secrets of their seemingly willing victims. Television is turning us into a nation of voyeurs to whom nothing in other people's lives is sacrosanct, for whom people's necessary privacy, hitherto fiercely defended, is up for sale. But even in the most candid of television interviews, the candour is always on the side of the interviewer, to be expressed—God knows why—in rudeness and in questions evolved by a hierarchy of form-fillers. I long to see some celebrity turn and smite one of these insolent products of the new nihilism. But no, they nearly always take it all with routine humility and earnest propitiation, like captives ordered to do a funny dance before being shot. I have seen just three men and one woman turn and rend their ill-mannered interlocutors: John Osborne, Lord George-Brown, Sir John Nott, and Bessie Braddock. I suppose they valued their self-respect more than the money.

But before I leave the fifties, I have to record (as 'one who was there') the tragic occurrence of the very last and worst of London's particulars in December 1952, the worst fog I ever saw and by far the most lethal. The London particular of my childhood, for all its sulphurous and carbonic content, was innocuous and benign by comparison with what modern industrial and road-transport conditions could produce, given the right temperature and humidity. This one killed over 4,000 people, either through respiratory damage or accident. Jenifer and I were living at Blackheath in South London. We were three-quarters of a mile from Blackheath Station, in a restored Georgian crescent called the Paragon. On a train which left Charing Cross at 6.30 p.m. I got to Blackheath Station at 9.15—nearly three hours to cover about six miles. I remember trying to imagine the thoughts of the motorman driving that crawling train, with hundreds of lives dependent on his blind responses to an automatic and entirely aural signalling system. But the moment I had alighted at Blackheath Station and cannoned into a platform seat, in a visibility of no more than a yard in any direction, I would have given much to be back on metal rails and going anywhere. During the further hour and a half that it took me to walk, or shuffle, from the station to my home, I realized that I was more frightened than I had ever been in my life, including the commonly shared anticipation of violent removal during the air raids on the City of London. By feeling my way along village shop-fronts, house railings, gateposts, and privet hedges, hampered by streaming eyes and bursting lungs, I arrived after about an hour at a street corner where a teenaged couple were huddled under a street lamp, coughing and spluttering and helpless. They were able to tell me that I was at the Standard, the name of the local pub. I had groped my way much too far. At that moment a shop door opened and a man called to us to go in and shelter for a time. The couple gratefully went in and I, having thanked him, resumed a house-clutching progress now made slightly easier for knowing where I was, though I was half a mile off course. Eventually I was home, exhausted and feeling rather ill.

It soon transpired that many hundreds of people out of doors in London that night never saw their homes again. I remember too that the only outdoor public service that could function that night was the police. In my part of South London no road traffic could move, even the trams were stranded by other helpless vehicles, not even an ambulance went out, and people in the streets died where they gave up. The outcome, which took four years to materialize, was the Clean Air Act of 1956, one of the most beneficent statutes that ever needed a four-year campaign by a small and determined pressure group to bring it to birth. In the end it was a Private Member's Bill, foisted onto Gerald Nabarro by the Housing Secretary Duncan Sandys, and based on the report of a Committee on Air Pollution chaired by Sir Hugh Beaver, an eminent consulting engineer. It must have saved many thousands of lives, as it ruled a line under the history of the London particular, which had convinced everyone at long last that if London didn't kill it, it would kill London.

It was towards the end of the fifties that I perpetrated the Great Imposture. Well, perhaps I can plead, as the initially reluctant imposter, that I allowed it to get born and begin its horribly rapid growth because smothering it might have done more harm than good. This is my opportunity to make the confession that has long been seeking a way out, and this is me making it.

In the mid fifties Kingsley Martin allowed himself to be persuaded that the *New Statesman*, now a very prosperous weekly, should pay some occasional homage to its altruistic beginnings. Its socialist conscience was uneasy. Kingsley himself, when he was appointed editor in 1930, had had the perspicacity to stipulate that his salary should go up (or, I suppose, down) with the paper's income, and it had been going up for twenty years. He was now very comfortably off. The thing to do, it was decided, was to run an 'occasional series' of long articles on matters of serious import which most people wouldn't really want to read: the kind of article belonging to the Drains and Democracy flavour of the pre-1920 *New Statesman*, when the Webbs, and Hubert Bland, and G. D. H. Cole were contributing their long, unhurried, and barely readable Fabian theses, worthy rather than spell-binding. In 1913 when Bernard Shaw, the Webbs, and Arnold Bennett put their money into it, they were thinking about political discussion, not about profit; and here it was, coining money that it didn't really want. There was always a feeling among its contributors that it could have suitably eased its conscience by paying them a bit more; but they could be set off against people like Douglas Cole, who was able to write so prolifically for next to nothing because he was nicely sustained by a Magdalen fellowship. But Kingsley now thought it might be politically decorous to do some political 'vanity publishing', reviving our lost crusading image with some long pieces, 12,000 words and upwards, which would be called 'Supplements' and which no one but their authors would really want to read. When my turn came, I was to do a 12,000-word piece about penal reform. It appeared on 2 February 1957, in the form of an open letter to Mr R. A. Butler, the Home Secretary, and it was called *Prisons and Prisoners*. There were twenty-four packed columns of it, and I remember being appalled to find that it had been printed without a single subheading — it *looked* unreadable, and I thought this was carrying verisimilitude a bit too far. I was told that to make room for subheadings it would have had to be cut down, and no one wanted to cut it at all. It looked like a long extract from *The Times* of 1795. I have just reread the whole thing, chin on fists, trying to recapture the frame of mind in which I must have been working at the time. In vain. Certainly it touches on all the familiar problems, all of which could have been (though I don't think they were) dredged up from long-forgotten government blue books. Sadly it confirms that they nearly all remain untouched — with a few little changes here and there it could reasonably be addressed to the Home Secretary today. It uses all the clichés of the period. The words 'massive' and 'widespread' and 'purposeful' occur throughout. ('Massive' had just arrived, in its new meaning that has nothing whatever to do with mass.) It is didactic and opinionated, and its peroration is full of things that poor Rab Butler 'must' do without further delay.

The sequel was truly comic. Kingsley was so pleased with it, or perhaps with the fact that he had given up valuable space to it, that he sought opinions about it everywhere. Naturally he got enthusiastic responses, because only a secret few had found the time to read it. Among the *cognoscenti* the enthusiasm sprang from the fact that all the recommendations I pressed upon the unsuspecting Rab Butler were those they had all been urging for many years. Among the non-reading majority, it reflected the belief that the article must be good because it had been allowed to go on for so long.

But when, two years later, the Home Office published its still famous White Paper, *Penal Practice in a Changing*

Society (Cmd. 645 of 1959), I found that everyone was congratulating me on being virtually its unacknowledged author. Nothing I could say would disabuse them. The Home Office, they said, had adopted all my points and simply expressed them differently. But they were totally mistaken. The points the Home Office had 'adopted' had been lying around in numberless blue books, White Papers, and research reports for at least fifty years. (It all reminded me of Tommy Trinder's discovery that 'Shakespeare and me use a lot of the same words really, only he puts them down in a different order.') In fact Cmd. 645 of 1959 has acquired a number of ghost authors, among them Sir Lionel Fox, who was then chairman of the Prison Commission. The Home Office Assistant Under-Secretary who actually did write it happens to be an old friend of mine and I shall not betray him. But even in the authorized 'history' of the *New Statesman's* first fifty years (Edward Hyams, *The New Statesman: The First Fifty Years*, Longman, 1963, pp. 144–5), there appears this reference to myself:

One of his most important contributions to the paper was the writing of a Supplement on crime and punishment in which suggestions were made whereby the Home Secretary could improve the quality of justice without amendment to the Statutes. Mr R. A. Butler used this Supplement almost as a programme, taking it point by point in a major speech.

Well, that was the gossip of the time, even (I found) among the experienced campaigners in the field of penal reform, who really ought to have made more enquiry. Poor Rab Butler couldn't have appeared to do otherwise: the 'point by point' presentation would have had to be made if my *New Statesman* Supplement had never been written. The 'points' he made had all been in Home Office ministerial briefings for four or five generations, their only difference that day being that they were all a bit older. But thus is history written. And once written, thus it stays. Nor all thy tears . . .

CHAPTER NINE

URING the late fifties I had come to know Arthur Koestler. I don't presume to say that we were friends, merely that he had long attracted my admiration as a writer, as a vigorous thinker and (I suppose above all) as a savage debunker of Soviet Communism, and that I knew I had his slightly uneasy esteem as a former policeman who was, however improbably, involved with him in the campaign for the abolition of the death penalty. We were members of the committee which, under the chairmanship first of Victor Gollancz and then of Gerald Gardiner, was working to bring that about.

Shortly before Christmas 1959 he telephoned me at the *New Statesman* office and said he would like to see me. He had to repeat this once or twice because, inherently unlikely as it would have sounded anyway, his pan-European accent needed very careful listening to. Anyway I think I must have regarded it as a summons, for I asked him where I should go. No, no, he said, he would come to my office. He came the next morning. He wanted to establish, beginning in a small way, an annual prize or group of prizes for the best artistic or imaginative work done by prisoners in lawful custody in Great Britain. He had turned to me because I was much involved in the development of what I was then seeing as a promising way of 'rehabilitating' discharged prisoners. (I was glad, years later, when the moralistic word 'rehabilitation' was dropped from the penal-reform vocabulary and succeeded by 'resettling'.) He had the best of personal reasons for knowing the tranquillizing and regenerative effect on a man in captivity of the opportunity to paint and draw, to model, to write, to compose verse and music, to sing and play and act. In 1936 as *News Chronicle* correspondent in the Spanish Civil War, he had collected much evidence about German and Italian Fascist aid to Franco and his rebels, and in February 1937 he was captured on the Andalusian front. The Fascists condemned him to death as a spy, and during the next three and a half months he expected daily to be taken out and shot. From his cell every morning he could hear the executions taking place in the courtyard outside. In May 1937, on the initiative of the British government, he was exchanged for another prisoner and came back to London. In September 1939 Hitler's war saw him back in France, where he was again arrested, this time as an apparently stateless refugee, and sent to the notorious prison camp at Le Vernet. After four months of that he was released, and joined the French Foreign Legion, from which he proposed to desert as soon as possible and get back to England. Back in England with a forged Swiss passport, he was at once imprisoned in Pentonville as an 'undesirable alien'. There he stayed for the six weeks that it took for the Great Fifth Column Scare to die down, and for the Home Office to decide who he really was. Whoever writes Arthur Koestler's 'definitive' biography will find few readers to believe what he has to tell them.

He had discussed his scheme with his literary agent A. D. Peters ('Peter' to all his friends), and decided that he could allocate £400 a year from his book royalties to a fund which might, he hoped, in due time attract support from other sources. (It was this reason, and not any undue personal shyness or modesty, that made him so determined at the beginning to exclude his own name from the title of the award. He gave way on this with great reluctance. What was modest about this was his belief that the name Koestler was not spoken happily in British official circles and that it might, accordingly, saddle the whole scheme with a totally unnecessary handicap.) How should he go about it, he said, and how did I think the Home Office would react?

Why did he want to do it at all, I asked him, interested always in motives and their staying-power? I can remember his answer much more clearly than my question. 'I vill put it like zis;' he said slowly, 'zat it is becoze I vish a leetle cheap immortality.' And he grinned, as well he might. He always said 'becoze' and talked about 'the cozes of crime'. His astonishing fluency in about six languages (in addition to his native Hungarian) had never been accompanied by much interest in their pronunciation. I suppose it was a concession that he didn't say 'becowze'. A week later we went to the Home Office and met an interested and courteous Assistant Prison Commissioner named Charles Cape who, as it happened, was an ardent Koestler devotee and had himself published a book of verse. He was in charge of Prison Education, and Education was the only official slot into which Arthur's unexpected notion seemed to go. It turned out that, welcome as the proposal might be in principle, there would be many details and difficulties to be surmounted first. Mr Cape ran through them — not, I thought, discouragingly, but I was wrong. Arthur came away fuming and inconsolable. He made me feel I had let him down badly, but I defended my Home Office man with all the resentful anger (which I think I concealed) of the ridiculed impresario.

He next addressed himself to David Astor, then editing (and in effect owning) the *Observer*, and a man in whom he had, as I think everyone had, boundless trust and confidence. If you got the sympathetic ear of David Astor in any such scheme, an early outcome was usually a lunch-party in a private room at the Waldorf Hotel in Aldwych. This lunch was attended by Arthur and 'Peter', his agent, Cynthia Patterson, his secretary and companion who later became his wife, Hugh Klare of the Howard League for Penal Reform, a lady whose identity I never discovered (or, if I did, forgot), and me. We appointed a committee of eight people, of whom only David, Hugh Klare, and myself are still living. A couple who came into the scheme very early were John Grigg (who renounced his peerage as Lord Altrincham) and his wife Patsy — and from the first these two were among the most active organizers and planners. We decided to call ourselves the Koestler Award Foundation. We all wanted David Astor to be chairman, but the Home Office, whose co-operation was of course absolutely vital, said they could not approve of a newspaper editor in that capacity, so A. D. Peters took it on for a time, and eventually, to everyone's delight, Sir Hugh Casson took over from Peter. He was then lecturing at the Royal College of Art, and he was later President of the Royal Academy. This gave the whole thing a new prestige, access to a Royal Academy room for committee meetings, and a rapid spread of public interest among the influential people whose arms Sir Hugh Casson so skilfully twists in good causes. And in 1982, when he decided that at last he must give it up, David Astor was no longer editing anything and he became chairman once again.

The prize money gradually climbed and the reserve funds swelled as various industrialists, philanthropists, and grant-making bodies took us up. Every year, for example, one of the best entries is an elaborate model made from glued match-sticks, the model of a cathedral, a four-masted barque, a caravan, a musical instrument, a bouquet of flowers. There is something about these eternity-filling jobs that touches the hearts of people who normally wouldn't give much thought to the prisons, the 'black flower of civilized society'; something specially illustrative of imprisonment's endless hours and of prisoners' desperate patience. It wasn't long, accordingly, before the match manufacturers Bryant & May were among our regular financial supporters. Then the Reed Paper Group kindly allowed us to use their well-appointed picture-gallery in Piccadilly for the annual exhibitions, until circumstances made that difficult for them, and then we were accommodated in similar splendour at BP House, Victoria.

I have to confess that the prize for the best painting or drawing was usually awarded, by our distinguished panel of art critics, to the precise pictures which I myself would have hurriedly put back in the van in case somebody saw them. Not that I favoured chocolate-box pictures, but I think I have the populist concept of the functions of art as the communication of pleasure and excitement rather than the 'making of a statement' which most normal people would want hushed up. And at one of the annual exhibitions Arthur Koestler, making one of his very rare appearances for the occasion, whispered in my ear (to my unholy and unforgettable glee) that if the first and second prize-winners that year were artists he himself was an all-in wrestler. His seeming shyness about the whole thing was encouraged rather than lessened when the necessary details of organization and financial planning made it seem to him harder to give money away than to earn it.

On 6 July 1981 Sir Hugh Casson threw a huge party at the Royal Academy to celebrate the twentieth anniversary of the Koestler Award's establishment, by which time more than 4,000 creative inmates of the prisons and special hospitals had earned Koestler awards. The guests were a dazzling lot: former prime ministers, peers, judges, members of the Cabinet, MPs, financiers, editors, publishers, artists, writers. But they did not include the founder, the man whose imagination had brought the scheme to birth and who will, despite his hopeless suicide in 1984, long sustain it. 'Koestler the polemicist', wrote Alan Hamilton in *The Times* of 6 July 1981, 'has been curiously self-effacing about his prison awards. It is as though he was so well aware of his reputation for opinions, even arrogancies, in other directions that he needed something to keep quiet about.' It seems to me a strange misreading of the man. I do not profess to have understood him, and indeed I believe that Cynthia, his wife, was the only person who ever did. But I know that at the centre of his unchangeably distorted nature was a hatred of authority, a distrust of the officials who represented it, and a certainty that all the authorities hated him. He thought the very sound of the Koestler Award must impinge upon the ears of officialdom as if it were the Lenin, Crippen, or Myra Hindley Award; and in view of what he had said to me, the ex-policeman reborn as a barely credible recusant, I was astonished that he ever consented to the use of his name. He may have had a few more things than most of us to keep quiet about. After his wretched death, there began the inevitable quest to find out whether he did, and what they were. And it may well turn out that he has furthered this process by leaving £700,000 to Edinburgh University—because it proved to be the only university

in Great Britain prepared to establish a professorship in para-
psychology. That was the subject in which his restless mind
had become gradually more absorbed in his last few years.

Late in the sixties I wanted to talk to Arthur Koestler about
Kingsley Martin for the purposes of a biography. He invited
me to lunch in his tall, opulent corner house at No. 8
Montpelier Square, Kensington. Cynthia, who was not then
his wife, got the lunch and looked after us. She was one of
those women who, throughout the ages, have accepted without question the role of 'looking after' men. She was also one
of the sweetest-natured creatures I have ever met, and I was
to meet her many times. It is a permanent scar on my memory
that when, in 1984, he took his life because he was incurably
ill and intolerably depressed, she went with him though she
was much younger, in good health, and loved by everyone.

Kingsley Martin had many followers and admirers, but
Arthur Koestler (I was credibly informed) was not among
them. There were no grey figures in Arthur's world: they
were black, or white, or invisible. Kingsley, I was told, was
firmly among the black. I found that this was grotesquely
untrue. When you are prompting a man to talk to you
frankly about his knowledge of some well-known person,
and he is as fluent and vituperative as Arthur Koestler was,
the picture he gives you will contain some sharply drawn
sketches of other people, acquaintances mutual to him and
to your subject. It was thus that I discovered Arthur's bitterness and spite, and the deftness with which he reduced
reputations to tatters. It's one of the less happy tricks of
the memory that the kind of thing you hear at such a time
stays indelibly in the mind, and despite all that you can do
colours your pictures of the people defamed, warping your
judgement of the good that they have done. Thus my memory
retains drops of Arthur's poison about people I have known
and liked, many of them good friends; and I wish the poison
were not there. To paraphrase Mark Antony:

> The hatred that men tell lives after them.
> The love is oft interred with their bones.

I do not know how a man should be expected to endure what Koestler endured and retain much love for human kind. But he did; and through the furrows in his ravaged outer surface there gleamed a vast generosity. Those who loved him must have known his faults, and loved indulgently.

He spoke warmly about Kingsley Martin, and said that his influence in the thirties, that first decade of his *New Statesman* editorship, had been beneficent (I am not quoting him, for I forget his words). He certainly didn't share the general disapproval, represented by George Orwell and Malcolm Muggeridge and even the left-wing intelligentsia, for Kingsley's decision not to publish an Orwell book review exposing the atrocities of the Spanish left in the Civil War. Everyone was lying about the Spanish Civil War, he said. No editor could possibly know who was telling the truth. Let an editor choose his own lies — the whole of Fleet Street was open to Orwell if he wanted to write.

I had never met George Orwell, of course. My wife Jenifer had known him in his BBC days, and often told me how she remembered him as a gentle, quiet, and unassuming person with a wry sense of humour and (according to her) the slightly 'lost' look that calls up the mothering instinct. But, with an envious regard for his literary craftsmanship and his sensitive reporter's eye, I have always felt that this apostate Etonian, whose enemies affected to see him as an inverted snob, was really a snob the right way up, writing about drab and boring people with a singular lack of understanding and empathy; nevertheless pouring scorn upon all social reformers as 'sandalled progressives'; and succeeding marvellously in dramatizing what was in fact a brilliant imposture.

'Swinging Sixties' had, I thought, no firmer foundation as the title of a decade than a surrender to the lure of alliteration. We had lived through the Hungry Thirties just

as, under Queen Victoria, there had been Hungry Forties.
Our Twisting Twenties had greeted the Charleston, with
which Britain was said to have gone suddenly mad, our
mysteriously flat-chested womanhood dancing jerkily from
the knees downwards. But the swing associated with the
sixties was what *Longman's Dictionary* calls 'jazz played
usually by a large dance band and characterised by a steady
lively rhythm, simple harmony, and a basic melody often
submerged in improvisation'. It seems to me an unusually
careful description of the music that was damaging ear-
drums forty years before the Swinging Sixties. 'Swing'
seems to have been one of those periodical rechristenings
to which jazz has always resorted when tin-pan alley is
worried about the till.

In these respects the really eventful time, for me at any
rate, had been the fifties, the rock and roll decade which
I now leave (no rock and roll man myself) with an
affectionate glance back at the kinds of entertainment for
which it deserves to be remembered: *Under Milk Wood*,
The Boy Friend, *Look Back in Anger*, *My Fair Lady*. I
remember it too for the huge Aldermaston marches (to
which I shall return), and Roger Bannister's still incredible
four-minute mile. It was a decade that began, as all decades
now seem destined to finish, with *The Mousetrap* and *The
Archers*.

For me the sixties got off to a bad start. It was, as I
have sadly noted, in 1960 that the *News Chronicle* and
the *Star* were wantonly and needlessly killed off, and
editorially they were the habitat of nearly all the journalists
I felt really at home with: people who seemed less élitist
than the average *New Statesman* writer. (*Average*? What
am I saying? How would you arrive at an average with
such material? Not even 'typical' will do, and why should
it? No one would ever look for such a word in relation to
the *New Yorker*. I know what I mean, but the word eludes
me.) I suppose that every well-established paper has its
mystique. The late Edward Hyams, in his didactic ramble
of a book about the *New Statesman*'s history, said that
the paper possessed a 'whatness', a word he coined because

the word he wanted eluded him. The *News Chronicle*
possessed it too, as everyone who worked for it would
agree. Its lighter side was exemplified by F. W. Thomas,
who contributed a daily shaft of sunlit lunacy called 'Merry
Go Round'. And here I want to help in the perpetuation
of his memory, and his paper, by reproducing his timely
and philosophical reflections, dated 6 October 1934, on
'Putting the Clocks Back':

One other little thing before we part.

DON'T FORGET THAT

At 2 a.m. by G.M.T.,
Or what in Summer Time is 3,
Herbert Morrison, Evelyn Laye
Nervo, Knox and Ian Hay,
Lord Baden-Powell and Walpole (Hugh)
Mr Gordon Selfridge too,
H. G. Wells and Thalben Ball,
Winston Churchill, Henry Hall,
C. B. Cochran, Christopher Stone,
G. B. Shaw and David Bone,
Hore-Belisha, Zena Dare,
Sir Kingsley Wood, the New Lord Mayor,
Larry Gains and Ramsay-Mac.
Must wake and put their watches back.

ON THE OTHER HAND

Cleopatra, Julius Caesar,
Dirty Dick and Mona Lisa,
Liszt and J. Sebastian Bach,
Morny Cannon, Mungo Park,
Farragut and Francis Drake,
Milton, Shelley, William Shake,
Garibaldi, Gibbon, Gray,
Guy Fawkes and the Vicar of Bray
Charles the First and Rin Tin Tin,
Mickey Mouse and Gunga Din,
Samuel Pepys and William Pitt,
Needn't bother a single bit.

No doubt it was through the influence of the Cadburys
and Sir Walter Layton that 'the Cocoa Press' had always

shown an interest in pragmatic criminology, a concern
which went much deeper than the buying and selling of
current murder stories. I mention criminology here because
it was in the course of the sixties that I began to shed some
comforting illusions about the prospects of understanding
and 'controlling' crime, and to record some of my
perplexities in the *News Chronicle*. I had been an executive
committee member of the Howard League for Penal Reform
for fifteen years. I had listened respectfully to the views
and proposals of colleagues who knew far more than I about
penology. I knew that my election to membership had
come about (a) because I was always writing about what
people called penology, and must therefore know a lot
about it (false), and (b) because I had come through the
experience of being a policeman without losing my faith
in humanity (true). I had studied prisons and prisoners
in Britain, America, Australia, and New Zealand—
perhaps when I say 'studied' I should say 'puzzled about';
and had tried to communicate to others my optimisms,
perplexities, and hopes in countless articles, discussions,
lectures, and radio programmes. I had watched the
emergence, or it may have been the revival, of an official
theory that a man in prison usually reaches a kind of moral
zenith, a psychological peak, at which you must catch him
if you are to have any chance of helping him to benefit from
his 'treatment'. The Home Office and the prison service
were presented as thinking like this collectively, though
to my knowledge there were many in the probation and
prison services who knew it to be an illusion. Most of the
current research was directed to 'evaluating' this
reformative effect in different types of prison regime. These
didn't really differ much, but depended to an extent never
officially recognized on the personality of the prison
governor. The theory was that if a man were kept in prison
beyond his 'zenith', he would begin to go downhill and
you had lost him.

It was nonsense, of course, and always had been
nonsense. I had begun to distrust it as a result of getting
to know men who had served (or were serving) long

sentences. They were little different inside prison from
outside it. Typically, I recall a conversation with a man
in Alcatraz, the dreadful USA federal prison on an island
in San Francisco Bay (now long closed). He had been a
prisoner for thirty-two years—not all the time in
Alcatraz—and was about 53 when I met him. He had
become an assistant to the so-called Education Officer, and
spent much time teaching illiterates to read. In his cell
he had a pile of copies of the *Listener*, which someone in
England sent him every week. He was as rational and well-
informed, as socially concerned and thoughtful, as anyone
you meet outside prison, and much aware of the myth that
the human personality breaks up irreparably after about
ten years inside. It seemed to me that if it did, and was
known to do so, this must be what the penal systems of
the world desired and consciously set about achieving . . .
And incidentally if Alcatraz couldn't do it, nothing could.
The prisoners' cells in Alcatraz were like zoo cages, of
which the entire front wall was a grille through which the
captive could see (and be seen by) nearly all the other
captives on his landing. There was no privacy whatsoever
day or night. And it was thus that many of the inmates
were spending the whole of their lives. One man thus caged
up was a would-be artist whose pictures all represented
the Madonna and Child, and the walls of the Warden's
office were covered with them—dozens of them. The
Warden must have liked them? 'Like them?', he spluttered.
'They're just God-awful, but if it stops the guy going crazy
it's OK with me.' It is fair to say that in the subsequent
twenty-five years America, and particularly California,
have been in the vanguard of imaginative and experimental
penology.

   And it is that phrase which brings me to the confession
that has been half-heartedly trying to find its way out for
some years. I do not believe that, in the seventy years I
am now reviewing, all the 'imaginative and experimental
penology' in the world has made any significant difference
to the incidence of crime, anywhere. In the 1940s I made
the discovery that whatever punishment (or 'treatment')

was given to a first offender, 15 per cent of such offenders came back for more. Whether it was prison, Borstal, fine, detention centre, probation, conditional discharge—for 15 per cent of beginners it was ineffectual. For the other 85 per cent *the effectiveness of each was the same*. And, apart from some changes of nomenclature for the treatments meted out, the position is still unchanged—except in one respect, and that is the state of mind produced and nourished in the active theatre of punishment and 'correction'. Any change in the method or apparatus of punishment makes the punishers *feel* better, and their supporters feel better with them. Something is being done. And this, I must suppose, is a good thing. If people are to go on believing that their leaders or representatives are *trying* to find a solution, there must be periodical changes in the official rhetoric. The room in which I am writing this is crammed with government blue books, White Papers, Green Papers, draft bills, Hansard reports, Royal Commission reports, criminal statistics, annual reports by chief constables and prison authorities and innumerable reformist movements. They have been a part of my required reading for fifty years. Most men would have burned the lot years ago. I cannot do it. They are a part of history, the earnest testimony of concerned people who meant well, taking up the slogans of previous generations (like the ridiculous 'short sharp shock') as if they were new coinages or inventions. From among them all there may even emerge, one day, something to reinforce the belief to which I stubbornly adhere, the perfectibility of man.

I once heard Kingsley Martin assert at an editorial meeting that anyone who concerned himself with that particular pipe-dream was probably an intellectual pervert. Dick Crossman at once told him he was quoting Hugh Kingsmill and getting him wrong; and an argument ensued which, I should have thought, was a considerable waste of everyone's time, both men growing stridently and comically cleverer as they went along. I didn't know then, but Hugh Kingsmill was a favourite source of disagreement between them, Crossman (it seemed) approving of his bitter biographies and Kingsley Martin hating them. The meeting was held up while they traced the words attributed to him, which appear in his life of Matthew Arnold:

A concern with the perfectibility of mankind is always a symptom of thwarted or perverted development.

To me, then as now, it was a wisecrack from the thin air of academic lucubration. But it rankled, and I decided in later years that perfectibility had at least two meanings. Mine saw it as a progress *towards* perfection, a state of being perfectible. No lower target, no watered-down aim, could ever be agreed or identified; perfection was what men must keep their eyes on. They might know, they must know, that it is unattainable, but they must 'love the highest when they see it', even if their approach to it can never be closer than 'decimal nine recurring'.

And it was in this frame of mind, admittedly half-baked as I have now shown it to be, that I was asked to serve on the parole board for England and Wales, then newly established under the Criminal Justice Act of 1967. The whole concept of parole for prisoners — we fell into a way, at our meetings, of calling it 'the philosophy' — was based on this idea of a mental and moral 'climax' in the prisoner's mind, which the prison 'training' was supposed to anticipate, recognize when it came, and then beneficently exploit. When did it happen, this white-hot moment in the squalid and monotonous life of a captive in one of our crammed and impersonal sin-bins? Conveniently, its arrival varied with the length of the sentence. If a man was doing three years, you looked for it at the end of his first twelve months, like watching for a chrysalis to split open. If he was a lifer, it could happen between ten and fifteen years, though some lifers seemed to 'climax' earlier. And since most lifers were murderers without other crimes to their names, they were difficult to classify in the league of redemption.

I'm certain that we members of that first parole board half believed all this, and took our duties and our instructions very seriously. But a major consequence of this 'prison climax' business was the coining of a whole new vocabulary of unconscious humbug. It spread throughout the prison and probation services, infected all the usual public spokesmen and writers on penal affairs, promoted every prison to the notional status of a re-educational establishment. We all spoke a language in which prisoners were making steady progress, finding things difficult, responding (or not responding) to treatment, nearly ready, better orientated, showing (or, disastrously, not showing) remorse or contrition, co-operating, settled, forward-looking, resentful, and (cruellest of all) 'still denying guilt'. The logical extension of this last one was that a man couldn't have parole until he admitted his offence, whereas many prisoners are sustained in their residual self-esteem only by the continual attempt to convince themselves that they were wrongly convicted. The prisoners themselves caught it. In the statements they sent in when they were asked if they wanted to be considered for parole (as they became eligible for it), those who wrote out their own statements used the language suggested to them at the prisons. A surprising number didn't want to be considered at all: they welcomed even so self-damaging a means of bucking the system. But I remember one man at Gartree who said he thought he would now be likely to benefit by removal from a structured environment, another who reckoned he had now reached the optimum moment, and a third who felt that his new-found morality represented an ongoing condition.

In all this we had helped to create, with unintended cruelty, an atmosphere in which prisoners were obsessed with the subjective value of conformity and (for a time) performed miracles of good behaviour. Fine for the long-suffering prison staff—the most maligned and misre-presented body of men and women in the entire social service structure—but among the prisoners it built up an ugly backlog of disappointment and bitter cynicism, giving much encouragement to those prisoners who refused parole out of defiance. The reckoning came when it was first suggested that prisoners refused parole should be told why.

It seems a rational and humane idea, and the Press and other media were loud in their demand that reasons must be given when a man was being told he had to stay in prison.

From the first I was against giving reasons, but opinion on the parole board was divided, and I believe it still is. I thought I saw all too plainly that any panel of parole board members, even if they agreed on some necessarily stereotyped reason in an individual case, would all have different explanations for having arrived at it. If the whole machine were not to be brought to a standstill, you couldn't have a comprehensive 'case report' on every prisoner, to be added to the mass of papers already on his dossier. The reasons given would have to be stereotyped. (In fact a two-years' experiment in 1978–80 resulted in the production of sixteen 'standard causes for concern' which were expressed in precisely the kind of telegraphic jargon that had seemed to me as inevitable as it was cold-hearted.) I imagined chief prison officers having to say 'Sorry, Jones, you haven't got it this time — you'll see why, it's numbers 3, 8, 14 and 22.' The prisoner wants to know what he can do, how he can change his conduct or demeanour, to cure or modify whatever defects might be thus cryptically imparted to him. No one can tell him. They may not even be prison defects. It may be that his family dread his return to hearth and home, drink, and wife-bashing.

So there would have to be some means by which he could challenge the 'given reasons', the 'standard causes for concern'. While he then prepared his arguments and the Home Office its answers, the hitherto confidential reports of probation officers, police, social workers and prison officers would perforce be supplied to the prisoner himself. Can you not imagine the effect of this possibility upon the compilers of such reports, and on the people from whom they sought their information? The quality and utility of all such work would get near to vanishing-point. Appeals would take their place in a lengthening queue, and people would spend longer in prison than if they hadn't bothered to appeal; just as some prisoners get their convictions

quashed or sentences set aside by the Court of Appeal long
after they have served their sentences anyway.

The whole well-intentioned parole scheme subsumed
the mystic process by which bad men were changed into
good ones by being in prison, and a trained eye which could
recognize the moment when they were . . . By the time
I left the parole board I was convinced that the whole
scheme needed drastic changes and that the best and
simplest change, likely to result in the least suffering, was
to abolish it. One evening in a House of Commons
committee room I said so to a meeting of a Labour Party
Penal Affairs Group chaired by the genial and courteous
Sam Silkin, QC. It made roughly the same impact as a rose
petal dropped into the Grand Canyon; and, I discovered
later, it didn't even get into the minutes of the meeting.
But it is now advocated by our leading criminologists,
among them Professor Norval Morris and Dr D. A. Thomas.

I should admit, of course, that I observed the system at
close quarters only in its first two years, after which I went
off to Australia and New Zealand to look at their systems.
But they were the formative years, in which our parole
system was going through its awkward infancy and we
were blazing some sort of trail. We almost made it up as
we went along. It seemed to me that we got an absolute
minimum of information about individual prisoners, and
it was expanded slowly (sometimes, I thought, almost
grudgingly) by the permanent officials when we kept on
pressing for more. In the first few months, the heavy brown
parcels containing as a rule the dossiers of thirty or forty
prisoners, and sent to our private addresses by post a few
days before each weekly meeting, sometimes arrived burst
open, obviously dispatched by someone who didn't know
how to do up parcels. Then the Home Office acquired some
very strong plastic brief-cases, stout enough to withstand
anything that the postal service could do to them. But the
next thing was that some of the prison governors, long used
to the business of protecting their charges from public
nosiness, began refusing to include certain prison
documents in the parcels at all, and there were a few

awkward delays. In the end they had to be told by the Home Office that they must obey orders whatever they thought about them . . . Incidentally I was astonished to find that in New Zealand in 1968 the national parole board had absolutely no opportunity to look at the prisoners' files until the very day of the meeting, and were expected to make their agreed assessments there and then, which seemed to me to involve a farcical rubber-stamping of the views sent up to them from the prisons.

By contrast, most of us spent at least two and a half days a week studying the dossiers and making notes on which to base our personal recommendations. But at first our information, when it did come, was poorly documented, improvised, and tentative. There were barely legible photocopies, themselves often taken from faint carbon copies; unsupported expressions of opinion; irrelevant letters seemingly stuffed in to pad out a dossier, so that it could at least look adequate before you went through it; and, where a man had been in several different prisons while serving one sentence, a succession of prison reports so different that they could have related to a number of different men. Sometimes it was clear to us all that, even if a man did get parole, it would get him out of prison only two or three weeks before his normal discharge date. And accordingly some of us would think the period too short to justify all the formalities of release and supervision, while others said you simply must not prolong a man's imprisonment for a single unnecessary day. We were constantly reminded that we were not a part of the 'sentencing process', passing further judgement on offenders already dealt with by the judges; but some of us simply couldn't see what else we were.

The whole experience confirmed my belief that if any good effect is ever produced by imprisonment, it happens because the prisoner has been brought into contact (for the first time in his life) with someone in authority whose nature is unusually sympathetic, understanding, patient, and above all unorthodox. Two such men were John Vidler and C. A. Joyce.

When I met him in 1955, John Vidler was Governor of Maidstone Prison, and it was his last job because he was unwell. He was already a legend. So far as he could, he would establish a personal relationship with every man in his prison, and he made a point of knowing as much as he could about them all. This was not at all usual: I have known governors who quite deliberately knew nothing personal about their charges, preferring to be 'emotionally uninvolved', concerning themselves only that the prescribed number of men could be accounted for at any given moment. But John Vidler's achievement in knowing them all by name was not unique—anyone so minded could do that in a long-stay prison. What was unique was his perception of their characters and temperaments, his capacity to short-circuit disciplinary trouble, his skill in detecting the 'sickness' that was really malingering, and his aptitude for soothing (and in many cases converting to his own viewpoint) the prison officers who were predictably upset by an unorthodoxy which depended on everyone else's being orthodox. Of course he had a charmed life, and I never knew what the Home Office really thought about him. I do know that he once absented himself from the prison for nearly two days while he drove a prisoner across three counties to visit a dying wife. And I suppose that if anything had gone wrong with that little enterprise it would have ended the Vidler career. I often heard that when the Prison Standing Orders were called in for amendment, Vidler's copy could never be found; but that if anyone had found it, he would have discovered also that its margins bristled with ribald comments in Vidler's handwriting. What I also came to know was that men who had served their sentences under Vidler, even if they were not genuinely 'reformed characters', kept out of trouble as a kind of tribute to 'old John Vidler'. In many ways he was a saintly man, but honesty compels the admission that his unorthodoxy could be tolerated only because no other prison governor tried it on.

'Saintly' is not the word that would present itself in describing C. A. Joyce, headmaster of the Cotswold

Approved School (since 1969 these schools have been called community homes—I never understood why). Salty, perhaps, rather than saintly. And yet his methods and characteristics were like Vidler's. He knew every boy in his school's changing population, studied him, sought and found the best in him. He operated a system which could be described, not unkindly, as a sort of loving megalomania. He had been a Guards officer, an assistant prison governor, and a Borstal housemaster. I have known a number of ex-prisoners who had been through his hands and who, when they came to decide (as many did) that the criminal life was stupid, cruel, and bloodyminded, traced their change of heart to the influence of 'Mr Joyce'—never 'old Joyce' or any nickname; an influence which had flickered in their minds for years as a kind of solitary inextinguishable lamp.

He always said that the man who might have been his most spectacular success was his most horrendous failure. This was Neville Heath, a sadistic, sex-crazed murderer hanged in 1946 who had been one of Joyce's 'more promising' boys at Hollesley Bay Borstal Colony in the late 1930s. He knew all about Heath's record as a cheat, liar, swank, imposter, and pervert, but believed he had 'got through' to him. In the following few years I met Joyce a good deal in BBC studios, and saw in him a growing cynicism which could have been attributable to his shattering disappointment about Neville Heath. He seemed to develop, under the nourishment of broadcasting, a more flamboyant and extravagant persona, becoming (as Gilbert Harding did) a professional character 'famous for being well known'. But I liked and admired him, and would have been glad myself to be more like him.

The success or failure of such a man in dealing with offenders is seldom, if ever, officially reported or even appraised. What is officially appraised is the system in operation at the relevant time, and men like Vidler and Joyce operate in defiance of systems. So their appraisal stays in the minds of their charges; and I have met enough of those to be quite certain that Vidler and Joyce had a wholly beneficent influence. Both were vigorous-thinking men, both were born leaders and managers, both saw much that was amusing in life (and told good stories well). Both were Christians. Joyce's Christianity was the more muscular and articulate, but he was no fundamentalist, nor was he demanding except in one imposed daily ritual. Every afternoon at 4.00 in the Cotswold School an angelus bell was rung, everything in the school and grounds came to a dead stop, and there was utter silence for one minute. Every day, he said, it made them all wonder, himself and his staff included, what it was all in aid of; and then they remembered that it was a sacred bell and would perhaps start wondering what sacred meant. This was true whatever kind of religion they had been taught, and true if they had been taught none. 'Be still, and know that I am God' was the idea of it. Whose idea? 'Oh, mine', he said. 'Home Office know nothing about it — or if they do they've never interfered'. The boys seemed to me to go along with the idea. And if there was something other than porridge in their brain cavities, said Joyce, it spent at least half a minute every day groping towards the light.

He had other ways of assisting this struggle. At 4.15 p.m. every day there was a school assembly, and he invited me to sit at a sort of high table with him. When everyone had settled and was quiet, he pointed to the door, which the last arrivals had left open. 'Shut that fucking door', he said loudly. A startled youth rushed to do his unexpectedly phrased bidding and then sat down again in an uneasy silence. 'None of you liked that much, coming from me, did you?' he said. 'Well, I don't like it from you either, and there's a lot too much of it. So let's all start disliking it together, shall we?'

I suppose it may seem a simple thing to say, but both men taught by example and not precept, both were good men, and both (to my own knowledge) were remembered by old lags as well as young ones who professed, at any rate, that they forsook the criminal life because of one or the other. Neither would have wanted any better epitaph, but I doubt that either would have believed it.

And apart from all that I have said about him, I have further cause to remember C. A. Joyce in the fact that when he died in 1970, my wife received three messages of condolence because the radio news-reader, announcing his death, managed to make 'C. A. Joyce' sound like 'C. H. Rolph'. Jenifer learned of my death when her former BBC secretary phoned to express her sympathy. Of course it happened while I was away from home, and Jenifer had to wait a day and a half before she and I, happily reunited, were able to agree that the report of my death was, on the whole, an exaggeration. There were two other messages of condolence, both written; and since I was the household letter-answerer, it was I who sent their writers the reassurance which, it may be rashly, I felt they might like to have.

CHAPTER TEN

IN the City Police, which I left in 1946, I hadn't had
the privilege of serving with Col. Sir Arthur Young, the
Commissioner from 1950 to 1971, who turned out to
be so great an improvement on Sir Hugh Turnbull, the
awful man he succeeded. Nor did I meet him until 1960,
when to my astonishment he invited me to lunch with
him at the Athenaeum. I think that by this time I had a
none-too-enviable reputation as a kind of double agent,
a scribbling one who knew the defects of the service
and, to his lasting disgrace, failed to keep quiet about
them. Sir Arthur Young, on the other hand, was himself a
ruthless reformer, and went reforming all over the world
at the bidding of the Home Office, the pleasure of the
Commonwealth Office, and the eager request of assorted
far-flung police authorities — in the Gold Coast, Malaya,
Kenya, and Northern Ireland. He had had the kind of career
which, because of an ancient belief that meteors move
faster than anything else, is usually called meteoric.
He was a constable in Portsmouth at 17, Chief Constable
of Leamington at 31, Assistant Chief Constable of
Birmingham at 34, and Chief Constable of Hertfordshire
at 38. At 40 he was Assistant Commissioner of the
Metropolitan Police. And then with his KBE, his CMG,
and his CVO he was combining the commissionership of
the City of London Police with advisory appointments that
took him all over the world and left the City Police to look
after itself.

At the Athenaeum I was a bit alarmed to find that he
was about six inches taller than I. Talking to taller men
has always robbed me of any possible advantage, even of
equality. This is because as I look up to see what effect
I am producing (if any), I can feel my Adam's apple going
up and down ridiculously. Luckily we were soon seated
at a table and looked roughly the same size, while he was

making every effort (rather noticeably) to put me at my ease. We had what the diplomats call a wide-ranging discussion on matters of interest to our two, er, factions, at the end of which he asked if I would like to meet the Commissioner of the Metropolitan Police, Sir Joseph Simpson. Was there any reason to suppose that Sir Joseph would want to meet me? Oh yes, there probably was. At any rate I was quite mistaken if I supposed (as I rather did) that he regarded me with some sort of distaste. I saw the necessity to smother my astonishment, and my host said he would arrange the meeting.

A week later I had a phone call from Sir Joseph's secretary. He said Sir Joseph understood that I would like to see him; not, I noticed, that Sir Joseph would like to see me. We made an appointment and at 11.30 one morning I presented myself at New Scotland Yard (which in fact was the old Scotland Yard, the one on the Embankment at Westminster). I have the clearest recollection, the more vivid because despite Sir Arthur Young's assurances I felt that I was 'on the carpet', of a feeling that the various policemen who then passed me from one to another on my way to the Commissioner's sanctum had all been carefully trained in how to look inscrutable. Not even twenty-five years in the police service have weakened my preference for policemen whom I can scrute. But as it turned out I was deceiving myself in supposing that any of them had the smallest idea who C. H. Rolph was. Their job was simply to ensure that no one was ever allowed to wander about on his own inside Scotland Yard unless he belonged or had lawful business there.

I found Sir Joseph Simpson easier to talk to than Sir Arthur Young. There was no atmosphere of social effort, and if the laughter was rarer, it was more natural. We began in rather the same way, because when he got up from his desk to greet me I found that he too was a head taller. This kind of thing was not supposed to happen to City of London policemen, whose standard height of six feet (I'm a little less now) had been decided on for reasons of prestige. But he was completely disarming and unfussily friendly. On the left side of his desk there stood a foot-high pile of *New Statesman* issues. I wanted to find out if his inscrutable entourage had had to read them all and mark up passages for his attention. 'Well, occasionally someone does', he said. 'I find they mark up all the things I don't want to read.' This made it impossible not to ask him if these included my own articles? 'Well, you write about all sorts of things, don't you? I have to draw the line somewhere.' He said he was a bit surprised that no one wrote about Rugby or cricket. We were a pretty gloomy lot, weren't we? The one thing he always looked for was a piece by Arthur Marshall, with whom he had been a boy at Oundle School in the twenties.

Now I had gone to the Yard with plans to turn this meeting into a searching interview, but I'm afraid we spent the rest of the time talking about cricket and Arthur Marshall. I wonder how it would go today? Today's *New Statesman* is a far more dyspeptic weekly burp*, with a trendily ill-written and hastily constructed demonology which puts the police on about the same level as Himmler, Count Dracula, and the KGB. (I hope, by the way, that it goes on thumbing its nose, now that its one-time constructiveness has been taken over by rivals; no one has to read it, but there is a constant need for some kind of socio-political graffito which can keep us comfortably aware that its authors still don't have to dread the 3 a.m. knock on the door. To paraphrase Logan Pearsall Smith's *Last Words*, denunciation of the police is a necessary part of the hygiene of the dissenting, and greatly assists the circulation of the blood. It may also do something for the circulation of a weekly paper.)

Sir Joseph saw me out at his office door, which (I reflected) was far more than my own Commissioner would have done. And as we shook hands in the doorway, he said 'Well anyway, I suppose I can take it that you have the interests of the service at heart?' I tried to look like a man contemplating his heart. 'Right up to the point where they

---

*Written in 1985. Today (1988) it's no longer true and is happily disowned.

start conflicting with the interests of the public', I said, and hunched my shoulders as a man does when he is waiting for the heavens to fall. I can see him now, towering above me with his shock of grey hair and his rugged, frontiersman sort of face, as he leaned slightly backward with his hands hanging limply at his sides. 'You're pretty nearly incorrigible, aren't you?' he said, precisely at the point, if he had but known, where he had got me feeling unusually corrigible. And then he took the sting out of it with a broad and disarming smile.

I met him several times after that, at Press conferences and criminology seminars. And once we debated something before the assembled Medico-Legal Society—I think he won, but I have forgotten about it with the convenient amnesia that wipes out defeats. But I should have liked to serve under him.

It was at about this time that I got involved in the field of mental health, and particularly in the treatment, or perhaps I should say the prescribed and organized neglect, of discharged mental patients. It seems to have been common knowledge but it came to me as a tremendous shock that we had in our midst a huge number of people, possibly two or three millions, who had come out of mental hospitals half-cured, or perhaps even worse than when they went in. They were being 'cared for in the community', the phrase which had been officially adopted as the rationale for closing down a lot of mental hospitals, and in particular mental wards in general hospitals. I ought to have been prepared for it, because in 1957 I had been commissioned by the National Association for Mental Health to write an explanatory pamphlet ('Mental Disorder', NAMH, March 1958) about the *Report of the Royal Commission on the Law Relating to Mental Illness and Mental Deficiency* (1954–1957).

I became a member of the NAMH (it now calls itself MIND, which is a little cryptic but not in any way acronymic), and after a time I found myself elected to its Publications Committee. The chairman at that time was

the able and urbane Kenneth Robinson, who in the next
Labour government was to become Minister of Health—
and of that, more anon. I had learned much about the sharp
distinction, unperceived by most people even today,
between mental illness and mental deficiency, the former
often curable, the latter no more curable than an amputated
leg. I had followed and reported on the parliamentary
debates that preceded the Mental Health Act 1959, which
set the seal upon the principle of informal admission to
hospital to be treated for mental disorder. Anyone mentally
disordered was now to be regarded as an ordinary member
of the public going to hospital for treatment in the same
way as for any other illness. In all the publicity surrounding
the passing of this well-intentioned Act, much was made
of the notion (it was little more) that it got rid of the
'stigma' attaching to certification and the old status of the
'certified lunatic'. In fact the new procedure wasn't much
different. A near relative, or a mental welfare officer, could
in those days apply to the 'manager' of a mental hospital,
produce medical evidence, and ask that someone be taken
into the hospital forthwith for treatment—with his
consent if possible, and if not, then without it. Normally
there were to be two doctors' recommendations, but in
an emergency one was enough. And whether or not you
called this a 'certification' depended on whether you were
inside the system and adopted the changes of terminology
thought up by the legislators, or outside it and went on
calling spades what you had always called them.

For me, this new involvement led to some conflicting
interests which I shall describe in the order in which they
arose.

First, my *New Statesman* editor Kingsley Martin began
receiving long and pleading letters from a woman in a big
provincial mental hospital who swore that she had been
wrongly 'certified'—before the 1959 Act changed the
terminology. The letters were literate, cogent, and (we
thought) totally convincing. They were not written in
green ink, or on brown paper, or in block capitals. Kingsley
had received three or four of them, sending the non-

committal replies which must be bitterly familiar to patients in mental hospitals—and to their medical staff. Finally he sent for me. 'I can't stand this', he said. 'I worry about it every night, when I should be thinking about something else. There's something terribly wrong here. I'd like you to find out, if you've got nothing else on at the moment?' (This meant whether I had or not.) 'These people,' he went on, 'thousands of people, all suppose this paper can do something dramatic and magical about these things, which we can't—unless she's right in what she says. Then we can raise the roof, and you're one of our resident roof-raisers.'

So I wrote to the medical superintendent of the hospital, who telephoned me next morning as soon as he had opened my letter. He had read my articles for years, he said, and he seemed still to regard them with approval. He knew that Mary had been writing to my editor (I shall call her Mary, which is not her name) and that the letters were all beautifully written. They weren't really, but such praise is readily bestowed. If I would like to go down and see her, she would meet me at the station. And perhaps I would make a point of seeing him too? He would be pleased to put me up for the night. There was a train from London every morning at 9.10.

A few days later Mary met me as I got off the London train. She took me to a little neo-Georgian cream-bunnery in the High Street. She was about 45, small and spare, with a rather shiny but keenly intelligent face, large spectacles, and a Yorkshire accent. A copy of the *New Statesman*, protruding from her handbag, proclaimed her identity in the way I had rather expected. She was instantly likeable, and you could tell that she had known much suffering. Her story was disturbing enough but, looking back on it after thirty years, what is more disturbing is that it could all happen again under current legislation and procedure.

I still think there is little doubt that she was mentally ill and that her unfortunate husband, alarmed (it seems) by her exhibitions of rage over unimportant things, feared for the safety of their three children. He had her 'certified' and taken to a vast and famous hospital just outside the town. Her description of the scene when she was forcibly removed from her home and children was nightmarish. Her hospital detention was as escape-proof as if she were in Parkhurst as a 'Category A' prisoner. After some months the doctors must have thought she was sufficiently improved to become a 'voluntary patient'; and then she was able to get out and go to see her children at home. Her husband soon decided (I still don't know on what ground) that the doctors were wrong, and he took to refusing her admission to the house. The hospital became the only place where she was sure of a bed. As I listened to her I found myself doing battle with the familiar hallucination that besets the social worker and the case-book or agony-column journalist, namely that for the time being he is God. I don't know what I thought I could do; I merely understood that for the time being I was enabling my editor to suppose that something or other was actually being done.

I walked with Mary back to the hospital, and in the huge grounds she directed me to the superintendent's house and then left me . . . Dr Evans and his wife were hospitality itself. I spent a happy evening in the bosom of his family, and I remember that just before dinner and the children's bedtime he put on the gramophone a stentorian recording of the Berlioz 'Symphonie Fantastique' and, in the march theme, stamped round the dining-room table with his children, all of them using rolled-up newspapers as trumpets. Later he talked to me seriously about Mary, and seemed to know already that she was preparing to sue him, and other doctors, and the Regional Hospital Board for false imprisonment, wrongful certification, and a number of the related injuries that lawyers can always think up. And he was right.

She discharged herself a few days later, and hurried to London, partly (I think) to be nearer to me and the *New Statesman* and partly to prepare herself for what was to be a long battle with the law. She had no money. She had borrowed a little from friends, and had signed on at the

Holborn Employment Exchange. She got herself a bed at a convenient Cecil House (for single women) in Red Lion Square, found a temporary (and woefully ill-paid) job with a small charity organization, and set about applying for legal aid in her anti-hospital campaign. When this was refused, no doubt because the legal aid committee thought she had no case, she came into my office in a state of far from speechless indignation.

It was of course impossible to convince her of the likelihood that legal aid had been refused because the committee thought she had no chance of succeeding. It was because the whole world was against her, she said. The legal aid people had doubtless made enquiries at the hospital and had been supplied with the usual tissue of lies. Never mind, she would become a lawyer herself and conduct her own case. Barrister? Oh no, barristers had to be engaged by solicitors. She'd be a solicitor. But, she wondered, would that give her the 'right of audience' in the High Court? No, but she wouldn't need it, I said, if she was going to argue her own case as a 'litigant in person'. No, no, she would be arguing the case as a lawyer, on equal terms with the other lawyers. I imagined that the High Court, always indulgent to the litigant in person, would treat her as such whether she was a lawyer or not, and allow her the small unofficial privileges that a lawyer wouldn't get.

Very well, she would start with an LL B. That would necessitate some A levels. She enrolled at the LCC Evening Institute in Princeton Street, Holborn, and duly equipped herself with three good A levels. Then she homed in upon me one day to announce, with her eyes shining and her whole body shaking with excitement, that she had been admitted to a redbrick university and was to read Law. Three years later she had her LL B, and was applying to the Law Society for permission to take their examination for admission to the roll of solicitors.

Then to my great surprise I had a long telephone call (at the *New Statesman* office) from the Vice-Chancellor of her university—who, it seemed, knew of my interest in her progress and was worried about her future. He thought she was unstable, clever, socially isolated, embittered, and likely to ruin herself emotionally in the obsessional pursuit of a hopeless claim against the mental health service. Her LL B. papers, though not brilliant, were of a quality that comfortably earned her the degree. But she would now want to be a solicitor, and the award of the LL B. (unavoidably, he thought) would make it difficult for the Law Society to stand in her way. Everyone liked her, but liking her was irrelevant. Confidentially, did I think she was a suitable person to be a solicitor?

I did not. I believe I had seen this coming for some time, and I knew in my heart what the honest answer was. She was too unstable, excitable, vulnerable. Would I ever want her to be my solicitor? I felt I had to convey this to the university, and as I thought of Mary I felt like Judas himself. A sequel to this was a phone call from the Law Society, who wanted to know if I could confirm the university's misgivings. So to Mary's heart-broken indignation she was not allowed even to sit for the exams.

Anyone who supposed that this would put an end to her campaign would need to be a total stranger to Mary and all her ways. She stormed off to the High Court and issued writs (at long last, and only just within the statutory limit of time) against the Hospital Management Committee, Dr Evans, several other doctors, social workers, and an assortment of lesser fry concerned in her 'wrongful' detention. In due course — and 'due course' in this kind of case means a long time — a Queen's Bench Divisional Court dismissed her claim and complimented her on the skill with which she had presented it. She promptly gave notice of appeal.

The judges in the Court of Appeal (again 'in due course') were equally complimentary about her skill as a litigant and advocate, dismissing her appeal none the less. At once she gave notice of her intention to appeal to the House of Lords, at that time her last chance — the European Court of Human Rights did not yet exist. In those days an appeal to the Lords was a kind of Bleak House scenario. The statement of the appellant had to be inscribed on vellum (probably Their Lordships had not yet heard about photocopying and were still marvelling uneasily about carbon copies); but for some reason she got herself excused this expense and had the documents typed. In due course she appeared before Their Lordships in a committee room of the House of Lords, where (she told me incredulously) she was not called upon to say a word but had to listen to the Lord Chancellor explaining why her appeal must fail. I believe, now, that she found this rather more satisfactory than she made out, cherishing the attention devoted to her case by the Lord High Chancellor of England, for so long a mere figure in her textbooks.

I was sorry for her from the beginning, partly because I thought I saw the final result as inevitable, and partly because she was the first and remained the most poignant example in my experience of what a discharged mental patient could expect from the new regime of 'care in the community'. Community care for such a person was simply non-existent. The social services were not to blame. Like many discharged mental patients she would have absolutely nothing to do with them, and they couldn't force their care upon her. She distrusted authority of every conceivable kind, and in every official context or gesture she saw the threat of further detention in what she called 'the bin'. No matter how ill she was, she would never go to a doctor or have one summoned to her aid. Any doctor, she said, would have access to her mental health record (as, if he took enough trouble, he surely would); and he would thereupon inform the police, or the 'so-called mental welfare people', and she would be put away. Such people, she assured me, would always say she was hallucinating.

She then embarked on another long campaign, this time for access to her children: not access in the usual litigious meaning, for by this time they had all grown up, but access as a woman who wanted to reinstate herself as a mother, in which she faced endless family frustrations. She got a job in a Midlands hospital (!), and when I finally lost touch with her I think we had been corresponding for about

twelve years. I do not know the end of her story, which
deserves a far happier ending than it probably got. I do
know that for me she had been the beginning of a long
acquaintance with the procedures and deficiencies of our
mental health service, which I found progressively
horrifying.

In the course of it I made the acquaintance of Barbara
Robb, the very remarkable woman who was to become a
thorn in the flesh of certain hospital authorities in whose
flesh a thorn was long overdue. She mounted a highly
efficient campaign in aid of old people detained (well or
ill) in State mental hospitals, and it became known as
AEGIS, which meant Aid for the Elderly in Government
Institutions. I had written an article in the *New Statesman*
in 1966 about the plight of the aged in mental hospitals
where they didn't belong. As a sequel, I was invited to
lunch by Charles Clark, of Penguin Books (he is now
copyright adviser to the Publishers Association), who was
an active member of the National Association for Mental
Health. The purpose of the lunch was that I was to meet
Barbara Robb, and in due course I became deeply involved
in her campaign. I chaired Press conferences, vetted letters
she wrote to the media and to Members of Parliament, and
acted in the capacity which she was pleased to call 'legal
adviser' (though she had the priceless assistance of Theo
Fitzwalter Butler, the editor of *Archbold*, the bible of the
Criminal Bar, and a former Recorder of Newark. I felt a
decent diffidence in his company at AEGIS meetings, but
he was an indulgent man.)

Almost by chance Barbara had come across the growing
practice of confining unwanted (but perfectly sane) old
people in the geriatric wards of mental hospitals. Of course
she knew that in the general hospitals, too, there were
thousands of old people who needn't be there, but the fact
that their presence was 'voluntary' was little talked about:
in a mental ward it was more significant, and its
significance was a matter of record. When Barbara came
to collect her experiences and the outline of her campaign
in a book which she called *Sans Everything*: *A Case to*

Answer (Nelson, 1967), she told the story of a Miss Wills whose 'rescue' from a big mental hospital was contrived and effected by herself and her AEGIS friends. I thought this story was a trifle overdrawn, since Miss Wills was a voluntary patient and was not disabled. She could have walked out when she wished. Barbara and her friends certainly got no encouragement from the staff, but discouragement is not the same as a locked ward; and whichever side Barbara was seen to be on, the staff would be unlikely to suppose that it was theirs. But it was the case of Miss Wills, and her need for friendly concern, that started the whole thing off.

These old people, said Barbara Robb, in hospitals of both kinds, were 'the most unvisited of all hospital patients — among the relatives and friends who might know of their plight there are many who despairingly don't want to know'. The publication of *Sans Everything* brought her campaign to a climax. A number of distinguished psychiatrists were among its contributors, in addition to the nurses I mention later, and I wrote a first chapter. The book was widely and sympathetically reviewed. As I write this brief account of the campaign, the full story is the subject of a proposed thesis by a research student at London University, who for the time being has possession of my AEGIS papers. Its completion may well reopen the whole problem, and enable us to judge how the hospitals are coping with it today. I have reason to believe that if Barbara were alive today, she would find that little has changed.

It is now almost twenty years since *Sans Everything* was published. Looking at it again now, I can recall the shock of misery with which I read the letters that came to me after the *New Statesman* article. The ones from nurses, some of whom later repeated their revelations in sworn affidavits, were the despairing cries of decent, ordinary people unable to get a hearing in the hospital world. These nurses told of the pitiless neglect of the helplessly old, and of the common practice of 'stripping' old patients of their teeth, spectacles, hearing-aids, toilet tissue, combs, writing materials.

I have nursed for the last seven years in a well-known geriatric hospital here. It has a growing reputation, largely due to self-advertisement, for the humanitarian and 'new approach' conditions under which the aged patients live. The actual treatment of these helpless old men and women is such that I have taken out an expensive insurance policy in order that I may never find myself a patient there. With the help of another nurse, who feels as I do, I have made a detailed list of the things from which our 'confused' old patients suffer most. If you are interested I should like to send you a copy of this. I think you would hardly believe how much roughness, laziness and dirt can go on unchecked in these days.

The rest of the letter appears in *Sans Everything* under the heading 'They Cannot Defend Themselves'.

Barbara Robb had friends in Parliament, anxious and willing but largely powerless, notably Lord Strabolgi, Lord Amulree, and Mr (now Sir) Geoffrey Howe, QC. She found no friend in the then Minister of Health, Mr (now Sir) Kenneth Robinson, or in the excellently organized National Association for Mental Health, to whom the mere existence of AEGIS was of course an implied criticism. But she found an unexpected ally in Richard Crossman, who had recently given up the leadership of the House of Commons in order to become Secretary of State for Social Services. In this capacity he was Kenneth Robinson's nominal boss without the power to direct the way he was to run the health service. In his new capacity, Dick Crossman insisted on receiving and studying some scarifying reports from AEGIS, reports which his permanent officials would have been glad to suppress. Barbara was widely regarded, and in official circles I had heard her vehemently described, as a 'bloody nuisance'. Crossman invited her to go and see him, and to his eternal credit he was soon insisting that the truth about these mental hospitals must be dug up and revealed. I'm in a position to say something about the personal impact of these two people upon each other, during an interview at which I should have loved to be a fly on the wall. For Barbara had an effervescent and mischievous sense of humour which she could indulge without ever giving offence; while Dick, so far as I can recall, had almost none—what took its place was an aptitude for making people not only look but feel foolish or inadequate. I find it difficult to imagine the kind of man who could make Barbara Robb look inadequate (however she felt), though Dick could always do it effortlessly to me, even when both of us knew he was talking rot, as he sometimes was. Barbara gave me her account of the interview on the following day. Dick gave me his about a year later, when I spent a weekend at his house near Banbury to discuss a projected biography of Kingsley Martin.

'What makes you disposed to trust me more than other politicians?' he asked her. Twinkling under a wide-brimmed hat bought carefully for the occasion, she asked him why he supposed that she trusted him at all. Did he not know, she went on, that he was known as 'Double Crossman', manifestly unfair though that was? He didn't know that, but seemed not to mind it. (She had been told that the shrinking violet act, which she could do very well indeed—she began as a ballet-dancer and an actress—would merely annoy him and that she would get nowhere with it.) He had read her report, he said, and my *New Statesman* piece, and the nurses' affidavits, and he saw that there would have to be an official inquiry, or maybe a number of official inquiries concerning different hospitals. She was greatly relieved at this clear possibility that her case against six different hospitals would not be referred to just one inquiry.

I asked him whether he had been impressed by Barbara. 'Impressed?' he said. 'Have you seen the hats she wears?' Even if it were possible to forget Barbara, it would not be possible to forget those extraordinary, carefully chosen, and obviously expensive hats, with which she seemed to transmute every occasion into a kind of one-woman Ascot. None the less, as Sir Edward Boyle said of Dick Crossman in the *New Statesman* on 12 November 1976, 'no one could have insisted more firmly than Crossman that the truth about our mental hospitals must be revealed and the necessary money found to put things right'. So it was

really Barbara, not the hat, who left the effective
impression. Whenever she had such an interview, or a
chance conversation that seemed to offer scope for
advancing her cause, she made and typed a full report of
it, and always sent me a copy for filing. These reports, plus
copies of newspaper cuttings and news items, rapidly filled
many filing jackets, and she kept me supplied with
expensive-looking binders to the contents of which, at
regular intervals, she sent me an index. Whenever she
wrote a letter to *The Times*, the *Daily Telegraph*, or the
Guardian, which was often, she sent me a draft and invited
comments. An invitation from Barbara had the same effect
as a command. Features editors asked her for many articles,
and before submitting one she always sent me a draft or,
if time was short, read it to me on the telephone. Every
statement of fact, every attributed comment, would be
footnoted with a reference to the source of it, and whenever
possible that source was photocopied and supplied with
the article. I have been told by more than one features
editor in Fleet Street that they never saw manuscripts so
overwhelmingly supported by authority, and never had to
feel uneasy about any statement that Barbara made. And
she made some hair-raising statements about the plight
of the old in hospitals.

In the basement kitchen of her tiny Hampstead cottage
she amassed so many files that she and her husband (Brian
Robb, the artist, illustrator, and lecturer) had to eat out.
Together they spent most of their income on AEGIS, and
though they are both dead their social compassion and
inexhaustible energy are a vibrant memory for a great
number of people.

She and I once prepared a television programme, in the
series *Man Alive*, about the fate of these forgotten old
people; and two of the nurses involved, who had by that
time left their jobs in despair of effecting any improvement
from inside, told their horrifying stories in interviews. It
was a live programme — there wasn't much pre-recording
in those days — and its final shape and content therefore
remained very much in the hands of its experienced and

highly efficent producer, Desmond Wilcox. To our utter dismay there appeared at the very end of the programme no less a person than Mr (now Sir) Kenneth Robinson, Minister of Health, who proceeded to dismiss all the nurses' evidence as a pack of lies, a 'smear campaign', as he called it. No one suggested why all these wretchedly worried people should concoct such horrendous stories, but the Minister's contemptuous dismissal must have left any reasonable TV audience with the feeling, no doubt comforting but extremely puzzling, that the lying nurses had an unfounded grudge against someone in authority.

I wrote a letter of astonished protest to Desmond Wilcox, not about what the Minister had said (for which the producer was in no way responsible and which was in any event fairly predictable) but for giving him the last word when it must have been known that he was going to dismiss the whole programme as a pack of lies. We had a mildly acrimonious correspondence which, of course, led nowhere. His attitude, the traditional one no doubt, was that if you try to produce a 'balanced programme' you can never please everyone. Mine was that a balanced programme didn't end with an unchallenged pronouncement (from a Minister of the Crown on the defensive) that everyone else was lying.

On the other hand, the report of Mr Geoffrey Howe QC on the Ely (Cardiff) Hospital scandal in 1966, which had been touched off by precisely similar revelations to those made by our nurses on television, showed that these and similar allegations were only too well-founded. Other inquiries followed, all the hospitals being named in the ensuing inquiry reports. Some were exonerated (a bit too easily), others denounced. There was much public distress, much angry eloquence from the professional angermongers in both Houses of Parliament (irrespective of party); a hospital ombudsman was appointed and a 'monitoring service' was set up. And as I write this twenty years later it is still possible for the following report to appear in the *Daily Telegraph* of 22 June 1985 — and go completely unanswered:

Pictures of a hospital for the mentally ill where cockroaches scuttle around the kitchen, and patients' beds are inches apart, shocked a conference of English and Welsh Health Authorities in Cardiff yesterday. Mr. John Yates, a research associate at the University of Birmingham, told the health officials: 'We are asking nurses tonight to bath 27 patients on their own. Institutions like this should be closed down, as the end of a 250-year failure story in care for the mentally ill and handicapped.'

The hospital, whose identity Mr Yates refused to disclose, had dripping, dirty and dark corridors 'because the authority prefers to save money to spend on patient care'. The rooms were empty of movable objects, and the lavatories had no paper . . . Worst of all were the cockroaches, a dozen of which had been photographed swarming on tables, around the sink and on the floor in the hospital kitchen. 'These pictures were taken not twenty years ago but just this month', said Mr Yates.

In a paper presented to the Conference he argued that the 'horror stories' about mental hospitals of the last 20 years were not isolated incidents but signs of a system of management and monitoring that did not work. 'Given the fact that monitoring mechanisms are specifically designed to prevent such occurrences, monitoring is clearly ineffective', he said.

If I say that I am glad Barbara Robb didn't live to read that, I shall be aligning myself with the don't-want-to-know majority that she spent so many years (and so much money) in attacking. But I end this chapter with an anxious, almost despairing enquiry about the integrity of politicians, at least of those who accept ministerial office. There were men in ministerial positions in 1965, and there are others today, knowing all about the appalling conditions in which old people are living out their count-down in some of our hospitals. They know that these conditions could be cured with money. They have instead adopted the facile and escapist doctrine that 'you can't cure these problems by throwing money at them' — and they know that it is untrue. Why then doesn't some Secretary of State for Social Services, some Minister of Health, some Chief Medical Officer, perhaps some Church Commissioner, suddenly resign his office with organized and reverberating publicity, denounce what he has discovered about the hospital service, and then devote his whole time to a campaign for its reform? All these officials allow themselves to be persuaded, no doubt, that they can best serve the cause of hospital improvement by staying in office, accepting the assurances of their minions that 'everything possible is being done', and drawing their £30,000 a year plus emoluments. Each of them has a superb opportunity to blow the whole miserable conspiracy sky-high. No one ever does. What happens to their consciences?

CHAPTER ELEVEN

I HAVE a theory, and I trace it back to my school-days and the use of examination verbiage in the shrouding of ignorance, that the art and practice of writing are esteemed far beyond their social value. 'With the art of writing,' said Carlyle in *The Hero as Man of Letters*, 'the true reign of miracles for mankind commenced.' And, in a way, it did. Writing got me the sack from my first job, but in the second and subsequent ones it concealed a comfortable and rather lazy mediocrity from nearly everyone, easing me into what my father used to call 'competencies' with various employers. From the time when it got me on to the staff of the *New Statesman*, I found that it had established me as a man of wisdom, vision, justice, compassion, and (funniest of all) learning. The whole concept of course was phoney, to a large extent embarrassing, and apt to establish me in postures which could have been sustained only by a trained mental acrobat.

I suppose I came across the most startling illustrations of all this when I went to Australia and New Zealand in 1968 as an inwardly incredulous, but I hope outwardly convincing, British Council lecturer. It is relevant to recall that in the mocking sixties, when Bright Youth was at the helm and we all knew less than usual about where we were all going, much fun was being had at the expense of the British Council. Its job was, and still is, 'to promote wider knowledge of Britain and the English language abroad'. The cast of almost any contemporary stage comedy or funny novel about 'abroad' had to include a British Council lecturer.

And I was to lecture about what, and to whom, and with what authority? The Council had in mind the things I had been writing about for years in the *New Statesman* and the daily papers, talking about on the radio, and lecturing about when I had rather desperately padded out an inadequate income fulfilling engagements through the Maurice Frost Lecture Agency. These were to be expounded to university social science departments, students' associations, schools, police and prison officers, and the great Australian public. The subjects included civil liberties, censorship, free speech, public order, the jury system, the death penalty, and about ten others which were really variants of those or virtual repetitions of them, billed as something else. All this I could sustain without much anxiety, for the lectures were about matters I was supposed to be familiar with; and there are probably some lecturers who are not writers to begin with. (Come to think of it, I'm sure there are.) Moreover even if, as I should have argued, I was standing up there merely because I could write, my views were deemed valid only so long as I stuck to my subject, which I tried hard to do. Yet a man who is compendiously known (and sent abroad to lecture) as a 'writer' is commonly given limitless opportunities — indeed obligations — to hold forth on subjects of which he knows absolutely nothing. And he holds forth. Thus throughout my three months' circuit of the antipodes, because of the British Council's advance publicity I was met at every airport by newsmen and camera teams and television crews. And thereafter in each successive hotel bedroom, with my morning coffee I sat in my pyjamas contemplating Press cameramen's versions of my own face, usually with its mouth wide open and eyes squinting in the hard sunlight (or screwed shut in the flashlights), as I pontificated about student riots, nuclear energy, miniskirts, the Pope and the pill, homosexuality, animal welfare, flogging, royalty, bodyline bowling, and topless sunbathers. My immediate predecessor on that British Council lecture round had been Mr A. Alvarez, the distinguished poet and critic, who has always seemed to me (I'm judging from reports, and hope he will forgive me) enviably quick-on-the-draw with pressmen; and I have often wondered how he got on. 'The reason why so few good books are written', said Walter Bagehot in his *Literary*

Studies, 'is that so few people who can write know anything.' George Stonier at the *New Statesman* used to tell me about Bagehot, by way of dispelling my misgivings that I hadn't yet read enough to be much shakes as a writer. They would both find today that, on the contrary, those considered able to write are judged *ipso facto* to know absolutely everything.

When I think of the eminent men and women in the world who owe their eminence to their scribbling, particularly this powerful *fin de siècle* tribe of 'instant pundits' on television, I feel anxious and frightened; frightened, vicariously, for a future I shall never see. Admittedly it is among the demagogues, not among the tyrants (for they are still distinguishable) that you find this coincidence of penmanship and power. Leave out aberrant demagogues like Hitler, whose writing was about as good as his painting; and Mussolini, who could turn out a decent script, wrote some poems, and is at least credited with the long article on Fascism in the *Encyclopaedia Britannica*. Each of them was able to dramatize a feeling of common purpose in a demoralized and hungry people, but they did it by Barnum and Bailey methods. It seems to be true that history's tyrants have not usually been good writers, anyway since ancient Rome. But in the democracies the way to the top has often been through the well-turned phrase, the neat and cogent essay, the flow of epigram; above all, the political best-seller. It had always seemed to me that I had little to offer the world but scribbling, and I knew that 90 per cent of all scribbling is imitative. So I had become a successful imitator. My copy-book masters had been Macaulay, Hazlitt, Tom Paine, Wells, Shaw, and Bennett, and I took care to remind myself that among these only Macaulay, being a legislator, a statesman, a judge, and a historian as well as a poet, had to be regarded as a man of power.

However, my selection by the British Council as one of Britain's short-term 'cultural ambassadors' had no other basis than what the Council had seen of my writing, though its interest may have been sharpened by the importunacy of Dr J. L. Robson, the New Zealand Secretary for Justice, who had been a pen-friend of mine for many years, and wanted to get me out there to 'do some lecturing'. It was a development which suddenly hoisted me to an eminence wherefrom I was to get at least a brief illusion of importance, which other people then proceeded to nourish into a sense of power. I mean that it was busily fostered everywhere by Press, radio, and television people, and by the many transport officials who proceeded to hustle me through New York–Chicago–Los Angeles–Tahiti–Auckland–Wellington–Sydney–Canberra–Melbourne–Adelaide–Perth–Singapore–Bangkok–New Delhi–Cairo–Geneva–Paris and home. The experience took its level from the fact that I was a first-class passenger throughout, with VIP treatment at all airports, and in hotels of the kind I had previously seen only from the tops of buses. This VIP business at airports I found most instructive, for it was clearly based on the daft assumption that a VIP is *ipso facto* completely trustworthy and that there is no need to search either him or his baggage.

My bags, in fact, were opened at only three airports out of about sixty — New York, Auckland, and New Delhi. At the first two the search was both perfunctory and apologetic. At the third it was offensive, ham-handed, insulting, and carefully humiliating. I find it impossible to forget the greasy little Indian official at the New Delhi customs counter, the home-made cigarette disintegrating on his pendulous lower lip, and his manifest enjoyment in exploiting every last ounce of authority to be found in his job. The best I can say about him is that he treated his own countrymen rather worse, and that they seemed to expect him to. One of my bags contained about a dozen long typewritten theses on penology, pressed upon me at various universities by their none-too-diffident authors. When these had been turned out on to the customs counter, the nasty little man told me that there would be 240 rupees to pay on them, solely because of their weight, not their possible content. I hadn't got as much as 10 rupees. The chap had delayed me so much that I could now see I was on the point of missing my Air India plane. I shut my bag, hurried away, and left all the theses for him to read with his evening curry. I've often wondered what happened to them, and entertained hopes about what happened to him. It's sad but I suppose normal that I should remember him more clearly than anyone else I met on that round-the-world scamper. The episode underlines a principle I tried mightily to instil in the minds of young bobbies when I was a training instructor in the police service, namely that any alien visitor's first contact with an official could stamp in his memory for ever the conception he was to have of the country in which he was newly arrived. I wonder what kind of instruction our own customs officials get? I find them unfailingly polite.

I had undertaken, when the parole board released me for the British Council assignment, that I would take every opportunity to observe the parole systems operated in Australia and New Zealand. I had few such chances in America, where there are almost as many different systems as there are States of the Union (some States allowing their prisoners no parole at all, nor am I now prepared to criticize them for that). But there was at that time (1968) a healthy impetus, originating in California and rapidly spreading, to develop alternatives to imprisonment (the most costly and futile of all punishments). These varied from 'cost-effective' probation schemes, which swelled the funds allotted to the probation departments to the precise extent that they saved money on prison systems, to the 'updating' of fines to reflect modern money values. (It seems odd that although the great majority of offenders are punished by fines, criminologists and penal reformers seldom even mention the fine as a weapon of crime control or, therefore, as a subject demanding research.)

Thirty years ago I might, in writing something of this kind, have had some profound observations to offer on the subject of American penology—which in my lifetime has always been experimental, daring, and exemplary. But those thirty years have battered me into the traditional frame of mind in which an old man longs to be as certain of anything as he formerly was of everything. Since the overall state of US crime seems not only about the same as in most other observable countries, including all the 'progressive' and experimental ones, but also rather worse than it was thirty years ago, the perceptible changes have to be seen as mainly cosmetic.

I saw only the 'better' prisons on my fairly direct route through the States: I didn't want to see the others. I knew by repute that Illinois, Ohio, Tennessee, Georgia, Alabama, Mississippi, and Louisiana had some of the worst prisons in the western world (and were so described by American observers), but I was concerned to find out what was good and developing, not what was sensationally bad. Among the British papers expecting articles from me when I got home, the only one that would want horror stories was *John Bull*—and it was going to be disappointed. It was more useful to be able to report that, for example, in prisons such as Vacaville, Chino, San Quentin, and Corona there were extensive grounds accessible to the prisoners for games, and that they had decent sanitation, civilized visiting conditions, and well-equipped educational classes held in suitable rooms (not in adapted cells as in Britain). Admittedly it seemed to me that all the cells were too small—and even at that they sometimes had two occupants. But they all had individual toilets with press-button flushing systems; and whereas our Prison Department always maintained that prisoners would (for some presumably British reason) plug the U-traps with their own clothing and then proceed to flood the building, no American prison guard I spoke to had ever heard of such a thing. I suppose it must once have happened in a British prison, somewhere and at some time during the past century; and if it did, the offending prisoner has been a boon and a blessing to the Home Office ever since, an ever-ready answer to critics and an imperishable reason for Doing Nothing.

The all-women prison at Corona left two lasting impressions on my mind. The first was that 90 per cent of the women (nearly all young) were serving sentences for cheque frauds, and represented the concealed aspect of America's credit-based economy, the have-it-now-pay-later recklessness induced by high-pressure salesmanship. The second was that all the women (at least all those I saw) were wearing pretty summer frocks which they had made themselves in the prison. They had twenty printed materials and six paper patterns to choose from; and whereas some of them had finished their dresses in a day, others took weeks of try-and-try-again before they had produced anything which, in or out of prison, was 'fit to wear'. (There was a limit to this, and it was set by the amount of dress material officially deemed expendable. When this was reached, a volunteer from among the better dressmakers would finish the job.)

I was at Chino on a visiting day, and hundreds of visitors were sitting at white garden tables under the trees talking to their captive relatives and friends. Idyllic, you may say: why wasn't there an orchestra playing? But there was. On a permanently built bandstand the prison orchestra was playing the overture to *Zampa*, though it seemed rather nicer when they had stopped. There is always something desperately sad about a prison, and there is certainly something perverse in my own nature which finds a special sadness in all these well-intentioned ameliorations (the ultimate example being the ladies' orchestra in Auschwitz). They are typical of the 'better' American prisons, whose orchestras (for example) actually broadcast on public radio. But at the least it can be said that participation in them is voluntary, and that some attempt is being made to ensure that prisoners come out no worse, if no better, than they went in. As I walked about (or was driven around) Chino and Corona I seemed to be the only person aware of this sadness, and at Corona, which holds about 500 young women and where it did *not* happen to be a visiting day, the quietly cheerful atmosphere simply could not have been a charade . . . I could weary you, and myself, with accounts of 'progressive' prisons in the USA, Australia, and New Zealand; but before you actually drop off I want to tell you about the still new, ultra-modern and massive maximum-security prison at Auckland, New Zealand.

Its actual site is at Paremoremo, and it was built to receive what in Britain we call 'Category A' prisoners. They come from both islands. The prison took about seven years to build (it was unfinished when I was there), and the following entry from a diary I was keeping during my travels — a unique exercise for me — is a convenient way of recalling my reactions to it.

23 September 1968. Auckland. 11 a.m. Mount Eden Prison (soon to be relieved of its overcrowding by the massive new prison at Paremoremo, nearby). Mount Eden Prison was partly burned down during a riot in 1965, when a pistol had been smuggled into the prison during visiting hours and some men got loose. Unable to shoot their way out (because no one presented himself to be shot), in their rage they set fire to some curtains and there was a serious blaze. The surviving part of the prison is old-fashioned and cramped and ill-designed, *BUT* every cell has its own sanitation and the prison is not pervaded by the familiar British prison smell of latrines, carbolic, and 'frying-tonight' cooking-fat. Nor do the prisoners (I'm told) smash up or foul their lavatories. The superintendent, Mr E. G. Buckley, is likely to get the new job at Paremoremo in due course. (PS He did.)

This has been in process of building since 1963. (Estimated cost $6,900,000, about a seventh of the cost of the new Sydney Opera House, which I shall soon be seeing.) Chubbs have made the locks and grilles, most of them in tool-resistant (manganese) steel and all of them electronically controlled — all the cell doors can be opened and shut from a central control tower. The architect proudly showing me round the unfinished building assured me that he deplored as much as anyone the need for an institution of this kind, 'but until there's some other way of protecting the public from the worst criminals, what else can we do?' (Which is partly what I'm over here to talk about.) 'We've tried to combine maximum security outside with maximum freedom of movement inside.' And that's what they seem to me to have done, though it has been the subject of much controversy. It's a very clever compromise. Every possible escape route and device has been anticipated and every possible use made of intra-mural space for movement and recreation. Opening

January 1969? I wonder. There was something uneasily infectious about the enthusiasm of the prison architect as he showed me round, indicating with genuine pride how a chap couldn't get out here, couldn't lie concealed there.

I think I always want to see one possible avenue of escape from a prison, however hazardous and daunting; so that every inmate has, or thinks he has, the one remaining scintilla of free will — 'Do I attempt to get out that way or not? No, not worth it.' But this prison has been maliciously misrepresented by the New Zealand yellow press, which (like ours) is full of right-wing sloganizing, all out for Laura Norder, but bound to attack any and all Laura Norder measures introduced by the notoriously left-wing Dr J. L. Robson, Secretary for Justice, graduate of the LSE in London, friend of the criminal. For once in his political life, and I found that he was immensely enjoying it, he was being presented to a probably bewildered public as the man responsible for a soul-destroying, cruel, vindictive, abandon-all-hope mausoleum of the damned. These are some of the epithets in papers which are normally busy demanding the fiercest possible sanctions against the criminals whose stories sustain them in business.

Paremoremo, I decided, could hardly fail to have one good effect: it would transform the functions of the prison officer from that of turnkey and head-counter into that of custodian with more time for the treatment of his charges as human individuals. When a party of prisoners arrived at a workshop door they went in in groups — they weren't marching in single file. And if the roll-call showed that one was missing, the discovery didn't touch off a dozen clanging bells and an atmosphere of general alarm. OK, there was a man adrift for the moment, but he was in the prison somewhere.

I thought that on the whole the New Zealand Press had crippled its writers, though there is always a chicken-and-egg problem between a national Press and the supposed demands of its intended public. 'Popular' journalism in New Zealand (which none the less has some fine papers) may have been the work of a subservient generation of anything-for-money scribblers, but their standards were far below what New Zealand could have on demand—the writers are there, and the vision, urgency, and optimism. As it was then—seventeen years ago—they had the job of reporting to the world what was going on in about the most exciting socio-political crucible to be found anywhere. For the most part, they sneered at it all.

When I was given leave from parole board duties to depart on my world-trip, by the Home Secretary (Mr Callaghan) and the parole board chairman (Lord Hunt), I promised that on my return I would put in a report about my findings and impressions, comparing especially the parole systems of New Zealand, Australia, and Great Britain. Because there is no other record of it and because by this time it has almost certainly been shredded, I have decided to include it here, and to reveal for the first time that, although the Home Office made a considerable number of pale grey photocopies of it for selected distribution, I have never known from that day to this whether it was ever read by anybody, anywhere. In other words, for aught I know it was a total waste of time. Here it is.

The New Zealand parole board serves the whole country. Its chairman is a Supreme Court judge (Mr Justice Henry), and the other members are the Secretary for Justice ex officio, a psychiatrist, a stipendiary magistrate, a personnel manager from industry, and a well-known employer. The board visits each prison (there are only ten) and conducts its business there. The prisoners are brought before it in person, to make their representation but *not* to listen to its deliberations. When I was there it had just been decided that the prisoners should in future be allowed to sit down instead of standing to attention; and, in sharp contrast to everything else about New Zealand penology, which is experimental and fast-moving sometimes to the point of apparent recklessness, there was an air of suppressed excitement about this innovation as if some major step into the unknown had been taken.

The board does *not* see the prisoners' dossiers before the meeting, 'except' (said Mr Justice Henry) 'in any difficult or special case'. This difference from the British procedure is felt to be accounted for by the fact that the New Zealand board sees every six-years' man fairly frequently, particularly the very long-sentence prisoner, who is seen at six-monthly intervals; and each member of the board makes his own notes about the prisoners, keeping his own set of files. He brings these notes to the meeting, where much comparing of notes goes on.

No prisoner is eligible (at present) unless he is serving a six-year sentence. Anyone serving a life sentence for murder has the *right* to be seen at the end of ten years, and at the present time the board is seeing all lifers at the end of five years. But any member of the board has a statutory power to recommend that any prisoner's case be specially considered at *any* time. (No such recommendation, so far, has borne fruit.)

The board always has copies of the Court of Appeal judgements; and if any judge in the court below has made any significant observation, in passing sentence or otherwise, the Department of Justice always brings it to the notice of the board. These judicial observations are recorded in court, as is every other word of the proceedings, by an 'associate'; and the associate merits a special paragraph to herself.

For it is nearly always a woman, and she is *not* what we call an Associate in the High Court (i.e., in effect, the Clerk of the Court). She is the judge's personal amanuensis. She books his hotel accommodation, does all his secretarial work, deals with the Press if they want to talk to him, and—most important and onerous duty of all—types every word of the proceedings at the trials.

She sits next to him on the Bench, but on a slightly lower level by way of indicating (I suppose) that she is not sitting in judgement; and on an allegedly noiseless typewriter, with an amplifier standing next to it and picking up the evidence and speeches, she types *everything* that is said—using, it must be explained, a kind of cablegram language composed largely of familiar contractions. Thus there is always a record (as there is not in this country) of what a sentencing judge has said. She tears off each foolscap page as she finishes it, and the judge reaches down and takes it from her. There are other copies for counsel. In the court library there are thousands of roughly bound foolscap volumes of these verbatim reports, all immediately accessible for reference. Periodically the older ones are removed to a records office, but they are *never* destroyed. It seemed a fantastic system to me, but its advantages are obvious, and are without benefit of either shorthand writer or tape recorder. (The associate sometimes resorts to shorthand—instead of the typewriter—in taking down what the judge is saying; and I remember wondering whether this was because some judges had wanted to get things expunged from the record after saying them, for it would be easier not to include them at all than to amend a report already typed.) At intervals the parole board chairman asks for a full report on all parole cases that the Department of Justice has under control—the parolees frequently reoffend in a small way and are not recalled to prison. Small breaches of parole conditions are often dealt with by varying the terms of the licence, without necessarily bringing the man back for the occasion. The Minister of Justice (but no one else) can recall a parolee to prison without any court proceedings.

In New South Wales my guide and informant was Mr John Moroney, formerly Controller-General of Prisons for New South Wales and now a member of its parole board. The board, meeting once a week (oftener when necessary) has its own room in the new 30-storey City Building in Macquerie Street, but meets from time to time in prisons to see long-term prisoners whose movement about the State presents special problems. It does *not* see every prisoner. An important contrast with the English practice is that the 'non-parole period' is not fixed by statute in general terms, but by the sentencing judge in specific terms. This is true of all the other Australian States. If the judge does *not* fix a 'non-parole period', then the question of parole never arises—parole is regarded from the outset as an integral part of any sentence when it is mentioned, but not otherwise. The Justice Department assembles all the information relating to a prisoner two months before his date of eligibility, and photostat copies are supplied to each member of the board. They have little time to study all this material. They don't get it, for some reason, before Wednesday afternoon and the board meets on the Friday morning. Mr Moroney seemed to think this was ample time, but other members of the board thought it was not. There may be thirty-five or forty dossiers to read, and some of them are even bulkier than ours.

The dossier does *not* include a police account of the crime 'unless the board thinks it is relevant'; but the secretary of the board has a standing instruction to have ready at the meeting, in all cases of violence or sexual crime, copies of the depositions and the transcripts of trials and appeals. The board has never yet had a 'majority decision', but would record it as such if it did. These small boards in New Zealand and Australia confirm my own impression that, if I may say so, our own experimental three-panel system is inhibiting minority views. It may be that a man who is one of eight or ten members will 'stand his ground' against the rest—and win converts—if he starts with the comfortable feeling that what he is saying doesn't really matter much.

New South Wales (and, so far as I could discover, only New South Wales) has a follow-up research scheme in operation. It records all the objective factors known, and they bring into account a series of subjective factors in the parolee's mode of life that are reported on by the parole officer and others, and recorded on punch cards. The board includes, with Mr Moroney, two judges, the permanent Head of the Department of Justice, an independent employer, and the Registrar of the University of Sydney (this is Miss Margaret Telfer, and she is the 'statutory woman', whose appointment was widely approved by women's organizations and by the Press).

In Victoria the parole board chairman is the Hon. Sir John Vincent Barry, a judge since 1948 of the Supreme Court of Victoria (and a much respected criminologist throughout the English-speaking world). He invited me to sit in during a session of the board, whose proceedings were agreeably informal. All the prisoners appeared personally—and this involves air transport for most of them, the distances being enormous by our standards. They sit at the table with the board, unaccompanied by any prison officer. They are brought from their prisons the day before, and for the occasion they are allowed to wear what they like— presumably within some kind of limits. One youth with very long hair was wearing a long gold-coloured silk tunic buttoned tightly at the neck.

'What's that called?' asked the chairman.

'It's a Nehru', said the prisoner.

'A Nehru? Are you an admirer of his, then?'

'Who?'

'Nehru'.

'Who's that, sir?'

'Pandit Nehru. Come on, you know who that is. Pandit Jawaharlal Nehru.'

'Never heard of him, sir.'

'All right. Where can I get one?'

The youth named a local emporium (I forget its name), which greatly amused the board; and the episode was prolonged to an extent that began to puzzle me until I realized that they — and even I — were getting to know the boy. I recount the episode because (in Victoria) it was typical of the interviewing I saw; though this may mean no more than that the interviewing was typical of that very extraordinary and perceptive man Sir John Barry. 'We never consider whether a sentence was too harsh or too lenient', he told me. I suggested this called for an almost Olympian detachment? 'We are not a reviewing authority over judges' sentences', he said. 'I happened to examine in America the papers about Tokyo Rose. [This was the US Press nickname for an American telephonist, employed in Tokyo when the US–Japan war began, who broadcast treasonable messages to American forces in the Pacific war area.] She was convicted of treason, before a sensible judge, who passed a sentence of about ten years or so. Her conduct in prison was not only exemplary, but she exhibited a devotion to humanitarian activities which was entirely admirable. When she came before the US Federal Parole Board, which was then presided over by Paul Tappan, he to his great credit was in favour of her being released. The others thought her sentence had been too lenient. Those others were utterly and completely wrong, because that is an arrogation to itself by the parole board of a function that is not committed to it.'

The parole board in Victoria, as in most of the other States, does not think a 'no drinking' condition is enforceable. But some of the parole licences I was shown bore the words 'to abstain from all alcoholic liquor', whether or not drink had had anything to do with the offence. This means, said Mr Justice Barry, that in theory the man must not have a drink *at all*. But in practice it means that 'although we can't supervise what a man does in his own home, if he comes in to see the parole officer and smells of drink, the parole officer will report him, and we will send for him and reprimand him, warning him that on any repetition we will revoke his licence. It's a condition we *always* impose on Aborigines.' (The Aborigines do a disproportionate amount of Australia's drinking, mainly, they say, because the Whites leave them little else they *can* do.)

In South Australia I had no time to look at the parole system, my five days there being entirely filled with lecturing and other engagements. By that time I had been reluctantly pontificating in radio and TV programmes in New South Wales, Queensland (where I had only two crowded days, crammed in because Brisbane seemed to resent having been excluded from my itinerary), and Victoria. And the cameramen and newsmen now converged upon me everywhere as though I were U Thant or a Beatle, even flying after me from towns I had just left. I kept on saying the same things, but they all seemed satisfied and happy. I gathered, however, that the South Australia parole system is not essentially different from that of Victoria or NSW; and luckily the Western Australia system, which I *was* able to see in operation at Perth, is precisely the same as Queensland's, the two States having codified their criminal law and procedure on almost identical lines.

The courts in Western Australia fix 'a minimum term, being a lesser term than the term of imprisonment imposed, during which the convicted person is not eligible to be released on parole'. The courts *must* do this when the sentence is twelve months or more, and may do it when it is less. There is an exception where the court considers that 'the nature of the offence and the antecedents of the convicted person render the fixing of a minimum term inappropriate'. I should have thought this exception destroyed its parent, but it was noteworthy, not merely in Western Australia but in every other State or country, that everyone thinks his own country has the best system. Everyone, in fact, listens to accounts of other systems with a faint smile. I have a mass of Australian and New Zealand documents, parole board reports, case histories, statutes, blue books, etc., which my parole board colleagues may wish to see. But I expect no rush of applications.

I wish, however, to conclude with a reference to one principle that unexpectedly underlies parole thinking in many of the places I have seen. I have thought hitherto, and have said at parole board meetings, that a prisoner who persistently protests his innocence right up to the end of his sentence is not showing either remorse or what we persist in calling 'a good response to prison' (whatever that is), and may be a bad risk. This is stated more clearly in a remarkable book called *Fall Among Thieves* [Currawong Publishing Co.] by L. H. Evers, Prison Psychologist at Long Bay Prison, Sydney; and this passage from it is in fact a development of an idea suggested by Alfred Whitehead, the American philosopher, in his *Essays and Recollections*: 'A person guilty of a crime may well change the nature of the act in his conscious mind, and ascribe a motivation for it more in keeping with a charitable fiction than the distasteful fact. None of this moralistic agility is the exclusive product of the criminal mind . . . Prison is probably the cruellest place of all in which to have to accept unsavoury facts about oneself, because the overwhelming reality of prison is the implication of guilt, and guilt is so savagely destructive of self-esteem that the human being will resist its onslaught with the same desperation as that with which he resists an attempt to choke him.

'There is no doubt that gaol is a place where love is not. If the human being does indeed have a need for tenderness he will find precious little of it within penitentiary walls. This explains for me why the prisoner, to a greater extent than any other, finds it so hard to support a feeling of guilt and the reason why he goes to such incredible lengths to defend himself against it; because love, or its manifest expression as tenderness, is a sort of proof of worth.'

I heard this expressed in different ways by people in the prison and kindred services in America, Australia, and New Zealand who had no contact with each other, could not have read *Fall Among Thieves* (it was not then published), and would be most unlikely to have read Whitehead. In its application to parole for prisoners, it stays in my mind as significant and salutary among the crowding impressions of an informative journey, and as something worth diffidently passing on to my colleagues.

The truth is, of course, that people like myself stand in constant need of an A. N. Whitehead to articulate for them the part played in the universe by 'love and tenderness'. I do not love criminals. I hate nearly everything they do, and there is a man inside me who demands that they be heavily punished, flogged, hanged, shot, or electrocuted. He is kept in schizoid and angry subjection by another man in there who knows perfectly well that punishment is usually futile as a means of changing character or future behaviour. And this is the voice that now keeps on telling me about the immense regenerating power of tenderness. I do not see how tenderness can be expected to achieve much in the hellish atmosphere of prisons, where the clanging corridors would echo with wild laughter at the mere suggestion. I know only that there are cases in which it does, though the words 'love' and 'tenderness' have to be kept out of it because of their rather happier association with Eros and the poets.

But I now realize that it was because of this, coupled with my writing obsession, that I came to be involved in so many movements for the promotion of this and the abolition of that. Among them all, though I was usually a committee member, I was never able to bring myself to the point of being an 'activist'. I would have proffered my services as a prison visitor, but I knew that (having served in the police) I was as irrevocably disqualified for this as if I had been a lifelong burglar or an enthusiastic rapist. In other respects, being an activist all too often seemed to mean shuffling about under banners, preceded by buglers or pipers, ignored by all except the ambiguous policemen marching alongside, by absurd groups of unwelcome and uninvited camp-followers, and by Press and television photographers concerned only to get comic pictures of the camp-followers. The main body would see its 'march' — it was in fact, and unavoidably, a straggling shuffle, with or without fist-shaking and the bellowing of slogans — as an organized means of advocating disarmament, the abolition of the death penalty, the relief of famine, the banning of the cane from schools, the release of some popular prisoner, or more pay for nurses. The camp-followers, on the other hand, who often had pink hair, tattooed foreheads, safety pins through their nostrils, and bare feet, would parasitically adopt the main procession as a way of promoting beliefs in the occult, the bizarre, the daft, or the downright nasty. Everyone seemed to believe in a 'right to march'; and this, I believe, merits a brief digression.

I suppose I was indelibly dyed with a policemanly acceptance of what the High Court had said in 1936 about a Mrs Kath Duncan. Mrs Duncan had been insisting on her right to stand on a box outside a Brixton training-centre for the unemployed, comforting any audience that gathered with assurances that their problems would all go away once we had adopted the benign principles of Marxism. One of these speeches led to a punch-up inside the training-centre. So one day the manager of the centre phoned the police to say that Mrs Duncan was about to get up on her box, and that he feared more trouble. The police arrived and told her she would not be allowed to speak there. She insisted on her right to do so, and was arrested and charged with 'obstructing the police in the execution of their duty'. The magistrate convicted her, and she appealed to quarter sessions (today it would be a Crown Court) on the ground that the police had no power to stop her doing something perfectly lawful, whatever consequences they might think it would have, and in doing so had exceeded their duty. What she had resisted was their conduct in exceeding it. She failed at quarter sessions, and appealed again to the High Court. There she failed again, Mr Justice Humphreys adding to the law of England, where it still remains shakily established, this astonishing proposition:

The respondent (i.e. the policeman) reasonably apprehended a breach of the peace. It then became his duty to prevent *anything* which in his view would cause it.

What, anything? I've put the word in italics because since 1936 there has been a police tendency to regard it, and an army of lawyers waiting for a chance to challenge it, as meaning that the police can prevent any quite lawful and innocent activity if they 'reasonably' suppose that there may be violent or rowdy objections to it. I thought from the first that this was a pretty extreme doctrine, and in 1936 so did a lot of my police colleagues. When I got to the *New Statesman* I found myself among 'civil liberty' zealots who, when I tried to explain it to them, swept it aside as 'absolutely monstrous'. An awful lot of those zealots have since died, but *Duncan* v. *Jones* still lives, awaiting some Denning who will lay it low. And yet, as the *Justice of the Peace* has just observed,

The Court, in effect, was stating that lawful conduct, however innocent, could be prohibited if a police officer feared a breach of the peace would occur. It mattered not that the conduct was lawful *per se*, nor that it was innocent. (*Justice of the Peace*, 29 June 1985, 403.)

None the less, in my personal support of the causes I hoped to further, I chained myself to no railings, sat on the ground in no public thoroughfares, and shook no fists, though all those are lawful occupations which sometimes provoke hostility in spectators. I quietly refused to go on any marches, even though a march—say from Aldermaston to Whitehall—is merely an exertion of our sacred and inviolable right to walk about instead of staying indoors or eternally sitting down. Instead I was allowed to write pamphlets and memoranda, the pen, in my case, being thought a little mightier than the long vigil outside a prison, the clenched fist, the heckling of opponents, and the organized point-to-point shuffle. I could never believe that the 'marching' did the slightest good (except as the traditional 'safety-valve') or changed the course of events in any way, and in this I was always in a tiny minority. At that time of course the marches were not televised, and there was little rivalry between assorted gospellers and terrorists in seeking the enormous free publicity now available to anyone 'claiming responsibility' for what can be seen by millions on television. But I am genuinely amazed, looking back at them now, at the number and variety of pamphlets, broadsheets, and circular letters which, particularly between 1950 and 1975, I wrote in support of 'good causes' which some people must have thought bad or insignificant. (I mean, if everyone thought them 'good' they would not be 'causes'.) I am also rather sobered by the reflection that in those twenty-five years I never heard, in one single instance, either that these compilations had any effect on anyone, or that they were even read by anyone other than the relevant committee, the printer, and me.

But I suppose that a man who 'wants to be a writer' is a man who secretly believes himself to be one already. The change from darkness into light must come at the moment when he moves over from being a would-be writer to the status of having got there. And when is that? As I sit writing these words in 1985 I realize that it is more than sixty-five years since I received my first cheque for having burst into print. In my case that merely serves to bring into contrast Dr Johnson's puzzling answer to Boswell, who was urging him to write a book about Italy — 'No man but a blockhead ever wrote, except for money' — with Kipling's sober vision in 'When Earth's Last Picture is Painted':

And only the Master shall praise us, and only the Master shall
    blame;
And no one shall work for money, and no one shall work for
    fame,
But each for the joy of the working, and each in his separate star,
Shall draw the thing as he sees it for the God of Things as they
    are.

For me it was always 'the joy of the working'. But I have always wondered if it was Boswell who put that comma after 'wrote', and if so why he did it. After all, it was his comma, not Johnson's. It seems to me one of the Great Commas in English literature. I believe in all honesty that I've written because I love doing it, half qualifying as a Johnsonian blockhead by doing much of it without pay. (But so did he.) And though I still have records from which I could compute how much money it has all earned me, sheer lack of interest in the matter will outlast the time I now have left to do it in.

CHAPTER TWELVE

JENIFER and I married in 1947 and for a few years occupied a tiny two-roomed flat in the reconstructed Regency crescent known as the Paragon, at Blackheath. In addition to the two rooms, we had a kitchenette in which one person could stand comfortably while the other received his take-away food in the doorway (which had no door). Originally built in 1798, on land belonging to Morden College (a 'retreat for Decayed Turkey Merchants'), the Paragon was a beautiful crescent comprising fourteen semi-detached houses, which together made seven blocks linked by single-storey colonnades. It really was, and externally still is, an architectural gem. To qualify as suitable neighbours for the Decayed Turkey Merchants, the Georgian tenants had to comply with very strict conditions, particularly about their jobs. Schoolmasters were to be as firmly taboo as fishmongers; an occupational coupling which greatly delighted Jenifer's father Philip Wayne, who lived nearby and was headmaster of St Marylebone Grammar School. But the people who occupied that lovely crescent during the next 100 years or so must have been even less sensitive about their surroundings than schoolmasters and fishmongers might have turned out to be, for the whole crescent gradually acquired extra rooms built like shanties on the top, even on the flat roofs supported by the elegant colonnades, and in the gardens at the back. When I first saw it, between the wars, the Paragon was already a pathetic, raddled reminder of past glory. It had the pathos of a vandalized masterpiece without the sanctity of a ruin. C. Bernard Brown, the architect who restored it with painstaking skill (and eventually became my landlord as I took up residence in it) deserves the thanks of everyone who loves his London. After very severe bomb damage in Hitler's war, the whole district had become seedy and run down; and in the next ten or fifteen years it became, once

again under Brown's direction, an attractive Georgian and
Regency village, thickly peopled with writers, musicians,
artists, and those who like to frequent them. Unlike
Hampstead and Chelsea it escaped colonization by the 'gin
and Jaguar' detachment, probably because few of its new
inhabitants had enough money. And it was a good place
to live in, full of exciting celebrities who, however
eccentric, when you got to know them were exactly like
people.

In the flat above us lived Denis Cannan, whom I have
always thought one of the cleverest playwrights of my
time. I should like to see every one of his plays, the best
of which is *Captain Carvallo*, revived as a television
series — so long as he were allowed to do the necessary
adaptation himself. But he will probably have to die first,
and so shall I, and what good will that be to either of us?

Thus began an inconceivably happy time, with a widening
circle of friends at and through the *New Statesman* and the
BBC, and the opening up of the writers' world I had dreamed
about since adolescence but never supposed I should
inhabit. It was a world in which, as it turned out, everyone
either loved or hated the *New Statesman*, never supposed
that it could be ignored, borrowed rather than bought it, and
privately held that whatever you thought of its politics it
was probably the best-written literary weekly in the English-
speaking world. And I believe that, for a time, this is what
it really was. The literary editors I had known and worked
for — Raymond Mortimer, V. S. Pritchett, T. C. Worsley,
Janet Adam Smith, Walter Allen, Karl Miller, Anthony
Thwaite, Claire Tomalin — between them span half a
century of distinguished critical writing. It is hard to think
of an eminent British writer who has not written for the
New Statesman, and this is because its literary editors
never hesitated to send a book anywhere in the world in
their search for the right reviewer. Of course this kind of
thing costs money; and let it be admitted that for a glorious
twenty-year period the money was there, for the paper was
prosperous. But the resources were in the right hands.

Kingsley Martin, editor for thirty years (from 1931 to
1961) had given me a small room to myself, with my own
telephone, typewriter, and basic 'office furniture'. In the
light of what I now know about the paper's domestic or
inter-office rivalries, I am astounded that I should have
taken this arrangement so much for granted. The only
other member of the editorial staff who had a room of his
own was the editor himself. An old police colleague, when
I told him, offered this explanation: 'If you go and work
among a lot like that, you can hardly expect them to share
rooms with you — they probably think you've got a hot line
to the Special Branch or M.I.5.' I brushed this aside. If they
had supposed I had a hot line to the Special Branch or M.I.5,
they would have been eternally in my room dropping contrived double-agent clues in the hope of starting something.
As it was, I did once impose upon a Scotland Yard friend,
a Special Branch sergeant, to find out for me whether the
Branch 'had a file on me'. On my behalf, he asked the
inspector in charge of records whether they had, and what
it said. 'Nothing', said the inspector unbearably the next
day.

After about ten years the office accommodation problem
at No. 10 Great Turnstile became so acute that I began
to see my eviction as inevitable. On Tuesdays and
Wednesdays ('Press day' was Wednesday) there were so
many contributors in the building at midday, with last-
minute pieces to type or correct, that there were people
balancing typewriters on their knees, sitting on the edges
of desks, or giving it up and going out to write on wet tables
in nearby pubs, among which the noisy and crowded
favourite was the Bung Hole in High Holborn. Some of
them, it seemed to me, were at least as entitled as I was
to a room of their own. And then suddenly there occurred
one of those intestinal upheavals which from time to time
convulse all office staffs, and this one involved the
conversion of my little room into a bedroom 'for the
directors', in case any of them should want to stay in
London overnight. This development, by the way, seemed
to me in itself symptomatic of the intellectual decay of

inner London. Just across the road, 100 yards away, there still stood the Bloomsbury of the Woolfs, the Garnetts, Maynard Keynes, the Nonesuch Press, and the Roger Fry entourage. But its inhabitants were now all solicitors, surveyors, building societies, small cafés, and betting-shops. 'Literary London' had moved out, either to the 'gentrified' one-time slums of my boyhood or to the country. In this growing desert, the *New Statesman* had decided to have an oasis, and its eye had fallen at last upon my little office.

Henceforth I would have to work at home? On the contrary, a better room was found for me, displacing two 'admin' people who had then to be crammed in elsewhere — and took it, I've always felt, extremely well. This lasted another five years. Then it was decided that the Literary Department should be transferred to the boardroom, which like most boardrooms stood empty when there were neither meetings nor visiting auditors to be accommodated. The Literary Department then had the mortification of seeing their old office transfigured as a rather splendid new boardroom, with a long and magnificent mahogany table and with large Vicky caricatures of former editors all round the walls. In this boardroom, by the way, there then ensued many weekly 'celebrity lunches' at which the Directors, including me, entertained a presumably careful assortment of public figures, among whom I particularly remember Mr Harold Wilson, S. K. Ratcliffe, Lord Hailsham, Sir Robert Mark, Mr Cecil Harmsworth King, and Lady Summerskill. The last-named I recall for no better reason than that when a waitress confronted me with a deep earthenware bowl with some Stilton cheese at the bottom, and stood over me while I dug about with the long-handled spoon provided, I was levering some out when the spoon slipped and projected a Stilton lump high in the air. It landed in Lady Summerskill's hair, and she either didn't notice or decided to pretend she hadn't. It may have been a recognition of her formidable reputation that none of us dared to tell her it was there, and I watched it, guilt-ridden and fascinated, for the rest of the meal.

But five years after that (this was 1970) there arrived from Washington, where he had been the *Observer*'s US correspondent, the peripatetic Anthony Howard, to be groomed for the *New Statesman*'s editorship in succession to Paul Johnson. The news was broken to me that this process was to take place in my little room, which at long last I might now care to vacate so that I could work from home? As it happened, the suggestion was more than welcome. For twelve years I had been living at Bramley, near Guildford, commuting (i.e., standing) to Waterloo every day, and thinking how nice it would be to stop. I had become a victim of my own lifelong inability either to start or to stop anything that entails a change in the pattern of my life, in sharp distinction from a kind of constitutional readiness to interfere in other people's. The idea of working at home was most attractive. After fifteen years of comfortable non-commuting, it still is, even though it is now done in the silent wilderness of the widower.

And I think this is the place at which I may be permitted to say that, of all the *New Statesman* editors and literary editors whom I have assisted in wearing out by going on too long, Tony Howard was the most *dependable*, in the sense that he always knew what he wanted and yet always seemed to know, when he found he had got something else, why he was none the less justified in using it. I have what is nowadays called a gut feeling that it was he alone among them all who had anything like Kingsley Martin's flair for editorship. I have no idea what it is. I suspect that Tony Howard may not know either. But it produces good work and some kind of team spirit among networks of wildly dissimilar and often difficult contributors.

I realize, as I end this book, that from the moment I began it I wanted it to contain, somewhere, some kind of statement of essential belief, much more for my own cathartic satisfaction than for consumption (or rejection) by such readers as might decide not to skip it. The thing is, mine has been a long lifetime of what might be called marginal and hesitant religious predisposition, informed by much reading of history and the less tortuously argued theology. For a long time I was defeated by John Robinson's *Honest to God*. I could understand what everyone was saying about it, and envied their percipience, but I could not really understand the book itself. (I shall come back to this in a moment.) Yet I was hungry for its promise of a freshly stated Christian doctrine accessible (this was the promise) to 'modern man'. I had supposed that the virgin birth and the empty tomb, those 'common-sense' stumbling-blocks either mysteriously surmounted or serenely ignored by my Christian friends, were essential to the faith. Since then, even the bishops have been saying they aren't essential.

So I had arrived at a rather comfortless conclusion; namely that mankind would have been collectively happier, more virtuous, far less cruel, and probably more loving if organized religion of every kind had been able to foresee the misery and devastation it was to nourish, and had then organized itself out of existence. This of course is a belief in itself, and one without proof. Moreover, it is one that subsumes the acceptance of an inherent goodness in man, perhaps dating the Fall from the time when he came down from the trees, or from his discovery that he could wonder who he was, or from his first use of instruments; from which point began his endless climb, with its innumerable and horrifying falls. Of course it stands the Adam-and-Eve story on its head, and his climb will be endless, with an eternal succession of phantom summits but with a mysterious (and, alas, incommunicable) purpose to sustain it.

Nearly all the mass murder, the torturing, the burning and lynching, the mutilation, the locking up, has been done in the name of some religion or other. They have stood throughout the ages between man and his God, exploiting man's sense of the numinous with manipulative skills which, beginning doubtless in love, have ended usually in frustrated, fanatical, and murderous hate. And as you look at the world today, every continent is riven with religious hatreds which mock the so-called perfectibility of man. At Easter 1969 I had a valuable correspondence with John Grigg, a prominent Anglican churchman whom I have known for many years as a Christian who does his own vigorous thinking — a fact which illumines his work as a historian, biographer and journalist. At the end of it he sent me the following declaration of belief, which I have just shown to him, to which he still adheres, and which he allows me to publish. It lies before me as I write, and for me it has been a theological lifeline which, as I cling to it and tread water, I want somebody to start pulling in. Nobody comes along, and the water creeps up:

I don't agree that there's nothing in Christianity unless the story of the empty tomb is true. Myth inevitably gathers around a great historic figure, even in times and places more given to rationality than those in which Jesus lived and died. But the greatness of the man surely transcends the myth.

Perhaps you would say that without his supernatural status he is more or less negligible, because his moral and metaphysical ideas weren't original. [I hadn't said this.] If so, I would reply that, where faith and conduct are concerned, even the most original ideas have little impact until they are projected with imagination, and communicated with the indefinable force that we call genius. Jesus illumined, popularised and dramatised a version of Judaism which, without him, could never have made such headway. For my money, it is still the most inspiring thing we have.

Moreover, I'm sure he was right to base his appeal upon a doctrine of immortality. Why should we tamely accept the necessity of annihilation? Considering what Man has achieved, scientifically, during my lifetime, I have no real difficulty in believing that he will in due course find the 'answer' to death, and apply it retrospectively. This rather confident humanism means that I can accept the Christian doctrine of resurrection, not in its historic form, but as something to be fulfilled in the future. To the dead, it makes no difference: they will be raised, as St Paul said, 'in the twinkling of an eye'. In other words, I see no necessary contradiction between the Christian spirit and the humanist spirit. On the contrary, I regard humanist ethics as logically untenable if combined with a belief that death as we know it is an immutable fact.

For fourteen years Jenifer played the organ in our village church. It began for no better reason than that she admired and respected (as we all did) the man compelled by ill health to give it up, who made it almost a death-bed request that she should take over from him. After a year of it, she decided to go to confirmation classes and was duly received into the Anglican communion. She would never discuss with me the new truths through which, after a relatively godless fifty years, she had at last been brought to see the light that dazzled Paul on his road to Damascus. I forbore to press her because I dread the possibility of destroying 'belief' in others. But I am in absolutely no doubt that it changed her life and irradiated her death, at both of which I was a forlorn spectator. Although she never asked or expected me to do so, I went to matins in the village church on Sundays because her unarticulated faith was a comfort to her and was (I knew) in some way strengthened by my being there. There was a tacit understanding that I absented myself from Holy Communion—on the principle that even altruistic hypocrisy must make a stand somewhere. And whenever the vicar, with his back to us, led his flock in the Apostles' Creed, I was relieved that his back was to us and that he therefore couldn't see how my lips stopped moving after the words 'I believe in God.' I believed, and believe, in none of the rest, and dared not stand there and pretend otherwise. And as I parted weekly with those who did, or had been saying they did, I tried to conceal from them my feeling of envious exclusion behind what was probably a sickly grin.

I could readily and happily believe in Paul Davies's 'grand unified theory of Nature', for which he argues in his book *Superforce: The Search for a Grand Unified Theory of Nature* (Heinemann, 1984) and in his conclusion about the existence of what we call theoretical physics:

The laws which enabled the Universe to come into being, spontaneously, seem themselves to be the product of exceedingly ingenious design. If physics is the product of design, then the Universe must have a purpose, and the evidence of modern physics suggests strongly that the purpose includes us.

In church I would listen to the voices of my friends and neighbours reciting the creed, and suppose that they were carrying each other along. ('Well, old So-and-so is saying it; I can see his lips making the right movements. Rather respect old So-and-so. Must be all right, perhaps.') During the sermons, too often inaudible and rarely interesting, I would covertly study the Thirty-nine Articles in the provided *Book of Common Prayer*. I must have read these through hundreds of times, always with a terrible, lonely incredulity. How *could* all those generations of scholars since the sixteenth century, men so much better equipped than I, accept the Thirty-nine Articles of Religion of the Anglican Church? And yet every bishop to this day publicly declares that he does, as a condition of taking office. How *can* a literate, intelligent, and honest human being do that?

Queen Elizabeth I, in her 1562 Declaration, described these Articles as 'The settled Continuance of the Doctrine and Discipline of the Church of England now established, from which' (she added ominously) 'We will not endure any Varying or Departing in the least Degree'. Thus, it seems, any man 'doing good works' without thereby consciously obeying the will of God is committing a sin (says Article 13); and in case this should seem to admit any ambiguity, he is declared guilty by Article 14 of 'arrogancy and impiety' if, as a voluntary do-gooder, he goes beyond what God requires of him — for he is then indulging himself in what Article 14 calls works of supererogation, which seems to mean impudently doing more than the Church actually asks him to.

I think I have often seen this spirit at work in the various reformist movements I have belonged to. All the voluntary social welfare organizations look upon each other with some distaste, the mere existence of each being seen as an implied criticism by all the others. In secular groupings, this does nothing but good. The friction produces the occasional pearl, and I think there ought to be a lot of little and highly active reformist and pressure groups, ready to combine every now and again in crises. But how can this sort of friction benefit a church which can go on printing and propagating the Thirty-nine Articles for more than three centuries, and which knows what it means by Truth?

I discussed all this once with Dick Crossman, staying with him in his Cropredy farmhouse and talking late one Saturday night, after his wife and two boys had gone to bed. We sat up later than we had intended, because when he stood up and announced that it was time for bed, he explained that he must be up 'sharp' in the morning because he had agreed to stand as godfather at the christening of a friend's baby. Since I had been arguing as a failed Christian and he as an implacable atheist, I couldn't forbear to ask if he had read the prescribed service for the Public Baptism of Infants. Probably, he said. Anyway, he'd heard it often enough. Did he remember that, as a godfather, he would have the entire Apostles' creed read aloud to him by the priest, and then be required, or anyway expected, to answer 'All this I steadfastly believe'? He sat down again. In a Christian country, he said patiently, as if dealing with a not-very-bright student who might nevertheless be open to instruction, a Christian country with an established church, the whole of public life, plus a great deal of what should be private life, was prescribed in this kind of formula. It was a part of the grammar of living. (These are not his actual words, but they are as close as I can remember after twenty years.) You either believed it, or you paid lipservice to it (as you did at prayers in the House of Commons or at the funerals of old friends), or you went away and dug a hole for yourself.

He simply astounded me. I begged him to read the whole baptism service, but I don't think he did. I suspect now that he regarded me (not for the first time) as a bit of an ass. Every curate will try to explain the Thirty-nine Articles if you ask him seriously, and how it is that he can voluntarily 'believe' what men and women once had to be tortured into believing against all the dictates of their common sense. But none of them will ever come near to admitting that 'I believe' can mean 'I want to believe, and if I go on saying publicly that I do, one day there will come a huge flood of light, a sudden splendid illumination of the mind, and I shall know that my Redeemer liveth and that I belong among all these others.'

I never thought this myself, but at one time I did suppose that every church congregation contained a proportion of honest but worried men and women who did. And I remember that in the fifties and sixties, when I was occasionally interviewing celebrities for radio 'profiles', a talks producer would sometimes suggest finishing with the 'good old pay-off' which said 'If you could have your time all over again, what would you want to be?' Sometimes it produced a revealing and wistful answer. More often it was just 'Same again, I suppose.' I have even had the question addressed to me, and then I have always lacked the courage to say, as I end this book by saying, that above all else I should like to have been a believing and committed Christian. The failure to do this is conspicuously the chief among my many failures. To acknowledge it here is, I suppose, to tug a forelock in puzzled homage to a legion of informed believers and twenty centuries of crushing scholarship, at the end of which I find myself fearfully and impiously uncrushed. I would have wanted to be a grateful, intellectually secure believer. Not a pretender, not a tub-thumper, not an evangelist, not a proselytizing bore, not a man whose friends would cross the road when they saw him coming. Just a quiet believer, like Jenifer in her last few years, and my mother throughout her long life, and many of my friends, and an imposing list of men and women with better mental equipment than any of us.

So to return for another few minutes to John Robinson, Bishop of Woolwich, and his bombshell of a book *Honest to God*, which sold in its millions and in many languages and was understood by everyone but me: years after I had put it away as 'a book for *them*', I discovered that its central theme was considered to be the one put forward by Professor Paul Tillich in his controversial book *The Shaking of the Foundations* (Pelican, 1962, p. 63), in which, having introduced the idea of God as 'the deepest ground of our being, the depth of life itself', he goes on

The name of this infinite and inexhaustible depth and ground of all being is *God*. That depth is what the word *God* means. And if that word has not much meaning for you, translate it, and speak of the depths of your life, of the source of your being, of your ultimate concern, of what you take seriously without any reservation. Perhaps, in order to do so, you must forget everything traditional that you have learned about God, perhaps even that word itself. For if you know that God means depth, you know much about him. You cannot then call yourself an atheist or unbeliever.

If so, it was an offer of rescue. In fairness to myself, I knew what John Robinson meant when he said that 'if Christianity is to survive it must be made relevant to modern secular man, not just to the diminishing company of the religious'. I was modern secular man, awaiting rescue from the old crippling concept of a huge invisible hominoid being either 'up there' (as in 'There is a Happy Land') or 'out there' (as in the worried thoughts of modern churchmen who knew about the space missions from Cape Canaveral, Florida). For many centuries this image had been tolerated, even fostered, by the saints and mystics, as a kind of Santa Claus for the masses, because it helped simple people who (like myself) 'wanted to believe'. Nowadays, instead of attracting us towards the truth, it repels us. Can we now take up that offer by Professor Tillich, and treat the word 'God' as a kind of algebraical expression, carrying whatever meaning has the most value for us? Ultimate reality, deepest truth, the creator spirit, the meaning and purpose of life, the Hebrew 'I am', the Hindu 'Thou art Thou', or the ever-mysterious Logos — i.e., 'the Word', as all the translators maddeningly go on calling it — from the first line of St John's Gospel? Or Einstein's 'central control of things and events'?

Paul Tillich in his day was no more popular with the Establishment (he died in 1965) than John Robinson was in his (he died in 1980). In 1985, in an initially exciting series of BBC radio talks entitled *Searching for God*, Sir Richard Acland drew upon them both in presenting all these meanings for the idea of God. I select Sir Richard

as one example, an eloquent and patently sincere one, of
the offers of help from Christian thinkers now to be
heard — though seldom, in my experience, from a church
pulpit. 'We need a new statement', he said, 'which must
not include the word "God", for the word is deeply
misunderstood.' God is a process. You and I are not
watching the universe any more than it is watching us.
All of us are involved in it, and without our involvement
it would not work. The scientists now tell us that the
human intellect ceases to be an impartial observer and
becomes a vital participant. So those who talk about God
as if the word is to have for us the same meaning as it had
for our great-grandparents 'are not helping us towards the
truth' (says Sir Richard); 'they are driving us away from
it — by offering us less than we are spiritually capable of
understanding'. We therefore sink back into the
anonymous mass of 'don't knows'. And any attempt to
show us the meaning of Jesus is like showing pictures to
the blind or playing concerts to the deaf.

But if you can look at the universe as a cellular whole,
he says, you may feel that

each of us may be perceived as a tiny conscious cell *within* the
whole. There is then a relationship of some kind between the
process going on in each of us and the far greater process moving
through the whole. If you see yourself as no less, but no more,
than a tiny conscious cell within a far greater whole, you have
turned in a religious direction.

Deflation. Where is Jesus in all this? Where, that is to
say, is Christianity? I should have thought there were now
very few thinking people, even (indeed specially) among
the scientists, who would not come as far as this with Sir
Richard Acland. But consider his final message, which he
enunciated after a short concluding anthology of the
sayings of Jesus: 'You will be more ready to accept Jesus
as the universal manifestation of ultimate truth in human
life.' It seems to me a complete *non sequitur*, an anticlimax
more disappointing than most of its kind because its
promise had seemed so bright — and you couldn't steal a

peep at the last page because it was a weekly broadcast. From cellular identity with the universe to the acceptance of Jesus as saviour—how does a man make such an enormous leap, even if (as in my case), he would fain do so?

That's where I stand, aged 84. So for me the quest continues, while it can.

INDEX